D1726922

European Yearbook of International Economic Law

EYIEL Monographs - Studies in European and International Economic Law

Volume 40

The European Yearbook of International Economic Law (EYIEL) is a Springer-publication in the field of International Economic Law (IEL), a field increasingly emancipating itself from Public International Law scholarship and evolving into a fully-fledged academic discipline in its own right. With the yearbook, editors and publisher make a significant contribution to the development of this "new" discipline and provide an international source of reference of the highest possible quality.

The EYIEL covers all areas of IEL, in particular WTO Law, External Trade Law of major trading countries, important Regional Economic Integration agreements, International Competition Law, International Investment Regulation, International Monetary Law, International Intellectual Property Protection and International Tax Law.

EYIEL publishes articles following a substantive review by the editors and external experts as appropriate.

The editors have published extensively in the field of IEL and European Law alike. They are supported by an international Advisory Board consisting of established scholars of the highest reputation.

Series Editors

EYIEL Monographs is a subseries of the European Yearbook of International Economic Law (EYIEL). It contains scholarly works in the fields of European and international economic law, in particular WTO law, international investment law, international monetary law, law of regional economic integration, external trade law of the EU and EU internal market law. The series does not include edited volumes. EYIEL Monographs are peer-reviewed by the series editors and external reviewers.

Juliana Marteli Fais Feriato

Legal, Political and Economic Strategies of Subsidies within the World Trade Organization

 Springer

Juliana Marteli Fais Feriato
Curitiba, Brazil

ISSN 2364-8392   ISSN 2364-8406   (electronic)
European Yearbook of International Economic Law
ISSN 2524-6658   ISSN 2524-6666   (electronic)
EYIEL Monographs - Studies in European and International Economic Law
ISBN 978-3-031-73868-5   ISBN 978-3-031-73869-2   (eBook)
https://doi.org/10.1007/978-3-031-73869-2

This Springer imprint is published by the registered company Springer Nature Switzerland AG
The registered company address is: Gewerbestrasse 11, 6330 Cham, Switzerland

If disposing of this product, please recycle the paper.

Dedication

To all women chasing their dreams, most importantly, my daughter Maria Beatriz.

"Don't let anyone rob you of your imagination, your creativity, or your curiosity. It's your place in the world; it's your life."— Dr. Mae Jemison, American engineer, physician and former NASA astronaut

Preface

Subsidies became the object of greater concern of governments after the gradual reductions of tariffs on international trade, which began to occur in 1947, through the General Agreement on Tariffs and Trade (GATT). Over the years, the agreement has developed through rounds of negotiations and has been expanded, both in terms of the number of parties and the subject matter. Free trade came to be seen as an instrument of development and peace among nations. In 1995, GATT obtained a more robust structure when it was inserted into the World Trade Organization, which, in addition to tariff barriers, regulated non-tariff barriers, as well as unfair trade practices, such as dumping and subsidies.

Once tariffs had been reduced, governments found subsidies to be a disguised way of safeguarding political-economic interests and protecting national industry. Subsidies have always served as government instruments, however, with the reduction of tariffs, competition has intensified, and subsidies have become a matter of concern among WTO members, because when, specifically, they allocate economic resources unduly, leading to unfair competition.

Due to their character as public expenditures, since they are granted by governments through tax incentives or direct financial investment, they are directly linked to the economic power of the countries.

For this reason, subsidies constitute a serious unfair trade practice that needs to be fought multilaterally, depending on global cooperation so that all countries can have access to international trade.

The WTO has regulated the use of subsidies, prohibiting those considered specific, export or import substitution subsidies, as it considers them harmful to free trade by improperly allocating economic resources. It also condemned those specific subsidies that have adverse effects on the interests of other members. While the former are considered specific per se and therefore prohibited, the latter are actionable if serious injury occurs.

In addition, the WTO provides its members with instruments to counter the use of these subsidies. It happens that both subsidy policies and the use of mechanisms to counter them are mainly used by developed countries. On the other hand, the delay in compliance with the decisions of the Dispute Settlement Body (DSB) by developed countries has been frequently questioned in the WTO. This makes the reduction of tariff barriers nothing more than mere speech since it is compensated by the practice of subsidies. This situation further accentuates the differences between members, leaving developing and less developed countries on the margins of the system.

The problem has become more acute with the new mode of production, known as global value chains, whose predominant characteristic is the fragmentation of production. As a result, poor countries have become more dependent on their exports, which are hampered by subsidies from rich countries.

Since 2001, when the Doha Round was launched, the organization's ability to promote the development of its member countries has been questioned. Although the WTO recognizes a more favorable treatment to the least developed and developing countries, the ineffectiveness of the system, especially for them, makes the organization less inclusive and very homogeneous, urging the need for changes. In this sense, the challenge was launched to seek a more inclusive and heterogeneous multilateral system in the fight against illicit subsidies applied by developed countries, in order to promote fair and stable prices for the development of countries.

Failures in WTO mechanisms allow governments to adopt economic and political strategies to maintain their subsidy programs. Once subsidies are granted, their damage is irreversible, since they deprive agents of achieving social welfare by not being able to compete in the international market with prices reduced by subsidies and may in the long run eliminate competition and generate monopolies or oligopolies.

There are two mechanisms for countering subsidies within the scope of the WTO: compensatory measures and retaliation. The first can be unilaterally imposed and constitutes an additional tariff charged on the importation of the subsidized product. The second can only be applied when authorized by the Dispute Settlement Body after all procedural rites have been completed.

It happens that compensatory measures, by the current rule, cannot be imposed when competing States compete for market in third countries. In this case, it remains for the government only to resort to dispute settlement, which, in turn, allows the granting state to take advantage of its loopholes to prolong its subsidy program, in order to gain time and market.

Poor countries affected by specific subsidies could still grant subsidies to their industry, gaining the time to maneuver until they are questioned at the WTO. However, in addition to being illicit, this can become extremely costly for countries with little economic power, triggering a race to the bottom. Another alternative would be to do nothing about it, which is in line with the liberal theory, since subsidies would be financing another country's consumption, which would be the purpose of all production. However, if the subsidy is causing harm to the domestic industry, countries can be pressured by lobbies to counter them. The important thing here is to expand the range of mechanisms for countering subsidies if necessary.

To understand how governments take advantage of these failures, it is necessary to study their rationality, as well as their conditioning factors. The WTO is the result of governments' rationalities, which in turn are limited by their rules. The way governments act in the face of such rules, whether in cooperation or not, will be studied through the Economic Analysis of Law, a movement that makes use of microeconomic concepts to study legal rules and their consequences.

Based on these premises, this thesis intends to show the ineffectiveness of the system of countering specific subsidies for developing and less developed countries. At the end, a preventive mechanism is proposed for these countries, to discourage subterfuge and opportunism of rich countries, in search of efficiency.

Thus, the possibility of amending the SCM will be verified to allow the imposition of a cross-compensatory measure, applied by less developed and developing countries against subsidies from rich countries, when these are preventing the exports of the former from being destined to the third market.

To do so, firstly, the economic theories that underlie free trade, the influence exerted by subsidies on the international economy, and the importance of its regulation through International Trade Law at a multilateral level will be addressed.

The second chapter presents the Economic Analysis of Law (EAL) approach, by which the problematic economic and political subsidy strategies of member countries will be analyzed. International organizations are institutions that influence the behavior of their members, providing the rules of the game that will be played according to the cost–benefit analysis of each strategy.

Furthermore, the WTO treaties are similar to contracts, whose breach can be either beneficial or costly, and it is up to the EAL to ascertain the efficiency of the system to prevent the violation of the Agreement on Subsidies and Countervailing Measures (ASCM) from being more beneficial. The internalization of social costs is added to the efficiency calculation, according to the *Principle of Social-Economic Efficiency* (PESE).

Based on the premises of the EAL, the third chapter aims to show how subsidies and countervailing measures are regulated within the WTO and in Brazil. To this end, the structure of the WTO, its guiding principles, and the WTO Agreement on Subsidies and Countervailing Measures (ASCM) will be studied, together with the jurisprudence on the subject and the organization's guidelines on subsidies in times of economic crisis. The impasses on the matter in the Doha agenda will also be studied. At the domestic level, the political-administrative structure of subsidies will be presented, with special emphasis on the procedure for imposing countervailing measures.

The fourth chapter will point out the failures of the WTO mechanisms to counter specific subsidies, which accentuate the differences between rich and poor countries, in order to propose preventive measures in order to put the latter on the same level of equality to negotiate efficient solutions and prevent the harmful effects of subsidies from materializing.

The method adopted is the deductive approach, aiming to analyze the systemic failures, to then be applied specifically to subsidies. The method of procedure is monographic, seeking to study the WTO factors that influence the adoption of political-economic subsidy strategies. Finally, the research technique of direct and indirect documentation will be used.

Curitiba, Brazil   Juliana Marteli Fais Feriato

Acknowledgments

First, I would like to thank God for having illuminated this journey and placed, in my life, people who supported and endured me throughout this period. To my parents, for all the struggle they faced to get me here. To Professor Doctor Carlos Araújo Leonetti, for trusting me and accepting the challenge of guiding me throughout my master's and doctoral studies. To Professor Doctor Everton das Neves Gonçalves, for having co-supervised me and introduced me to the discipline of Economic Analysis of Law with so much appreciation that instigated my curiosity and interest. I would like to thank Renata Vargas do Amaral for making herself available to discuss her thesis. To Welber Barral who has always helped me, even with a tight schedule. I thank my mentor, Graham Cook, who guided me during my doctoral internship at the World Trade Organization, for all the coffees and conversations that helped me conclude this work, for putting me in contact with the most knowledgeable and experienced in the field, among them, I highlight Victor do Prado, Director of the Board and Committee on Trade Negotiations of the WTO, professor at the World Trade Institute in Bern, Switzerland, specialist in subsidies and dispute resolution, with whom I had the honor of exchanging experiences. To Tatiana Prazeres for welcoming me to the WTO, to Celso de Tarço Pereira, diplomat and counselor at the Mission of Brazil to the WTO, for having received me on the mission, and to the Director General of the WTO, Roberto Azevedo, whom I had the opportunity to meet, listen to their experiences, especially in relation to subsidies.

Finally, I thank my husband, Viniccius Feriato, who supported me in every detail, who saw my anxieties and understood them, patiently, never letting me give up, on the contrary, he gave me the support I needed to succeed at the thesis and internship at the WTO.

Juliana Marteli Fais Feriato

Contents

Abbreviations

CAMEX	Foreign Trade Chamber
CGV	Global Value Chains
DEAX	Department of Statistics and Export Support
DECOE	Department of Competitiveness in Foreign Trade
DECOM	Department of Trade Defense
DEINT	Department of Foreign Trade Operations
DEPLA	Department of Planning and Development of Foreign Trade
DSB	Dispute Settlement Body
EAL	Economic Analysis of Law
ESC	Understanding on Dispute Settlement
GATT	General Agreement on Tariffs and Trade
GPE	Permanent Group of Experts
ICTSD	International Centre for Trade and Sustainable Development
ITO	International Trade Organization
MDIC	Ministry of Development, Industry and Foreign Trade
NAMA	Non-Agricultural Market Access
OCDE	Organization for Economic Co-operation and Development
OIC	International Trade Organization
OMC	World Trade Organization
OPA	Permanent Appellate Organ
PESE	Principle of Economic-Social Efficiency
SCM	Agreement on Subsidies and Compensatory Measures
SCM	Subsidies and Countervailing Measures
SECEX	Secretariat of Foreign Trade
UE	European Union
WTO	World Trade Organization

Chapter 1
International Economics: Overcoming the Subsidy for Free Trade

Abstract Considering subsidies economic effects, their regulation relies not only on the knowledge of their nature, concept, political and economic facts but also economic theories that underlie free trade once subsidies can divert economic resources impeding trade. To comprehend how subsides produce effects on international trade, it is crucial to go through the main economic theories that underpin current trade structure such as absolute advantage and comparative advantage in comparison to the Keynesian welfare state theory once governments migrate between intervening or not in economy according to their interests and circumstances. In the same way, trade law had been built based on those facts. By this, the chapter shows that free trade is not possible to accomplish fully because of markets failures that need to be corrected by law, in this case, by a complex multilateral law system. On the other hand, the system faces new challenges when governments compete for investment attraction by using subsidies to provide a more favorable environment for industries and companies.

Economic phenomena have influenced people's lives since ancient times. The discussion about opening trade has existed since the earliest Greek societies and involved political, philosophical, and ethical issues all together. At that time, little was dealt with strictly economic problems such as scarcity management.

The first attempts at commercial expansion that appeared in the fifteenth century, after the formation of the Modern State, gave rise to mercantilist ideas. As sovereignty is a fundamental element of the State, commerce came to be considered relevant to maintain its power. At that time, the regulation of commercial relations was exclusively internal, with the purpose of strictly controlling the production and exchange of goods.

The formation of the modern state brought up the discussion about its intervention in the economic domain. Subsequent events, such as the Industrial and French Revolution, two World Wars, as well as several economic crises, led to the development of the subject by economists, whose theories gave support to the current capitalist structure, of the neoliberal economic model.

© The Author(s), under exclusive license to Springer Nature
Switzerland AG 2024
J. Marteli Fais Feriato, *Legal, Political and Economic Strategies of Subsidies within the World Trade Organization*, European Yearbook of International Economic Law 40, https://doi.org/10.1007/978-3-031-73869-2_1

The intensification in production and the liberalization of trade brought concerns about its effects on the states with less productive economies, whose governments began to adopt interventionist practices to limit imports and promote exports.

The limits of this intervention have been the object of discussion of economic theories, and the concession of subsidies does not escape the observation of such theories. Magnus[1] even states that "as long as there are governments, there will be subsidies in international trade."

Although free trade is still a sensitive issue for the sovereignty of states, governments recognized, in the middle of the twentieth century, the need for cooperation, in an institutionalized way, for greater stability in international trade relations, which led the discussion to the scope of International Trade Law.

There is no way to deny the current economic reality and the importance of its regulation by Law, which, in turn, cannot be distanced from society, inserted in an economic model, in which subsidy concessions are operated.

Thus, subsidies, currently regulated by law, are political-legal manifestations with economic effects. For this reason, the analysis of its (in)convenience must be interdisciplinary, coming from the dialogue between Law and Economics. Economic studies cannot be discarded by law since they serve as an interpretative instrument or a foundation for the norm to achieve efficiency and the maximization of social welfare.

In this vein, this chapter aims to present the way in which the Economic Theory understands subsidies, justifying their regulation at the multilateral level. For this purpose, firstly, a historical approach to the international economy will be made in order to understand the current market structure in which subsidies produce effects and how they do so, covering the path followed to reach their regulation by the International Trade Law.

1.1   International Economics: Historical Approach

The current capitalist structure goes back to the mercantilist ideals that began to appear in the transition from the Late Middle Ages to the Modern Age. Although trade existed among ancient peoples, the economic foundation of trade, when it existed, was restricted to the pursuit of wealth.[2] The picture changed from the formation of absolute states, when governments came to see the benefits of expanding trade for the maintenance of sovereign power.[3]

---

[1] Magnus (2004).

[2] Dal Ri JA reports that the regulatory instruments which gave support to the trade expansion of Rome from the year 265 b.C. substituted the inflexible *jus civile*, but it still wasn't about an international universal trade right. These instruments' concern was exclusively the pursuit of revenue. In: Dal Ri (2004).

[3] According to Montchretien A "it's impossible to make war without men, keep men without pay, pay them without tribute, collect tribute without trade". In: Montchretien (1615).

An imperialist movement of expanding international trade began, which gave support to the current capitalist structure. The economy of the capitalist world at this time abolished the class division between feudal lords and vassals in favor of the interests of the merchants, also known as the bourgeois. There was a convergence of interests between the bourgeois and the government regarding the unification of the state. While the government needed resources to finance the centralization of power, which were obtained through the collection of taxes, they guaranteed the bourgeois security and stability in trade relations, through the determination of monetary standards and uniform laws.

Considering that the prosperity of the economy was measured by the accumulation of precious metals, the mercantilist logic preached the search for wealth in foreign lands while protecting, internally, its exit. The merchants were the source of resources, derived from the payment of taxes on the importation of goods. To this end, measures were adopted to encourage imports, while exports were discouraged.

Subsequently, the intellectual renaissance triggered inventions such as the telescope and the compass, useful to the expansion of trade through navigation, allowing the projection of maps and the exploration of new lands, inaugurating the colonial period,[4] which expanded the expansion of the world economy.

The new sea routes, the discovery of America and the consequent conquest of market colonies by the Europeans contributed to the transformation of trade. It was at this time that the movement that generated the current model of globalization emerged, disguised with imperialist elements.[5]

Due to the hegemonic European domination, the colonies were prevented from selling to other countries and were forced to buy the colonizers' products, creating a true commercial empire. On the other hand, no effort was spared to prevent the exit of these metals from the state treasury, which applied severe rules and even imprisonment to exporters of these materials, while the exportation was facilitated for goods considered irrelevant.[6] Spain even applied the death penalty to those who exported gold and silver.[7]

Thus, it can be said that the expansion of trade was the basis of mercantilism, reflected in the Law of the time. International trade and the international Law of war and treaties were tied to the sovereignty of states, which implied the legitimacy of the use of force in the case of abuses against the free circulation of goods on the seas.[8]

Through sovereign acts, governments encouraged exports and adopted protectionist measures for imports, even if they harmed individuals. By way of example, around the seventeenth century, France and England applied subsidies to promote

---

[4] Hunt and Sherman (1999).

[5] Silva (2010).

[6] Dal Ri (2004), p. 65.

[7] Hunt and Sherman (1999), p. 36.

[8] Dal Ri (2004), p. 70.

their exports, respectively of agricultural goods and textiles, but while England promoted its textile industry for export, France applied safeguards to protect it from foreign competition.

Also in England, the economic policy of internal monopoly was adopted, which prohibited English merchants from competing, which would increase the price of exported products due to the existence of a single seller. To balance out the trade balance, faced with the persistence of foreign competition, England adopted the policy of excluding such competition, forcing the colonies to sell raw materials at low prices and buy manufactured goods at high prices.[9]

In its last phase, the focus of state intervention ceased to be the accumulation of metals, as it was found to cause price increases. Therefore, it began to promote the manufacturing sector to stimulate the export of surplus production.

The international system of exchange of surpluses constitutes the basic element of the expansion of trade, linked to the central vision of States, serving as an instrument of economic exploitation.[10]

It is noted that mercantilism is marked by a movement of individualistic character and domination, centered on the strong performance of the State, based on commercial expansion through the exploitation of the territory of others.

However, the development of this commerce causes a restructuring in society, since it strengthened the bourgeois class, which started to contest the strong intervention of the State in commerce, around the end of the seventeenth century.

In this sense, thinkers such as John Locke, considered the father of modern liberalism, who began to challenge the authoritarianism of the State and to defend property, life, and people's freedom, stand out. For him, the State's interventionism obstructed trade which, in turn, was capable of self-regulation. Therefore, the price of inputs should be determined by the number of buyers and sellers.

In order to move the economy away from state interventionism, monetary theories emerged that converted metals into national currencies. It can be said that liberalism has a depoliticized character, constituting a movement of separation between economics and politics. Dal Ri Jr. explains that:

> The new "secularized" liberalism is distinguished by the liberal principle of the widest separation between the spheres of government and economic exploitation. And through these, it was possible to develop during the 19th century a logic that sought the realization and maintenance of an "almost-world government" of the economy, completely alien to the political world.[11]

Trade liberalization came to be seen as the best way to counter state authoritarianism. In the view of classical liberalism, represented in the ideas of Adam Smith, in his work "Wealth of Nations" of 1776,[12] the regulation of the economy by the State had the purpose of promoting specific interests of some and not the common good.

---

[9] Hunt and Sherman (1999), p. 37.

[10] Sanchez (2004), p. 54.

[11] Dal Ri (2004), pp. 101–102.

[12] Smith (1996).

Therefore, the best way would be to suppress state intervention and leave prices free to find their own point of equilibrium, what Smith called the "natural price".[13]

By leaving the market freely in the hands of merchants and industrialists, the common interest would be a consequence of the pursuit of individual interests, because by acting in their own interest, people would naturally choose the most advantageous and complementary investments. That is, merchants and industrialists, in order to increase their profits, would choose to produce what consumers are willing to buy while, on the other hand, competition for the consumer market would cause them to seek to develop better products, benefiting society as a whole.[14] Therefore, individuals were driven by the "invisible hand" of the market, which allowed the quantity of supply to meet effective demand.[15]

Note that by this time, the adverse effects of resource allocation that state intervention in the economy was capable of exerting were recognized, but at the same time, the important role of the state for certain functions was maintained. It was believed that it was up to the State to carry out public works and maintain certain institutions intended exclusively for public use and never to specific private individuals, in addition to guaranteeing security, condemning the practice of cartels and refraining from providing government support for the configuration of monopolies.[16]

The burden that the state exerted to meet its needs was too costly for trade and harmed the balance of international relations. Tyranny, wars, and arbitrary attitudes were incompatible with trade, which later came to be seen by Enlightenment thinkers as a means of social regulation and peace.[17] In this sense, it adds:

> Conceptions of international order in the Enlightenment period were the subject of intense debate. On the one hand, the idea of progress, allied to that of civilization, built by the pacification of tempers generated by commercial affluence and interaction, was current among a school of thought of the time, the Modernists, which included David Hume and Adam Smith. It was a thought that was the fruit of an ideology created around the strategy of valuing the cultural and economic modernization of the period. War, in this context, served only as a mere instrument of application of the Law, since the great transformations in the economic field increased the interdependence among nations and in this world war and armies have a price, financially considered, that is not worth paying.[18]

The strong presence of the State over commercial relations therefore confronted liberal ideas, and so there was a need to restrict its functions so that trade could flow freel.

It is important to point out that it is not possible to link capitalism directly to Smith, but his ideas were used by capitalists to suppress the strong role of the State over the economy.

---

[13] Ibid.

[14] Dal Ri (2004), p. 61.

[15] Smith (1996), p. 61.

[16] Ibid.

[17] Dal Ri (2004), pp. 84–90.

[18] Lupi (2001), pp. 89–90.

In the same line of reasoning, in opposition to the mercantilist ideas, David Ricardo,[19] Smith's disciple, in his book "Principles of Political Economy and Taxation" of 1817, criticized the barriers of trade and showed that all economies can benefit from free trade, even if one is inferior to another in the production of all goods. In this sense, Ricardo argued that the freedom of trade would allow the increase of profits without having to reduce wages, because it made it possible to import goods for workers for lower values than those produced domestically.[20]

Thus, to optimize production, the division of labor was necessary,[21] which would only be feasible in a free market environment. This led to the division of society into classes: the working class, the capitalists, and the landowners. The benefits would come from the clash of individual interests, which, in a free market environment, would provide for the welfare of society.[22]

It is important to point out that the free trade of the time was not yet linear, nor unanimous, since it coexisted with protectionist pressures, especially from more sensitive sectors such as agriculture and the expansion of industrialization. According to Garcia:

> At the beginning of the 19th century, throughout Western Europe, foreign trade was governed by very protectionist, prolix rules, inheriting from the trade standards of the previous three centuries. High tariffs and commercial monopolies began to be abolished from 1846 in England, and soon after in France, inaugurating - by imitation effect in other countries - a boom in free trade, which only began to diminish at the end of the century, as a result of the reaction of the partisans of protectionism.[23]

The landmark of this period was the repeal of the Corn Laws in England, which, since the seventeenth century, had subsidized the export of grains produced in that country, while imposing high tariffs on imports, causing prices to rise. For this reason, the movement for the liberalization of trade in the most sensitive sectors began.[24]

---

[19] Ricardo (1982).

[20] Ibid, pp. 104–105.

[21] In Smith's words: "[…] This great increase in the quantity of labour, which, in consequence of its division, the same number of persons are able to perform, is explained by three distinct circumstances: in the first place, because of the greater dexterity existing in each worker; secondly, to the saving of that time which, in general, it would be customary to lose in passing from one kind of work to another; finally, as a result of the invention of a large number of machines that facilitate and shorten the work, making it possible for a single person to perform it, which would otherwise have to be done by many". In: Smith (1996), p. 43. In this same sense, Ricardo supported industrialization to increase production. In: Ricardo (1982).

[22] For Smith, individuals, in pursuing their interests, do so in order to obtain the best possible result. In: Smith (1996), pp. 379–380.

[23] Free translation from: "A comienzos del s. XIX en toda Europa occidnental el comercio exterior se regia por una normativa prolija, muy prtecctionista, heredera de los critérios mercantilistas de los tres siglos anteriores. Los altos aranceles y los monopolios al comercio comenzaran a abolirse a partir de 1846 en Inglaterra, y muy poco despues en Francia, inaugurando—por efecto imitacion de otros países—un auge del librecambismo, que sólo empezó a perder fuerza a finales del siglo como resultado de la reacción de los partidarios del proteccionismo." In: Garcia (2002), p. 19.

[24] Ibid, p. 20.

The following period, from 1840 to 1873 (late nineteenth century), was known as the golden age of corporate capitalism, marked by a rapid commercial expansion on the European Continent for modern capital goods for industrialization, which caused a historic economic growth. Unfortunately, technology has allowed only the large corporations to enjoy this expansion, as smaller companies, unable to compete, have been eliminated.[25]

Marx[26] criticizes this model, due to the social injustices caused, demonstrating its harm to the working class, excluded from the economic development generated by capitalism. The specialization of work and the use of machines reduced production costs, but had perverse effects on society, such as child labor, long working hours, and unemployment.

The period was fraught with social conflict, which caused a great change in economic thought. Based on the assumption of the positive effects caused by free trade, neoclassical theorists sought to find the equilibrium point of the economic system. Thus, "every general equilibrium of economies in perfect competition, regardless of the initial distribution of resources, maximizes welfare".[27]

To this end, the standard of measuring the value of things was shifted from supply to demand, by which goods would be acquired according to their utility.[28] However, Smith's "invisible hand" still prevailed in neoclassical theories, a situation that began to change with Pigou,[29] when admitted the State's intervention in the face of negative externalities that cause costs to society, preventing the welfare from coinciding with the equilibrium point and the efficiency of the economic system.

Externalities can constitute benefits (positive) or losses (negative) appropriated by third parties. As an example of a positive externality, one can cite the technology invested by a company: even if it acquires the property right over it, the benefit can be extended to other companies, since it is not possible to fully appropriate the property. On the other hand, negative externalities cause damage to society and generate market inefficiency. Examples include environmental pollution from industry, the devaluation of real estate, the production of unsafe goods, etc. Thus, state interventions in the economy are necessary to prevent the negative externalities arising from free trade from materializing.

---

[25] Hunt and Sherman (1999), pp. 107–108.

[26] Mark (1980).

[27] Pareto (1996), p. 13.

[28] For the utilitarian neoclassicals, consumer choice was based on the utility of the commodity. Since the utility of a commodity was relative, as it depended on the subjective interests of consumers, Marshall adopted as a measure, the approximate utility, formulated by rational choice theory, by which he assumed that choices were made to maximize utility with expenditure. See: Marshal (1982). Pareto criticized the difficulties of measuring prices and sought a mathematical rather than psychological solution, creating the ordinal concept of utility, by which there was an order of preference of products. Thus, the loss of utility in one case was compensated by the other. See: Pareto (1996).

[29] Pigou (2013).

The end of the nineteenth century and the beginning of the twentieth century were marked by the hegemony of neoclassical thought, which believed in the market's self-regulation and in its ability to achieve a balanced economic system, including full employment.

The succeeding period was marked by a tragic economic crisis in Europe, caused by the outbreak of World War I, which practically destroyed European industry, forcing Europe to seek goods for its supply in the North American market. This situation allowed the American economy to grow rapidly and made the United States the world's great industrial and financial leader.[30]

However, the first war brought harmful effects to the economy, such as generalized inflation and exchange rate instability, which caused European countries to return to the adoption of interventionist policies, which made use of protectionist measures to seek greater export competitiveness.[31] According to Garcia: "the growing integration and globalization of the economy, which seemed unstoppable since the last quarter of the previous century, has ostensibly stalled and receded".[32]

In 1929, the United States faced its greatest economic crisis, caused by the lack of demand in the foreign and domestic markets. At the time, its main consumer market was concentrated in Canada and England, which, in turn, were going through a recession, which made it difficult for American goods to leave the country, nor could they sell in the domestic market.[33]

In this way, protectionist pressures began to appear and began a vicious cycle, as new restrictive measures were applied to counter protectionism, drastically reducing world trade in the first 4 years of the crisis. It is noteworthy that: "[…] To all was added the systematic use of competitive devaluations, with the aim not only of artificially improving the competitiveness of own exports, but also to curb imports[34]".

It is important to emphasize that, even equipped with factories, technology, and skilled labor, the North American entrepreneurs had no economic interest in starting them up, since the demand was in a situation of extreme decline. This fact showed that the idealism of the market economy was not focused on the welfare of individuals, but on profit,[35] leading to criticism of the neoclassical model.

There were two paths to follow: maintain the model of unbridled production or allow the state to intervene in the economy to circumvent the crisis and social

---

[30] Hunt and Sherman (1999), p. 164.

[31] Maia (2011), p. 93.

[32] Free translation from: "la creciente integración y mundialización de la economia, que parecia imparable desde el último cuarto del siglo anterior, se estancó y retrocedió ostensiblemente". In: Garcia (2002), p. 27.

[33] Ibid, p. 28.

[34] Free translation from: "A todo lo anterior se añadió el uso sistemático de las devaluaciones competitivas, con el objetivo no sólo de mejorar artificialmente la competitividad de las exportaciones proprias, sino tambien de frenar las importaciones. En las relaciones comerciales Este-Oeste desde 1945 y hasta la caída del muro de Berlin, el bilateralismo ha sido el sistema que las ha regido." In: Ibid, p. 29.

[35] Dal Ri (2004), p. 61.

problems, guaranteeing fundamental rights. In this way, the state had to deal with economic and social needs at the same time, which culminated in the *Welfare State* or Keynes' welfare state.[36]

For Keynes, state intervention was necessary in order to make socially useful investments, such as schools and hospitals, so as not to increase productivity and not to discourage future investments. The resources to carry out this policy would be obtained by borrowing excess savings.[37]

However, Keynes recognizes that, from a political point of view, the government would not make such investments if it were not to benefit the wealthier sectors, since these would exert pressure. Thus, faced with political obstacles, it would be more interesting to make such investments in favor of the wealthy, even if the benefits to society would be indirect, instead of doing nothing.[38]

The great challenge for the State was to reconcile both thoughts: Smith's liberalism with Keynes' policy of intervention in the economy for social purposes. In the face of popular pressure, the liberal state was transformed into a social state. About this transition, Bonfim states that:

> This economic stance, concomitant with the uncontrolled development of the industrial sector, generated serious side effects, certainly fostering the construction of an ideal aimed at the performance of the State as a positive agent in the achievement of fundamental rights and guarantees. The formal freedom enshrined by the liberal State did not have a broad scope, and it was essential that the State began to act as a positive agent in the attempt to materialize it.[39]

In this way, the neoclassical ideas were reformed and the State's intervention in the economy to correct the imperfections of the economic system was admitted. To this end, it was suggested, among other measures, that "special subsidies be applied to equalize social and private costs, whenever there was a gap between them".[40]

In the legal field, it was possible to visualize the inclusion of social rights in the federal constitutions, initially, in the Constitution of Mexico of 1917, in the Constitution of Weimar in 1919 and in Brazil, in the Constitution of 1934, remaining until the current Constitution of 1988, apart from the Constitution of 1937.

It turns out that the costs of maintaining the welfare state were high because of its duty to guarantee fundamental rights. This intense counter payment by the state and the internationalization of the economy[41]set off deep economic recessions,[42]

---

[36] Originated in Keynesian thought which, in opposition to Smith's liberal ideas, advocated the need for state intervention in the economy in order to promote full employment, given the possibility of reaching economic equilibrium below full employment. See: Keynes (1982).

[37] Hunt and Sherman (1999), pp. 189–190.

[38] Keynes (1982), p. 129.

[39] Bonfim (2011), p. 85.

[40] Hunt and Sherman (1999), p. 118.

[41] From the moment the economy becomes internationalized, it becomes more difficult for the State to maintain its national order due to the breaking of national barriers by internationalized capital.

[42] The high cost of the welfare state generated economic crises in several aspects: fiscal crisis of the state, crisis of the Keynesian model, structural crisis of capitalism, oil and interest rate crisis.

that incited the criticism of the Keynesian economic model and pushed neoliberal ideas.

Mises e Hayek[43] are the main critics of the welfare state and its excessive intervention in the economy. To Mises,[44] the economy is regulated by supply and demand, while the social system is based on private property and the division of labor. In the same sense, Hayek[45] maintains that only the market is capable of ordering social issues according to the price system.

In this sense, Hayek intended to demonstrate that fascism and communism tend to suppress individual liberties and democracy, elements that he considered essential to guarantee internal peace and individual freedom.[46] To this thought, Friedman added that individual and societal freedom is only possible if there is economic freedom.[47]

Under the influence of these economists, the neoliberal system was first implemented in England, under the command of Margaret Thatcher in 1979, and in 1980, in the United States, by President Ronald Reagan, to recover economic development. Neoliberal thinking was gaining hegemony with the process of globalization and with the recommendations of the World Bank and the International Monetary Fund, soon spreading to Latin America and the East.[48]

The main neoliberal ideas can be found in the guidelines of the Washington Consensus of 1990. At the time, Washington economists formulated a set of ten basic rules for adjusting the macroeconomics of struggling developing countries. To this end, it established "the lowest common denominator of economic policy recommendations that were being considered by Washington D.C.-based financial institutions and that should be applied in Latin American countries as their economies were in 1989".[49]

The Washington Consensus was based on two pillars: democracy and the market economy, but the second was a priority, because democracy was a consequence and not an objective. Moreover, democracy could even be an obstacle to the liberalization of trade.

---

[43] Ludwig von Mises in 1922 with "A Economia Comunal" and Friedrich Von Hayek in 1944 with "O Caminho da Servidão" presented the arguments against the ideas of Keynesian interventionism.

[44] Mises (1990), pp. 256–257.

[45] Hayek (1990), pp 68–69.

[46] Ibid, pp 25–26.

[47] Friedman (1995).

[48] China refused to follow the Consensus and chose to follow the example of England and Germany, adopting the Darwinian thought of competition, by which, in an environment of free competition, the less fit would be naturally eliminated. However, the Chinese state was still present in the economy and, therefore, only joined the WTO in 2001, when it was better prepared to adopt the measures required by the organization.

[49] Free adaptation from: "The lowest common denominator of policy advice being addressed by the Washington-based institutions to Latin American countries as of 1989." In: Washington Consensus. Center for International Development at Harvard University. http://www.cid.harvard.edu/cidtrade/issues/washington.html.

The recommendations were as follows: (a) fiscal discipline, through which the State should limit its spending to revenue, eliminating the public deficit; (b) Focusing public spending on education, health and infrastructure; (c) tax reform that broadens the basis on which the tax burden falls, with greater weight in indirect taxes and less progressivity in direct taxes; (d) financial liberalization, with the aim of establishing restrictions that prevent international financial institutions from acting on an equal footing with national ones, and the withdrawal of the state from the sector; (e) competitive exchange rate; (f) liberalization of foreign trade, with reduced import tariffs and export incentives, aiming to boost the globalization of the economy; (g) elimination of restrictions on foreign capital, allowing foreign direct investment; (h) Privatization; (i) Deregulation, eliminating barriers to entry and exit; (j) Intellectual Property.[50] About these proposals, Batista makes the following analysis:

> The proposals of the Washington Consensus in the 10 areas to which it has dedicated converge on two basic objectives: on the one hand, the drastic reduction of the State and the corrosion of the concept of the Nation; on the other, maximum openness to the importation of goods and services and the entry of risk capital. All in the name of a great principle: that of the absolute sovereignty of the self-regulating market in both internal and external economic relations.[51]

In Brazil, the Federation of Industries of the State of São Paulo (FIESP) published a document repeating the guidelines of the Washington Consensus, whose title exalted the modernity of the prescription and its relationship with the country's growth. This document was called "Free to grow – proposal for a modern Brazil".

Said document also added recommendations from the World Bank to foster the export of agricultural goods as a way of inserting the country in the world trade, that is, while developed countries dedicated themselves to industrialization, it was recommended to developing countries that they dedicated themselves to the agriculture, which, in its turn, was subsidized by the developed countries, causing the reduction of international prices..[52]

The contradictory interests in the decision-making process continued, which, at the same time as those countries that did not want to join free trade were relentlessly condemned, there was the fear that this liberalization would harm some sectors. Batista brings as an example the automotive sector, showing that:

> [...]This same press would register, with respect and without any corrections, statements of the president of the General Motors Worldwide when he came to Brazil to defend the need to contain the impetus of the trade opening, with the natural fear that GM North America would not be able to compete in the Brazilian market with vehicles of Japanese or Korean origin, if that process continued. Thus, it would be up to American and European investors,

---

[50] Negrão (1998), p. 41.

[51] Batista PN (1994) Consenso de Washington: a visão neoliberal dos problemas latino-americanos. http://www.fau.usp.br/cursos/graduacao/arq_urbanismo/disciplinas/aup0270/4dossie/nogueira94/nog94-cons-washn.pdf, p. 18.

[52] Ibid, p. 6.

and not national entrepreneurs, to assume the defense of the industry installed in the country through the import substitution policy condemned by the neoliberal wave.[53]

Stiglitz, in turn, referring to the neoliberal program for Russian reform, came to the following lesson:

> [...] the United States supports free trade, but often when a poor country finally finds a commodity that it can export to the United States, internal American protectionist interests are encouraged. [...] on the one hand, they received large doses of free market and economics textbooks. On the other hand, what they saw in their teachers' practice was far from this ideal. They were told that trade liberalization was necessary for a successful market economy, but when they tried to export aluminum and uranium (and other commodities as well) to the United States, they found the door closed. Evidently, America had developed without trade liberalization; Or, as it is sometimes put it, 'trade is good, but imports are bad'[54]

From this, it is possible to affirm that imperialism remains in current times, since "the globalized society is made up of proven imperialist elements, which makes it as cruel as in past times.[55] Thus, it is noted that, while free trade is encouraged in a foreign country, protectionism is adopted at home. These ideas have influenced the current multilateral trade system, causing it to be ineffective for poor countries.

1.2   International Trade Law: Historical Approach

International commercial relations have been regulated by International Law only since the middle of the twentieth Century when there was the first attempt at institutionalized regulation by an international organization. Until then, international law was limited to regulating the coexistence between sovereign states.

Despite the secularization of the state and the application of the most favored nation clause,[56] that emerged in the eighteenth century, fundamental to the expansion of trade in the Industrial Revolution in the nineteenth century, the state's presence in international trade relations was still strong in the sense of strengthening its sovereignty.[57] The regulation of international trade was predominantly done within the scope of its internal Law. According to Dal Ri Jr.:

---

[53] Ibid, p. 7.

[54] [57]Free adaptation from "The United States supports free trade, but all too often, when a poor country does manage to find commodity it can export to the United States, domestic American protectionist interests are galvanized." In: Stiglitz (2003), p. 172.

[55] Silva (2010), p. 34.

[56] The most favored nation clause determines that the benefits granted to imports of goods from one state should be extended to the others.

[57] The classic international law begins in the Modern Age, with the Treaty of Westphalia of 1648, which, based on sovereign equality, has the main objective of guaranteeing the political independence and sovereign equality of the States, having put an end to the Thirty Years' War. In this sense, see: Sanchez (2004), p. 56.

From the top of its tribune, the international legal culture of the late 19th and early 20th centuries insisted on not "getting its hands dirty", excluding any kind of possibility of analysis of international law in light of international economic phenomena.[58]

The regulation of international trade was for a long time excluded from international Law, which was attached to the sovereignties of States. Thus, even in the face of liberal ideas, the use of interventionist practices in favor of the sovereign interests of States was admitted. Therefore, while free trade was defended in favor of competitive goods, protectionist measures were applied to those less competitive, an inherent characteristic of mercantilism.

Until then, the opening of trade occurred unilaterally. The conception of multilateral economic legal order began to be considered after World War I in the creation of the League of Nations. The failure of liberalism has awakened a belief in the need to ensure stability and trust in international trade relations through multilateral regulation. According to Pureza:

The mourning of Westphalia did not bequeath us any determined institutional model but rather open horizons. Once the reference to absolute and exclusive state centrism is lost, our post-Westphalian time is both a time of experimentation with uncontrolled hegemony and an opportunity for a new regulatory culture.[59]

Trade needed a stable setting, with guarantees of ownership and enforcement of rules. For this, it was necessary that states stopped threatening with the use of unilateral force and entered into the movement of cooperation and reciprocity. For this reason, the reduction of barriers occurred mostly through international treaties.[60] A framework was also needed to provide transparency, predictability, and stability to international trade relations, which are currently underpinned by the WTO.

The fear that economic disorganization would trigger new conflicts increased after World War II, causing states to reach a consensus on the need for financial, economic and commercial stabilization in the world. Regarding this last aspect, there was already a concern to limit unbridled free competition that could threaten peace and social justice. Thus, it became necessary to establish a multilateral regulation of trade in a clear and precise way, to curb abuses by economic powers and private economic agents, based on the assumption that the economy can no longer go it alone, distorted of social and moral character.

However, consensus on the material issues of such regulation was not easily reached, as states still identified with the imperialist movement while revising the mechanism of coexistence to create international organizations.

Inspired by Keynes' ideas, in July 1944, representatives of the United Nations Alliance met in the city of Bretton Woods, in the United States, to define, at multilateral level, common rules for the States to achieve economic prosperity and full

---

[58] Dal Ri (2004), p. 113.

[59] Pureza (2001) Para um internacionalismo pós-vestfaliano. http://www.eurozine.com/articles/article_2002-04-26-pureza-pt.html.

[60] An example of a unilateral opening of trade is when England repealed the Corn Law in 1846, which restricted grain imports. See: Hoekman and Kostecki (2009), kindle edition, position 442.

employment. In this sense, Bechara points out that "the opening of international trade and monetary stability were essential conditions for economic development and for ensuring lasting peace".[61]

The result of this conference was the creation of two international organizations, the World Bank, and the International Monetary Fund (IMF), as well as the failed attempt to create the International Trade Organization (ITO).

The creation of the three international organizations would establish the tripod for the functioning of the New International Economic Order. While the World Bank was in charge of reconstruction and development through the provision of capital, the IMF regulated financial and economic issues damaged by the 1929 crisis and World War II.

The ICO, in turn, was designed to regulate trade relations between countries, but it never came into force. His project, proposed by the United States, constituted "a true code of international trade, an ambitious document that also incorporated provisions on employment and economic development, called the 'Havana Charter'".[62]

The victory of the Republican Party, known for its protectionist optics, the influence of American farmers and the difficulties in reconciling American interests with the Soviets, caused the United States, the largest power and promoter of the project of multilateral trade regulation, not to ratify the Havana Charter, making it impossible to advance. At the height of economic growth, the ICO could limit the United States' freedom of action in trade.

In this period, it was possible to identify the movement of international cooperation in the scope of relations between states only in the social space, once again leaving aside trade regulation. This is because, although there was consensus on the need to create international rules on world trade,[63] the states were not yet ready for the cooperative movement that could limit their sovereignty in this sense. The failure of the International Trade Organization (ICO) is an example of this discrepancy.[64]

Nevertheless, the recognition that it was necessary to regulate trade multilaterally, primarily for the purpose of reducing the negative effects of past protectionism, at least allowed governments to begin the expansion of international trade driven by rules of law. Although in a non-systemic and incipient way, they entered into a tariff reduction agreement, known as GATT/47 (*General Agreement on Tarifs and Trade*), ratified by 23 states in 1947, which still preserved the mercantilist view of reciprocity regarding the reduction of tariff restrictions on imports.

About the creation of GATT/47, adds Dal Ri Jr.:

---

[61] Bechara and Redenschi (2002), p. 65.

[62] Garcia (2002), p. 31.

[63] The Havana Charter, which would create the International Trade Organization, had this Keynesian inspiration, linking trade to the welfare state and development, that is, the expansion of trade would bring new opportunities for employment and income.

[64] Sanchez (2004), pp 59–60.

It is difficult to affirm that this whole tumultuous process, which concluded with the provisional use of GATT, was a mise en scène, a strategy to gradually and unconditionally release what interested a few. But it is also hard to rule out the possibility that, a few months after the conflictive Potsdam Conference, the absence of the Soviet Union from the Havana Conference, and the predictions of the Republican Party victory in the United States legislative elections, there was still a real interest in setting up a strong intergovernmental organization in the field of trade relations. Between creating an organization that could make commercial relations even more complex in a new bipolar world and instituting a simpler, less complex structure with fewer ties, the second option was chosen. It is hard not to think that, in the midst of the predicted collapse of a well-structured perspective such as the ITO, some have invested all their forces in trying to establish a second, more flexible entity, and therefore with more room for opportunistic maneuvering.[65]

However, GATT/47, as an international agreement, presented weaknesses when compared to systemic regulation within an international organization. It can be said that the lack of "jurisdictionalization"[66] of trade leads to its fragmentation and fragility, opening space for maneuvers. For Sanchez, the greater the degree of definition of the obligations signed in international treaties, the precision of the terms and the delegation of powers, the greater the "jurisdictionalization".[67] It is also pointed out that:

The interrelation of producer and consumer markets strengthens the perspective of interdependence among states, favoring the concept of cooperation, opening spaces for relationships beyond those of coexistence in the international arena.[68]

Given the opening of this space, new actors have appeared, favoring a pluralist and heterogeneous conception of the world, no longer restricted to the centrality of states and dispensing with their intervention. This reality goes beyond the national-international dualism, taking international relations to the transnational level, which creates difficulties for state control. According to Hobsbawm "[…] when the transnational economy established its dominance over the world, it undermined a great institution, until 1945 practically universal: the territorial nation-state, since such a state could no longer control more than an increasingly smaller part of its affairs".[69]

The weakening of the states' power of control brought about the fragmentation movement and boosted the organization of states in the form of cooperation. According to Sanchez: "The fragmentation movements of institutions and organizational forms favor - and to a certain extent force - the decision of cooperation by the states as a solution to the insufficient responsiveness of national and classical international systems".[70]

This does not mean that International Law has lost its classical bias, but that the movements of domination, coexistence and cooperation began to operate at the

---

[65] Dal Ri (2004), p. 136.

[66] By "jurisdictionalization" we mean the process of normalizing social relations.

[67] Sanchez (2004), p. 62.

[68] Ibid, p. 59.

[69] Hobsbawm (1995), p. 413.

[70] Sanchez (2004), p. 61.

same time, generating instabilities, which, in turn, provoked the search for greater "jurisdictionalization" of international trade.[71]

GATT/47 was a strictly diplomatic system, managed by political pressure from the countries with the greatest economic power, that is, GATT was "power oriented". As Petersman asserts:

> A power-oriented technique suggests discussions, negotiations, or litigation in which one party asserts or uses the relative power at its disposal in order to influence the conduct of the other party. In international trade negotiations, for example, a diplomat from a powerful importing country may indicate, subtly or otherwise, to an exporting, less developed country that the granting of development aid, trade preferences, or military assistance may have to be stopped unless developing countries "voluntarily" commit to limiting their competitive exports [...]This "power-oriented" policy tends to be "results- and conflict-oriented" because it aims at redistributing income to the "benefit of powerful protectionist interest groups."[72]

In view of the weakening of states, the culture of power is, to a certain extent, unviable, and there is an urgent need to implement a "jurisdictional" system. For the first time, international Law is concerned with regulating the international trade of goods and services in a systemic way.

To achieve this legal mechanism, seven more rounds of negotiations were held under GATT/47[73] until the WTO's systemic regulation of international trade was reached in 1995,[74] where it was established how free trade should be. At the time, then GATT Director General Peter Sutherland said: "Today the world has chosen openness and cooperation over uncertainty and conflict."[75]

It should be emphasized that this new order is not completely original and detached from everything that was achieved in the GATT/47 era, in fact, the WTO incorporated it, becoming known as GATT/1994.

In the Preamble of the Agreement Establishing the WTO, it is possible to see that its objectives are not strictly economic, but very similar to the objectives of the GATT, such as the "[...] raising of standards of living, full employment,

---

[71] Ibid, p. 69.

[72] Free adaptation from: "A power-oriented technique suggests discussions, negotiations or dispute settlements in which one party asserts or uses the relative power at its disposal in order to influence the conduct of the other party. In international trade negotiations, for instance, a trade diplomat from a powerful importing country may indicate, subtly or otherwise, to a less-developed exporting country that the granting of development aid, trade preferences or military assistance might have to be discontinued unless the developing country 'voluntarily' undertaken to limit its competitive exports [...] Such 'power-oriented' policy tend to be 'result-oriented' and 'conflict-oriented' because they aim at the redistribution of income for the benefit of powerful protectionist interest groups." In: Petersman (1997), p. 66.

[73] The rounds were: Annecy (1949), Torquay (1951), 1956 (Genebra), 1960/1961 (Dyllon), 1964/1967 (Kennedy), 1973/1979 (Tokyo) and1986/1994 (Uruguai).

[74] Instituted in 1995 by the Marrakech Agreement and internalized in the Brazilian legal system by Decree no. 1.355 of December 30, 1994.

[75] Los Angeles Times (1993) New Rules for global trade Reaction. http://articles.latimes.com/1993-12-16/news/mn-2416_1_global-trade.

considerable real income and effective demand, increased production and trade in goods and services, while allowing for the optimum utilization of world resources [...]".[76]

This has opened spaces for maneuvering in the regulation of the WTO, with the interests of the more powerful states prevailing. As in law in general, the construction of international trade law "has traditionally been instrumentalized by forms of power to assert their preferences in international economic organization".[77]

For the poorest countries to convert to the hegemonic economic thinking that prevailed during the WTO negotiations, the rich countries linked economic development to free trade, which in turn would naturally trigger social, legal and political development, reducing inequality among countries.[78]

There was also the idea that market economy, as dictated by the Washington Consensus, was the only solution to the economic crisis in developing countries caused by internal factors such as totalitarianism and nationalist policies.[79] This would only be possible if states transferred their respective sovereignty over fiscal and monetary policy issues to international organizations, since the image of developing states was tarnished because they were seen as the cause of economic crises.

In Sella's words: "the administration of the multilateral trading system resulting from this Round is now in charge of the World Trade Organization and was a response to the neo-protectionism that characterized the 1970s and 1980s".[80]

According to Batista's conclusions, the Washington Consensus "implicitly reveals the inclination to subordinate, if necessary, the political to the economic".[81] Therefore, if in liberalism the Law "did not get its hands dirty" to regulate the economy, in neoliberalism, it can be said that both Law and politics constitute its instruments.

Internal Law loses its space as society's sole regulator, since the State can no longer cope with the complexity of today's society, which pressures it to accept economic precepts that are in constant internationalization. On the other hand, there is still the rancor of sovereignty, which makes it even more difficult to produce norms at the international level.

In an interview, José Eduardo Faria points out that the result is a "decision-making pluralism, a situation of legal pluralism (multi-level legal governance)," a space in which customary Law, international Law, *lex mercatoria*, integration and domestic law will coexist, known in sociology as "semi-autonomous normative fields: the state provides autonomy but retains for itself the regulatory frameworks.[82]

---

[76] Marrakech Accords. http://www.wto.org/english/docs_e/legal_e/legal_e.htm#finalact.

[77] Sanchez (2004), pp 78–79.

[78] In this sense, see our work: Fais (2006) In: Barral and Pimentel (2006), p. 114.

[79] Batista (1994), p. 7.

[80] Sella   (2010)   http://www.anima-opet.com.br/pdf/anima4-Estrangeiro/anima4-Luis-Felipe-Sella.pdf.

[81] Ibid, p. 10.

[82] Faria   (2011)   http://rafazanatta.blogspot.com.br/2011/10/entrevista-de-jose-eduardo-faria-ao.html.

The end of the Cold War caused the restructuring of the state in the sense of deregulation, since it expanded the number of agents involved in international trade, which are no longer limited to the spheres of states. According to Sanchez, this restructuring:

> [...] provides an increase in the importance of regulation in the interstate space, from the perspective of cooperation. The WTO is therefore required to be more responsive when regulating the multilateral trading system and as a promoter of balance among its members.[83]

Given this scenario, it can be said that the contradictions of neoliberal thought have been transferred to the WTO, whose regulation has served as a backdrop for both the promotion of liberalism and protectionism. Barral acknowledges that "multilateral trade regulation has adopted, both throughout its history and in the current round of negotiations, simplistic assumptions about the effects of trade liberalization on development."[84]

After 5 years of the WTO, developing countries have not developed as their governments had hoped and so they have considered a new Round of Negotiations, the so-called Doha Round or Development Round, which began in November 2001, in order to consider the interests of the poorest countries.

Somewhat optimistically, former WTO Director-General Pascal Lamy stated that "[...] the challenge of the coming decades will be the convergence of collective preferences"[85] and that the globalized version of capitalism may cooperate to this convergence because of the approximation of values among members.[86]

Even in the face of the terrorist attacks that occurred on September 11, 2001, at the time, Robert Zoellick, United States Trade Representative reaffirmed the importance of free trade to the world:

> [...] new barriers and closing of old borders will not help the poorest. It will not feed hundreds of millions struggling for subsistence. It won't free the persecuted. It will not improve the environment in developing countries or reverse the spread of AIDS. It will not help the orphans I visited in India. It will not improve the livelihoods of the trade unionists I met in Latin America. It won't help the committed Indonesians I visited who are trying to build a tolerant, working democracy in the world's largest Muslim nation [...].[87]

---

[83] Sanchez (2004), p. 98.

[84] Barral and Pimentel (2006), p. 1.

[85] Free translation from: "l'enjeu principal des décennies à venir est désormais celui de la convergence des préférences collectives." In: Lamy (2014) http://entempsreel.com/wp-content/uploads/2014/07/Pascal-Lamy-En-temps-r%C3%A9el.pdf, p. 3.

[86] Lamy (2014), p. 4.

[87] Free adaptation from: "Erecting new barriers and closing old borders will not help the impoverished. It will not feed hundreds of millions struggling for subsistence. It will not liberate the persecuted. It will not improve the environment in developing countries or reverse the spread of AIDS. It will not help the railway orphans I visited in India. It will not improve the livelihoods of the union members I met in Latin America. It will not aid the committed Indonesians I visited who are trying to build a functioning, tolerant democracy in the largest Muslim nation in the world". In: World Trade Organization. Preparations for the fourth WTO Ministerial Conference (2001). http://www.wto.org/english/news_e/spmm_e/spmm72_e.htm.

Freedom of trade has already been consolidated as a common value among WTO members, since the market economy, in principle, enables fair competition, the elimination of price distortions, making the balance between supply and demand, in an efficient manner, without any intervention that leads to trade detour and, therefore, capable of promoting economic development and social welfare.

The opening up of trade serves as an instrument for the stability of relations between States, while its barriers destabilize them, promoting conflict. Montesquieu already said that peace is the natural effect of trade. For him: "[…] Two nations that negotiate become mutually dependent. If one has an interest in buying, [the] other has an interest in selling, and all unions are founded on mutual needs."[88]

However, the solution is not magic. It should be considered that international trade is dominated by large companies from developed countries, while in developing countries smaller companies prevail, which causes market imbalance. In addition, in the current scenario, the fragmentation of production allows leading companies to exert greater influence over the industrial policy of States, by seeking places where they can produce efficiently. This reality leads to subsidy competition between governments to attract investment.

To better understand what this means, the next section will discuss the theories behind free trade and then its shortcomings, as well as the influence of subsidies on free trade.

1.3   Economic Theories That Support Free Trade

Considering that resources are limited, states participate in international trade in search of benefits, producing what they do best with the factors of production[89] available. This allows them to produce on a large scale, exporting the surplus[90] and importing goods that they cannot produce or whose production would be extremely costly. Investing in scarce resources implies costs that could be used to produce other goods with comparative advantage.

In this sense, it goes back to the ideas of David Ricardo, who, inspired by Smith's theory of absolute advantage, introduced the concept of comparative advantage at the beginning of the nineteenth century. According to Smith's theory, a country should import the products of countries with an efficient industry, which would be paid for with the values derived from the exports of goods produced in an equally efficient way by its domestic industry. For Smith:

---

[88] Montesquieu (1985), p. 284.

[89] The factors of production are nature, labor, capital, technology, and entrepreneurship.

[90] Exporters, instead of exporting only the surplus, can choose to export the entire production to a market where it obtains better demand.

Table 1.1 Amount of work spent on production, in man-years

Discrimination	Portugal	England
Wine (barrel)	80	120
Cloth (piece)	90	100
Wine/cloth price	80/90 = 0.888...	120/100 = 1.20
Cloth/wine price	90/50 = 1125	100/120 = 0.8333...

Source: Author

[…] if a foreign country can supply us with a commodity more cheaply than we can produce it ourselves, we had better buy it from him with some part of the product of our own industry, employed in a way by which we have some advantage. […].[91]

However, the theory is not sufficient to explain cases in which the country does not have an absolute advantage in any product. If, hypothetically, one country produces cloth and wine under better conditions than another, there would be no trade between these countries because the former has an absolute advantage in both products.

The Ricardian model improved this theory, starting to compare the opportunity cost instead of the necessary inputs for production. The opportunity cost of a product A in relation to B represents how much of A could be produced with the resources used to produce B. Thus, a country could manufacture more of product A, using the resources needed to manufacture a smaller amount of B, which would give it a comparative advantage in producing A over B.[92]

The tendency is for countries to specialize in goods in which they have comparative advantages, allowing everyone to gain from trade, expanding consumer choice.[93] The classic example brought by Ricardo compares the production of wine and cloth in Portugal and England as follows in Table 1.1.

Considering that, in Portugal, the production of a barrel of wine requires only 80 days of work, while in England it would require 120 days, if compared with the production of cloth, it would be more profitable for Portugal to invest most of its resources in the production of wine, even if the cloth costs less than in England, since, by investing its capital in wine, it could obtain more cloth from England than if it used part of it to produce cloth. In this way, England would also benefit, since it would concentrate on cloth production and obtain the wine for 100 days of work, which would cost it 120 to produce it domestically.[94]

In this way, the producer, in this case, Portugal, which gives up less amount of fabrics to produce more wine, enjoys a lower opportunity cost of producing this good. Thus, the opportunity cost to produce fabric is inverse to the cost to produce

---

[91] Smith (1988), p. 424.

[92] This situation was regulated in the Methuen Treaty concluded in 1703 by England and Portugal, in which the Portuguese committed themselves to consuming British textiles, which, in turn, should consume Portuguese wines.

[93] Krugman and Obstfeld (2010), pp. 27–28.

[94] Ricardo (1982), pp. 104–105.

wine. It is these differences that, according to Ricardo, create the gains from trade. When each economic agent specializes in the good in which it has comparative advantage, the increase of total production in the economy occurs, benefiting people who can obtain the good at a price lower than its opportunity cost.

Note that Ricardo considers only one resource as capable of influencing the opportunity cost, labor. However, other production factors can also exert significant influence on this calculation, such as: natural resources (land, ores, rivers), capital (material and immaterial resources) and technology, but nothing prevents the application of the explicit theory.

In this way, Ricardo considered that international trade was beneficial to countries and the competitiveness it caused was positive. As a member of the British Parliament, he applied his theory in opposition to the law that restricted the import of grain.[95]

Regarding the Ricardian theory, Krugman warns that, although they have unrealistic aspects, the "[...] Its basic prediction – that countries will tend to export the goods in which they have relatively high productivity – has been confirmed by several studies.".[96] Thus, even considering two or more factors of production, "[...] An economy will tend to be relatively effective in producing goods that are intensive in the factors with which the country is relatively well endowed".[97]

In view of this, two reasons lead countries to trade: the different resources allow countries to specialize in what they do best and, consequently, to be able to produce in scale, which makes specialization of production or provision of services advantageous.

Stuart Mill refined the Ricardian model by showing that the true terms of trade are determined by the intensity and elasticity[98] of demand of each country.[99] The limits of the demand present in the terms of trade cause prices to change until the equilibrium point is reached.

Eli Heckscher and Bertil Ohlin sought to overcome the limitations of the Ricardian model, which was later consolidated by Paul Samuelson and became known as the Hecksher–Ohli–Samuelson model.[100] Both labor and capital are considered factors of production, whose endowment is relatively different in countries, justifying international trade. Thus, a country will export the product it uses intensively according to the factor it has an abundance of, be it capital or labor.

---

[95] Silva (2003), pp. 15–42.

[96] Krugman and Obstfeld (2010), p. 38.

[97] Ibid, p. 48.

[98] Concept created by Marshall which quantifies the variation effect of a variable in another. Therefore, the elasticity of the demand constitutes of the ratio between the offered demand variation percentage over the price variation percentage. When the offered demand variation is superior to the price variation, it is said that the demand is elastic, while it will be inelastic when the offered demand variation is inferior to the price variation. In: Marshall (1982).

[99] Ellsworth (1973), p. 74.

[100] See: Appleyard et al. (2010), pp. 127–134.

x	100	90	80	70	60	50	40	30	20	10	0
y	0	10	20	60	40	50	60	70	80	90	100

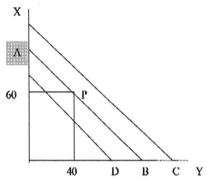

AB = possibilidade de produção
A = 100 de x e 0 de y
B = 0 de x e 100 de y
P = 60 de x e 40 de y
C = além da possibilidade (100)
D = aquém da possibilidade

Subtitles: AB = Production Possibility, A = 100 OF X AND 0 OF Y, B = 0 OF X AND 100 OF Y, P = 60 OF X AND 40 OF Y, C = over the possibility (100), D = under the possibility

Fig. 1.1 Opportunity cost of producing x and y. Source: Author. Subtitles: AB = Production Possibility, A = 100 OF X AND 0 OF Y, B = 0 OF X AND 100 OF Y, P = 60 OF X AND 40 OF Y, C = over the possibility (100), D = under the possibility

Modern international trade theory has replaced the comparative labor cost of Smith's and Ricardo's theories with comparative opportunity cost, ascertained through the simultaneous analysis of all factors of production. Suppose that country A is using 100% of its productive capacity to produce either good x or y. Depending on the opportunity cost, it can choose to produce more x or y, or produce only x and import y,[101] as shown in the Fig. 1.1.

To reach point C, it is necessary to increase production and make better use of resources. At point D, there is a drop in production and the economy is working with idle capacity. Finally, the substitution of x for y, and vice versa, depends on the opportunity cost.

However, the assumption that production takes place under the condition of constant costs and that factors of production can be substituted without loss of efficiency is a misconception, because in the real world, country A may be more abundant in one factor of production, such as land, which is suitable for food production, while capital, which is suitable in manufacturing production, may be more abundant in another country B.

Under these circumstances, even if all the land was already cultivated, food production could still be expanded in country A by the more intensive application of capital and labor, but production would not increase proportionately. In country B,

---

[101] Maia (2011) p. 355.

it would be possible to raise production by increasing labor in the absence of extra capital, but yields would be lower. Given this, it can be stated that the substitution of production factors does not generate proportional growth, nor is it perfect.[102]

It is important to mention that market prices are not only determined by means of the factors of production but are also based on demand. Thus, if for each unit of product x it is possible to produce one unit of y, but in the market 1 unit of x is exchanged for 2 of y, it would be more profitable to take off the resources for the production of y in order to produce x. Therefore, if country A is producing x at a ratio of $2y = 1x$ and country B produces at a ratio of $1y = 2x$, product y is cheaper in A and product x in B. In a situation of free trade between them, A would import product y in exchange for x and B, vice versa. The increase in foreign demand due to the opening of trade will cause the exchange value of cheap products to increase and thus a new price, determined internationally, which could be $1y = 1x$.[103]

Consequently, the increase in demand will raise the production of y of country A, while B will increase the production of x, until a new equilibrium point is reached, at which opportunity costs are equal to international commodity prices, provided that reciprocal demand is balanced.[104]

In this scenario, consumers would benefit from the lower prices of imported goods, which before the opening of trade, were higher, which restricted the consumer's purchasing power.

There is still a variable that deserves to be highlighted: generally, countries do not stop producing a commodity only to import it, since, in reality, costs are not constant, but increasing. Therefore, domestic production will compete with foreign production.

Considering that international trade has an influence on the relative prices of goods, as well as on the remunerations of resources and, consequently, on income distribution, the Heckscher-Ohlin-Samuelson model, when analyzing the influence of trade on income, added that the complete equalization of prices is not possible due to differences in resources, barriers and technology, which are variable from one country to another. Thus, in trade there are winners and losers, whose losses must be compensated.

In any case, market equilibrium is important and should be pursued by nations. According to Stigler,[105] this equilibrium is found when the quantity of supply is equivalent to the quantity of demand. As can be seen in Fig. 1.2, where price and quantity are P and Q respectively, while S is the supply curve and D the demand curve, any variable that is not on the supply/demand axis, such as subsidies and compensatory measures,[106] is able to shift the curve to the left or right.

---

[102] Ellsworth (1973), p. 87.

[103] Ibid, p. 92.

[104] Ibid, p. 93.

[105] Stigler (1977), p. 183.

[106] Compensatory measures are practices to counterbalance the effects of subsidies in the internal market and imply an increase in taxation on the import of subsidized products.

Fig. 1.2 Market
equilibrium (Source:
Author)

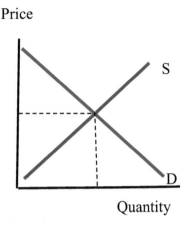

Given that not everyone gains from trade, although everyone, in theory, could win, Stiglitz[107] warns that both the economy and its regulation should not be projected into an ideal world, but into the real world. And in the real world, Krugman points out, "the existence of people who lose as well as those who gain from trade is one of the most important reasons why trade is not free".[108] To Bhagwati:

> If market prices reflect "real" or social costs, then clearly Adam Smith's invisible hand can be relied upon to guide us to efficiency; and free trade can correspondingly be the best way for trade (and associated domestic production). But if markets do not function well or are absent or incomplete, the invisible hand may point in the wrong direction: free trade cannot then be asserted as the best policy.[109]

Smith's and Ricardo's models could be useful in a market that operates under practically perfect conditions, with small companies and a single factor of production: labor. The reality of today's world, composed of large corporations, run by executives and no longer by owners, operates under imperfect market conditions. The scenario is much more complex, with the interventionist state coexisting with the "invisible hand" of the market.[110] In view of this:

> The assumption of the Washington Consensus would seem to be that Latin American countries would be able to compete in the export of primary products for which they have a natural vocation and/or in manufactured products on the basis of low-wage unskilled labor. As if it were possible or desirable to perpetuate comparative advantages based on a socially unjust and economically backward situation and, at the same time, confront the visible dark

[107] Stiglitz (2003), p. 194.

[108] Krugman and Obstfeld (2010), p. 56.

[109] Free adaptation from: "If market prices reflect true or social costs, then clearly Adam Smith's invisible hand can be trusted to guide us to efficiency; and free trade can correspondingly be shown to be the optimal way to choose trade (and associated domestic production). But if markets do not work well, or are absent or incomplete, then the invisible hand may point in the wrong direction: free trade cannot then be asserted to be the best policy". In: Bhagwati (2003), p. 12.

[110] Batista (1994), p. 19.

clouds of protectionism that are beginning to appear on the horizon of the markets of the developed countries, in the name of what they already classify as "social dumping".[111]

While Smith's and Ricardo's theories are still used by economists to support the argument for free trade, they are not sufficient to support today's economic reality.

Later, Schumpeter[112] He recognized that market freedom would produce side effects, such as monopolies, which, in his view, were not harmful. The monopolies only shifted competition to another level, in this case, innovation and management, which was beneficial for economic development and, therefore, state intervention was not desirable.

On the other hand, post-Keynesian theorists such as Joan Violet Robinson and Edward Chamberlin argue for the need for state intervention in situations of market imperfections to increase aggregate demand, creating a safe and stable environment for investment.[113]

However, today's economic reality is not driven by a completely free market structure or free of imperfections and, therefore, its study becomes much more complex than the assumptions of neoclassical theories.

1.3.1 Imperfect Market Structures

Despite the different impacts that free trade can have on society, it is still seen as a "game" in which everyone wins. According to the economic theories that underlie it, free trade could maximize the prosperity of countries.

The perfect market is one in which the goods offered are equals and the sellers and buyers are numerous to the point of having no influence on prices, for there is no single specific buyer or seller.[114] However, it must be considered that there are imperfections that can trigger adverse effects.

Considering that the perfect market does not exist, due to the influence of political and economic factors that distort its ideal conditions, it can be stated that these failures compromise the ability of the market to make efficient use of available resources.

Examples of economic factors that create market imperfections are transaction costs, information asymmetry, concentration of economic power, etc. As political factors, the following state interventions can be mentioned: subsidies, taxes, price and wage controls, etc., which, at the same time that they serve as instruments to correct market failures, can generate new distortions.

---

[111] Ibid, p. 22.

[112] Schumpeter (1982).

[113] See: Oreiro and Paula (2003) Pós-keynesianos e o Intervencionismo Estatal. http://www.ie.ufrj.br/moeda/pdfs/pos_keynesianos_e_o_intervencionismo_estatal.pdf.

[114] Mankiw (2009), p. 64.

Table 1.4 Main market structures according to J. Marshall. Source: Rossetti JP (1994)[a]

ATOMIZED STRUCTURE				
DEMAND/SUPPLY	MONOLITHIC STRUCTURE One Seller	MOLECULAR STRUCTURE Few Sellers	Many sellers with Viscosity	Many sellers with Fluidity
MONOLITHIC STRUCTURE A single buyer	Bilateral monopoly	Counterfeit monopsony	Viscous monopoly	Fluid Monopsion
MOLECULAR STRUCTURE Few buyers	Counterfeit monopoly	Bilateral oligopoly	Viscous Olipsonium	Fluid Olipsonium
ATOMIZED STRUCTURE many buyers with viscosity	Viscous monopoly	Viscous oligopoly	Twofold imperfect competition	Imperfect competition of buyers

[a]Rossetti (1994), p. 287

International trade gives consumers access to a wider range of goods for consumption. However, this model transforms the reality of the market, which now has to deal with imperfect competition, generated by the presence of market power, as shown in Table 1.4.

Monopolies occur when there is only one seller, while in oligopolies there are few sellers who do not always compete aggressively. In monopolies there is only one buyer, and in oligopolies there are few buyers. There are also competitive monopolies formed by many vendors offering differentiated products.[115]

It is noted that in all cases of imperfect market conditions, there is the influence of market power through one or a few agents, either in supply or demand. For competition to be perfect, both must be atomized, that is, market power must be absent in supply and demand.

Market failures, also known as market power, are caused by the economy of scale format that generates monopolistic markets and, consequently, the situation of imperfect competition. This is because the economy of scale[116] allows countries to restrict production variety by specializing in a few goods that will be produced on a larger scale than if they had to produce all consumer goods, which allows costs to be reduced.[117]

Economies of scale can operate in two ways: external and internal. The first occurs when the cost per unit depends on the size of the sector and not necessarily of the company, and the second occurs in exactly the opposite case. As an example of the former, suppose an industry with ten firms, each producing one hundred units. If the industry grows to twenty firms, each firm will still produce the same hundred units, but the cost may be lower, increasing the efficiency of the firms. In the second

---

[115] Mankiw (2009).

[116] By economy of scale, it is meant that by doubling resources, production would more than double and the cost per unit produced would be reduced.

[117] Krugman and Obstfeld (2010), p. 88.

case, suppose the industry's output is constant at one thousand units, but the number of firms has been reduced to five, with each firm producing two hundred units. By reducing costs, the firm will be efficient only by increasing its production.[118]

International trade will be mutually beneficial depending on the market structures and whether they operate in perfect competition or not. It is easy to identify the problem in internal economies of scale, since in external ones, firms are usually small and therefore may approach perfect competition. Internally, the existence of larger companies will make the market imperfect, since, by seeking to reduce costs and differentiate their products, they acquire advantages over smaller ones, influencing international prices, thus causing the situation of imperfect competition.

However, competition can also be imperfect in external economies of scale. This occurs when country A has sufficient capacity to supply all international demand at a relatively low price and sufficient to block the entry of the product of country B, which, in turn, could supply its domestic market at a lower price, if there were no trade in A. As a result, country B tends to adopt protectionist measures in favor of its industry.[119]

Introducing imperfect competition into the idea of comparative advantages means considering that, due to the economy of scale, even in the case of a differentiated product, that is, in monopolistic competition, countries do not have total productive capacity on the goods in which they obtain the greatest advantage and, therefore, intra-industry trade, in which there is a two-way exchange of goods, will remain.

Comparative advantage is most evident in inter-industry trade, where, for example, the country with abundant capital exports the goods produced by the efficient use of this resource and imports products from countries with abundant labor. This type of trade hardly ever takes place within the same sector due to the differences in production factors.[120]

The economy of scale, unlike neoclassical theories that presuppose perfect market conditions, recognizes that large companies have advantages over small ones and, consequently, those become monopolies or oligopolies, exerting direct influence on prices, presupposing the existence of imperfect competition.

These monopolies occur due to the specialization of companies in relation to products, turning them into unique, making each company take the prices of its competitors only as data and ignoring the effect of its own price on the prices of the others. Such a situation leads to market inefficiency since the average costs exceed the minimum costs.

However, international trade is not restricted to inter-industrial relations, but also refers to intra-industrial relations, that is, the country can export and import the same product. This is due to the economy of scale, transportation costs and the

---

[118] Ibid, p. 89.
[119] Ibid, p. 108.
[120] Krugman and Obstfeld (2010), pp. 98–99.

diversity of the same product, such as vehicles, as each company seeks to individualize them to the point of making them unique in relation to the others.

It is noted that the power that an agent or an economic group exercise over the market through monopolies causes significant impacts on prices, harming third parties external to the group. In this situation, it appears that the market does not operate under conditions of perfect competition.

In addition to imperfect competition, there are other failures that can compromise free trade. These are: a) public goods; b) asymmetric information; c) externalities. The problem with public goods, since they are not exclusive, that is, they are meant for everyone, the consumption of some does not harm the consumption of others. On the other hand, information asymmetry allows some to have greater access to it than others.

Thus, free trade is still desirable due to the benefits provided, but state intervention must be allowed, if they are intended to correct market failures.[121] State interventions become necessary to induce the occurrence of positive externalities and prevent negative ones, thus promoting social welfare.

However, new forms of production, arising with the development of globalization and the opening of trade, impose new challenges to the economic policies of countries.

1.3.2   Industrial Policy and the New Comparative Advantage

The economic reality of the twenty-first century challenges not only states,[122] but the WTO, due to the prevalence of the concept of sovereignty in its classical sense. While the WTO is still run by sovereign governments, trade is also influenced by *market actors.*[123]

In addition, the fragmentation of production, known as global value chains (*global value chains*), generated a new form of organization of the world space to produce goods, which is subdivided to achieve more favorable conditions for profit. The technology of production, communication, and transport, as well as the standardization of consumer goods, has made distances decrease and international business accelerate, making it increasingly interconnected, expanding the opportunities

---

[121] Krugman and Obstfeld (2010), pp. 180–181.

[122] In this sense, Souza points out that trade can no longer wait for national legal institutions, which do not "effectively impact investments by comparing, on a global scale, the relevant production conditions". In: Silva (2010), p. 55.

[123] According to Sanchez, market actors are those non-state actors that have specific interests regarding production and consumption, such as: producers, investors, traders, both small companies and large transnational corporations. In: Sanchez (2013) http://www.geocities.ws/cesario-pereira/mestrado/AtoresnaoestataiseaOMC.doc.

for participation in the international production chain.[124] Hoekman, points out that most of the world's growth stems from intra-industry trade in intermediate inputs.[125] For him:

> Ever-declining costs of trade and information and telecommunications have allowed companies to geographically divide their "production lines", to design international supply chains that allocate different parts of the production process to companies in different countries.[126]

In this sense, it can be said that the theory of comparative advantage takes on a new guise. Faced with the possibility of taking advantage of the best that each country has to offer, the industry no longer carries out the entire production process and begins to adopt the fragmented system. By focusing on specific jobs that form part of the international chain, fragmentation makes it possible to reduce costs and increase competitiveness.

In this new scenario, "the ability to participate depends not only on the capacity and competitiveness of companies, but also on the environment in which they operate".[127] This reality puts states in competition for foreign investment to expand their participation in international trade.

This search for a more favorable environment to achieve production efficiency puts States at the disposal of industry for the realization of its economic and social purposes, impacting on the adoption of industrial policies, either to attract investment or even to manage eventual market failures caused by the absence of criteria to legitimize efficiency in the adoption of these policies by competing States. According to Amaral:

> The evolution of GVCs reflects the international fragmentation of production and proposes considerations regarding the economic and trade policies adopted by the countries, since they directly affect the economic performance and the gain/loss of benefits derived from the participation or not in GVCs.[128]

Industrial policies can be horizontal or specific. The former are applied without favoritism, with implications for the entire economy in general and, for this reason, are more costly for the State. The latter stimulate and apply incentives in specific sectors, often with the justification of remedying market failures.[129]

---

[124]Low and Tijaja (2014) http://www.fungglobalinstitute.org/en/working-paper-effective-industrial-policies-and-global-value-chains.

[125]Hoekman (2014) http://papers.ssrn.com/sol3/papers.cfm?abstract_id=2406871, p. 27.

[126]Free adaptation from: "Steadily declining costs of trade and information and telecommunications have permitted firms to geographically splinter their 'production lines,' designing international supply chains that allocate different parts of the production process to firms in different countries". In: Hoekman (2014), p. 27.

[127]Free adaptation from: "The capacity to participate depends not only on the capabilities and competitiveness of firms but also on the environment in which they operate". In: Low and Tijaja (2014), p. 2.

[128]Amaral. https://bmj.com.br/cadeias-globais-de-valor-e-omc-win-win-game-2/.

[129]Low and Tijaja (2014), p. 4.

Examples of specific policies include import substitution, export-oriented industrialization, resource-based industrialization, export processing zones, and industrialization through innovation. All, without exception, depend on some form of subsidy, even if to varying degrees, producing, in turn, effects on free trade.

It is evident that this new reality leads to greater interdependence among States, which, to stay in the game, are forced to adopt new policies for the development of infrastructure and technology, as well as foreign investment. To this end, governments may change the tax system, adopt protectionist measures or grant subsidies.

References

Amaral RV. Cadeias globais de valor e OMC: win-win game. http://www.barralmjorge.com.br/pagina.php?id=965

Appleyard DR, Field JAJ, Cobb SL, Lima AF (2010) Economia Internacional, 4th edn. McGraw Hill, Nova Iorque, pp 127–134

Barral W, Pimentel LO (2006) Comércio Internacional e Desenvolvimento. Boiteux, Florianópolis, p 1

Batista PN (1994) Consenso de Washington: a visão neoliberal dos problemas latino-americanos. http://www.fau.usp.br/cursos/graduacao/arq_urbanismo/disciplinas/aup0270/4dossie/nogueira94/nog94-cons-washn.pdf. pp 6–7, 18–19, 22

Bechara CHT, Redenschi R (2002) A Solução de Controvérsias no Mercosul e na OMC. Customs, São Paulo, p 65

Bhagwati J (2003) Free trade today. Princeton University Press, p 12

Bonfim D (2011) Tributação e Livre Concorrência. Saraiva, São Paulo, p 85

Dal Ri JA (2004) História do Direito Internacional. Florianópolis, Fundação Boiteux, pp 61, 65, 70, 84–90, 101–102, 113, 136

Ellsworth PT (1973) Economia Internacional: teoria e prática, desde o mercantilismo até a formação do mercado comum europeu. 2ª ed. São Paulo, Atlas, pp 74, 87, 92–93

Fais JM (2006) The World Trade Organization and development. In: Barral W, Pimentel LO (eds) Comércio internacional e Desenvolvimento. Boiteux, Florianópolis, p 114

Faria JE (2011) O comercialista: a entrevista de José Eduardo Faria. http://rafazanatta.blogspot.com.br/2011/10/entrevista-de-jose-eduardo-faria-ao.html

Friedman M (1995) Capitalismo e Liberdade. Paz e Terra, São Paulo

Garcia JM (2002) International trade; theory and technique. Editora Universidad de Granada, Granada. pp 19, 27–29, 31

Hayek FAV (1990) O Caminho da Servidão. 5th edn. Liberal Institute, Rio de Janeiro, pp 25–26, 68–69

Hobsbawm E (1995) A Era dos Extremos. Companhia das Letras, São Paulo, p 413

Hoekman B (2014) Supply Chains, Mega-Regionals and Multilateralism: a roadp map for the WTO. http://papers.ssrn.com/sol3/papers.cfm?abstract_id=2406871, p 27

Hoekman B, Kostecki M (2009) The political economy of the world trading system: the WTO and beyond. Oxford, New York, kindle edition, position 442

Hunt EK, Sherman HJ (1999) História do Pensamento Econômico. 17th edn. Petrópolis, Vozes, pp 33, 36, 107–108, 118, 164, 189–190

Keynes JM (1982) A Teoria do Emprego, do Juro e da Moeda. Atlas, São Paulo, p 129

Krugman P, Obstfeld M (2010) Economia Internacional: teoria e política. 8ª edn. Pearson Prentice Hall, São Paulo, pp 27–28, 38, 48, 56, 88–89, 98–99, 108, 180–181

Lamy P (2014) L'Organisation mondiale du commerce. http://entempsreel.com/wp-content/uploads/2014/07/Pascal-Lamy-En-temps-r%C3%A9el.pdf. pp 3–4

Low P, Tijaja J (2014) Effective industrial policies and global value chains. http://www.fungglobalinstitute.org/en/working-paper-effective-industrial-policies-and-global-value-chains, p 4

Lupi ALPB (2001) Soberania, OMC e Mercosul. Customs, São Paulo, pp 89–90

Magnus JR (2004) World Trade Organization subsidy discipline: is the "Retrenchment Round"? J World Trade 38(6):985. https://doi.org/10.54648/trad2004041

Maia JM (2011) Economia Internacional e Comércio Exterior. Atlas, São Paulo, pp 93, 355

Mankiw GN (2009) Introdução a economia. Cengage Learning, São Paulo, pp 64–65

Mark K (1980) O Manifesto Comunista. CHED, São Paulo

Marshall A (1982) Princípios de Economia Política, Tratado Introdutório. Abril Cultural, São Paulo

Mises LV (1990) Ação Humana: um tratado de economia. Liberal Institute, Rio de Janeiro, pp 256–257

Montchretien A (1615) Traitè de L'économique politique

Montesquieu (1985) Do Espírito das Leis. Coleção 'Os Pensadores'. Abril Cultural, São Paulo, p 284

Negrão JJ (1998) Para conhecer o Neoliberalismo. Publisher Brasil, São Paulo, p 41

Oreiro JL, Paula LF (2003) Pós-keynesianos e o Intervencionismo Estatal. http://www.ie.ufrj.br/moeda/pdfs/pos_keynesianos_e_o_intervencionismo_estatal.pdf

Pareto V (1996) Manual de Economia Política. Nova Cultural, São Paulo, p 13

Petersman EU (1997) The Gatt/Wto dispute settlement system: international law, international organizations and dispute settlement. Martinus Nijhoff Publishers, London, p 66

Pigou AC (2013) The economics of welfare. Palgrave Macmillan, Houndmills

Pureza JM (2001) Para um internacionalismo pós-vestfaliano. http://www.eurozine.com/articles/article_2002-04-26-pureza-pt.html

Ricardo D (1982) Princípios de Economia Política e Tributação. Nova Cultural, São Paulo, pp 104–105

Rossetti JP (1994) Introdução à Economia, 16th edn. Atlas, São Paulo, p 287

Sanchez MR (2004) Demandas por um novo arcabouço sociojurídico na organização mundial do comércio e o caso do Brasil. Thesis, Law School of the State of São Paulo, pp 54, 56, 59–62, 78–79, 98

Sanchez MR (2013) Atores Não-estatais e sua Relação com a Organização Mundial do Comércio. http://www.geocities.ws/cesariopereira/mestrado/AtoresnaoestataiseaOMC.doc

Schumpeter JA (1982) A Teoria do Desenvolvimento Econômico: uma investigação sobre os lucros, capital, crédito, juro e o ciclo econômico. Abril Cultural, São Paulo

Sella LFC (2010) A Organização Mundial do Comércio: histórico e aspectos a reforma. http://www.anima-opet.com.br/pdf/anima4-Estrangeiro/anima4-Luis-Felipe-Sella.pdf, p 10

Silva KS (2010) Globalização e Exclusão Social. Curitiba, Juruá, pp 26, 34, 55

Silva TS (2003) Notas sobre a Economia Ricardiana. Revista PUC/SP 13:15–42

Smith A (1996) A Riqueza das Nações. Nova Cultural, São Paulo, pp 43, 379–380, 424

Smith A (1988) Riqueza das nações. Nova Cultural, São Paulo, p 424

Stigler GJ (1977) A Teoria dos Preços. Atlas, São Paulo, p 183

Stiglitz JE (2003) Globalization and its discontents. Norton, New York, pp 172, 194

Chapter 2
The Economic Analysis of Law (EAL)

Abstract The Economic Analysis of Law (EAL) provides those responsible for applying the law a method to verify how it works on individuals' behaviors and its efficiency. That means, based on the assumption that there is a certain rationality in the conduct of individuals, EAL makes it possible to investigate decision making in the face of a given legal rule. The EAL efficiency concept doesn't imply the substitution of the justice criterion by efficiency, but rather as an option for applying the law since it is known that every inefficient rule is unfair, although the opposite not necessarily occurs. Also, international institutions play a significant role when it comes to reducing costs and they influence negotiation and compliance. This way, EAL allows understanding the complex reality of political-economic subsidy strategies in the WTO and to rethink its mechanisms to counter distortive subsidies, specially, by least developed and developing countries. The study suggests that the social criteria should be added to efficiency by which negative externalities shall be considered in its calculation.

The EAL provides it with instruments of microeconomics[1] to better understand the implications of legal phenomena in society. Through these, the behavior patterns of individuals and states in the face of a given legal norm are verified. It can be defined as "the application of economic theory and econometric methods to examine the formation, structure, processes and influence of law and legal institutions".[2]

It is noted that the method adopted by Economics is deductive, that is, it makes assumptions about human behavior and deduces their implications on specific issues, applicable to any legal issue.[3]

---

[1] "Microeconomics is the study of how scarce resources are allocated between ends that are alternative to each other and [...] concerns the decisions made by individuals and small groups, such as families, companies and government agencies". In: Cooter and Ulen (2010), p. 35.

[2] Free translation from: "[...] aplicación de la teoría económica y de los métodos econométricos para examinar la formación, estructura, procesos e influencia de la ley y de las instituciones jurídicas". In: Roemer (1994), pp. 5–6.

[3] Stephen (1993), p. 2.

J. Marteli Fais Feriato, *Legal, Political and Economic Strategies of Subsidies within the World Trade Organization*, European Yearbook of International Economic Law 40, https://doi.org/10.1007/978-3-031-73869-2_2

Although the use of economic concepts by Law dates to the late Middle Ages and early modern times, with Machiavelli, Hobbes and Locke, the dialogue between Law and Economics began with Adam Smith, when he studied the effects of mercantilist rules on the economy. Then, Jeremy Bentham, when analyzing the laws that regulated markets, found that the maximizing rationality of individuals could be applied to all areas of law, including criminal Law.

However, the EAL movement developed among economists only at the end of the 1950s in the United States, and among jurists it became accepted at the beginning of the 1970s, and its expansion took place in the early 1980s, based on political economy and the doctrinal current of legal realism. The first came with Adam Smith, who conducted a study on the regulation of markets. The second appeared in the Law schools of the United States, because of the crisis of the *Welfare State* supported by Keynes, with the aim of studying the functioning of laws, recognizing the need for Law to be concerned with the practical implications of legal norms.

The change in the world scenario, especially from the 1980s onwards, brought to the fore the new liberalism, which, by preaching minimal intervention by the State, required a new model of analysis of the Law, more convergent to reality.

Economics, then, came to be seen as a method capable of providing Law with a "unique and rational criterion to achieve the possible task, according to given conditions, as opposed to the idealized but often unattainable task, due to its lack of commitment to the real world".[4]

Starting from the assumption that economic agents act rationally,[5] according to the normative stimuli, the EAL enables the inductive function of the norms, that is, of *legal-persuasive law*[6] and presents itself as a method for evaluating its effects on society, in line with the values of Law. This means that, based on the assumption that there is a certain rationality in the conduct of individuals, EAL makes it possible to investigate possible decision making in the face of a given legal rule, as well as whether the rule is efficient regarding the observance of legal values.

Considering that the reality studied by the Social Sciences is one, Economics, as an analytical science, is of great use for Law, by providing it with an analytical method that allows the investigation of interests, verifying the influence of norms on the conduct of both individuals and States.[7] The application of economic criteria to the Law implies attributing to it feasible criteria.[8]

---

[4] Gonçalvez and Stelzer (2009) In: Oliveira (coord) (2009), p. 38.

[5] By rational, microeconomics understands that humans and States act in a way to maximize their utility, in order to obtain the greatest possible satisfaction in their choices.

[6] Gonçalvez and Stelzer (2009), pp. 38–39.

[7] Ibid, p. 56.

[8] According to Gonçalves and Stelzer, legal positivism tried to incorporate feasible criteria to Law through the codification of principles, but these were still out of touch with factual reality. In: Ibid, p. 62.

The basic pillars of the EAL are found in the works of economist Ronald Coase[9] and the jurist Guido Calabresi.[10] The first study presented the transaction costs related to property rights and civil liability, while the last one addressed the issue of the distribution of risks in the civil liability law.

Initially, the method focused on specific areas of Economic Law, such as competition, trade, regulation, and taxation. From 1960 on, the movement spread to other fields of law, such as criminal, civil, procedural, etc. However, the discipline was still studied only by economists, until the American judge Richard Posner,[11] in the 1970s, defended efficiency as a criterion to guarantee the allocation of rights, thus implementing the interdisciplinary study also in the Law course.

In Brazil, the movement began in the 1980s, in Rio Grande do Sul, with the work of Clóvis do Couto e Silva entitled "A Ordem Jurídica e a Economia", of 1982, followed by the work of Guiomar Estrella Faria, "Interpretação Econômica do Direito", of 1994, both of critical content, however, admitted the applicability of the movement in Brazil.

Later, EAL studies expanded to the Universities of São Paulo, Rio de Janeiro, Brasília, Minas Gerais, Paraná and Santa Catarina, consolidating in 2007, with the XI Congress of the Latin American and Iberian Association of Law and Economics, in Brasília.

Despite criticisms of the application of economic precepts to Law, Cooter and Rubinfield[12] point out that "acceptance of the theory of economic analysis of law has been facilitated because of the structural similarities between economic and legal science." He also cites as an example the rationality of the individual not being very different for jurists and economists, in the same way that the fair division of risks matters to both sciences.[13]

EAL applied to International Law has also been the target of several criticisms. Among the main criticisms are the difficulty of measuring utility, due to the complexity of interests of the different subjects, and the positivism of International Law.[14]

SILVA NETO[15] rebuts these arguments, stating that, first, the EAL in International Law is applicable according to the neo-institutionalist current, considering that international organizations function as a system of awards and punishments that, by

---

[9] Coase (1960).

[10] Calabresi (1961).

[11] Richard Posner, the American judge who inaugurated the Chicago School, preached efficiency as the only criterion and objective of Law and the maximization of wealth as its ethical foundation. Later, due to criticism of this school, Posner abandoned this more radical vision. See: Salama (2008) In: GV Law Notebook (in press). http://works.bepress.com/bruno_meyerhof_salama, pp. 23–31.

[12] Free adaptation from: "It seems that the acceptance of economic theory into law has been eased by structural similarities between economics and law". Cooter and Rubinfield (1989), pp. 1067–1097, p 1068.

[13] Ibid.

[14] Silva Neto (2005), pp. 47–48.

[15] Ibid, pp 49–50.

implying new compliance costs, direct behaviors. And secondly, the positivism of International Law ceased to be Westphalian, which, due to the sovereignty of States, preached the non-subordination of these States to international norms, becoming based on the individual choice of these seeking to maximize their interests.

Furthermore, the applicability of the EAL to International Law is viable in an analogous way to the elements of Contract Law since international treaties are similar to contracts.[16] Therefore, its loopholes can lead to non-cooperative conduct if the costs of breaking them are lower than the benefits obtained by compliance. Thus, contractual logic can also be applied to the WTO, since its agreement has the legal nature of an international treaty.[17]

In international trade, transaction costs can be reduced, while contract-breaking costs can be raised by international institutions such as the WTO. Market failures need to be regulated, since the absence of institutions triggers the use of force by States. However, inefficient institutions lead to new failures. From this perspective, the study of economic neo institutionalism emerges, since organizations constitute institutional arrangements that will influence political and legal decision making.

Besides, Gonçalves and Stelzer[18] justify the application of the EAL as a method of interpreting international trade and as an option for a criterion of justice, since one cannot exclude the social coexistence of the market economy, in which individuals, economic agents and States seek to satisfy their interests.

Regarding the conduct of States, it is necessary to study the theory of public choice, together with the theory of games since they allow the investigation of patterns of state behavior in relation to negotiations and compliance with WTO rules.

The efficiency criterion is also of great value for this analysis, especially when it comes to countering distorting subsidies by less developed and developing countries. In this sense, Gonçalves and Stelzer state that:

> This legal-economic choice must be made according to an efficient decision, obtaining the best use of scarce resources and the social welfare, aiming at the desired development, the result of appropriate regulation of international trade.[19]

Thus, neoclassical microeconomic principles[20] used by the EAL serve as criteria for interpreting International Law in search of efficiency for development. We also add the viability of studying the neo institutionalist current, the theory of games and

---

[16] According to Congleton, "Treaties constitute Coase contracts between States. They are voluntary agreements between member States designed to promote common interests, including economies of scale and regulation of externalities". Free translation from: "Treaties are Coasian contracts among nation-states. They are voluntary agreements among member states designed to advance common interests, including economies of scale and regulatory externalities". In: Congleton (2007) http://ssrn.com/abstract=979459.

[17] "The WTO Agreement is a treaty, the international equivalent of a contract." Free Translation from: "The WTO Agreement is a treaty -the international equivalent of a contract". Appellate Body Report in the Japan case—Alcoholic Beverages (1998).

[18] Gonçalvez and Stelzer (2013) In: Barral and Pimentel (2006), pp. 45–54.

[19] Ibid, p. 39.

[20] Coelho (2007).

public choice for a more complete analysis of the complex reality in which international trade finds itself.

For the EAL, legal rules are like prices,[21] that is, they can encourage the conduct of individuals and States, whose decision-making is the result of an analysis of costs and benefits in favor of maximizing their interests. However, the interests of individuals do not always coincide with those of the state. For this reason, EAL uses two theories to investigate decision-making: rational choice and public choice.

Moreover, these choices occur within a game between all agents, with reciprocal interests or not, whose scenario will require the adoption of strategic behavior, as explained by the theory of games. Thus, EAL constitutes an important instrument for making political and legal decisions in the institutional sphere, applicable to international trade.

In sum, the EAL relies on three basic theses: (a) the maximizing rationality of individuals, (b) the view that legal rules resemble prices, and (c) the ability of legal institutions to promote efficiency.[22]

To this end, the EAL performs two types of analysis, the descriptive and the normative, both used in this chapter. The first, also known as the Chicago School, aims to analyze the effects of norms on the conduct of agents, while the second refers to the Yale School and intends to propose norms that promote efficiency.

The descriptive dimension seeks to understand the Law according to the economic elements and the normative dimension works in the plane of the duty to be, that is, in the formation of the Law, serving to determine the (in)efficiency for the realization of its values.

On the use of the concept of efficiency by Law, Posner[23] points out that "if the most efficient methods do not harm other values, they are socially desirable, even if the efficiency is considered low among the social values".

In this sense, EAL does not intend to place efficiency as the preponderant value of Law, but to help it seek its values in an efficient manner. According to Salama, "the question does not replace the discussion of justice with the discussion of efficiency, but rather, enriches the legal grammar by integrating the discussion of efficiency into the discussion of justice".[24]

To Caliendo,[25] despite the criticism, the EAL should be seen as a form of approach and not as a theory. Roemer states that, "the most important component of law and economics does not consist in specific economic concepts, but rather in how the analysis of the concrete case is carried out".[26]

---

[21] The word "price", besides the monetary expression, can also represent the positions of giver and receiver, not necessarily involving pecuniary movement.

[22] Roemer (1994), pp. 13–15.

[23] Free adaptation from: "If the more efficient methods did not impair any other values, they would be socially desirable even if efficiency were low on the totem pole of social values". In: Posner (1993), p. 27.

[24] Ibid, p. 6.

[25] Caliendo (2009), p. 16.

[26] Roemer (1994), p. 19.

Given this, it can be stated that EAL did not alter the traditional concepts of Law, but only clarified and increased the quality of legal argumentation. The generalization and rigorism of Economics allow jurists to understand aspects of Law that are still unknown. For this reason, there is harmony in the use by Law of economic premises.[27]

The proposal of Law and Economics is "to bring together the consequentialist ethics of Economics with the deontology of the discussion of the just",[28] since, considering the consequences produced by legal norms in practical terms, justice is more complete, effectively corresponding to social anxieties.

Therefore, the joint analysis of Law, Economics and Organizations will allow us to understand the complex reality of political-economic subsidy strategies in the WTO and to rethink its mechanisms to counter distortive subsidies by less developed countries. The EAL will serve as a basis for investigating States' decision-making in the face of the costs-benefits of asserting their interests within the WTO institutional apparatus, which may encourage or discourage the use of subsidies as it reduces or raises transaction costs.

The precepts exposed here will serve as a foundation for the analysis of the problematic political-economic strategies of subsidies in the WTO. Once the fundamental concepts for the application of EAL are presented, the issue of the (in)efficiency of the system for less developed countries in countering distorting subsidies practiced by developed countries will be addressed under the prescriptive aspect, while the normative aspect will serve as a basis for the proposal of this thesis.

2.1 Fundamental Concepts

Among the various postulates of the EAL, it was decided to present those most relevant to the analysis of the political-economic strategies of subsidies in the WTO, which are: efficiency, transaction costs, game theory, rational choice, public choice theory and neo institutionalism.

First, it is necessary to emphasize important concepts used by EAL, such as scarcity, rational maximization, balance, incentives, and efficiency.[29]

Scarcity constitutes the problem to be solved by Economic Science, since, if resources were infinite and everyone could have everything they wanted, it would not be necessary to divide them up. It is because of scarcity that individuals are forced to make choices and opt for one good over another, which has become known as opportunity cost.

These choices are made rationally to maximize the welfare of each individual. When making the maximization calculation, both monetary and non-monetary costs

---

[27] Ibid, pp. 19–22.

[28] Salama (2008), p. 22.

[29] Salama (2008), pp. 16–25.

and benefits are included. Thus, individuals tend to consume a given product again when the benefits are equal or greater than the costs. It should be noted that lack of information prevents individuals from making optimal choices. As a result, economics recognizes that rationality is limited.

Equilibrium constitutes the "interactive behavioral pattern that is achieved when all actors are maximizing their own interests simultaneously".[30]

Once the rational ability of individuals to make choices in their own interests is admitted, it can be said that they also respond to incentives, such as prices and laws. On the other hand, efficiency is understood to mean that the maximization of the welfare of individuals should be sought in a way that minimizes social costs, that is, one individual improves his situation without worsening that of the other, or by compensating for losses.

2.1.1 Efficiency and the Principle of Economic and Social Efficiency

EAL refers to the idea of efficiency, which means the maximization of some measure of value. For Economics, this measure is social welfare or the maximization of individual utilities.[31] Based on utilitarian theory, efficiency is composed of the greatest number of satisfactions in a society. Thus, efficiency is achieved when the result of the sum of the resources or values involved in a transaction exceeds the initial sum.

Both efficiency and effectiveness are ends pursued by EAL. While efficiency implies the possibility of achieving the best possible result with minimum waste of resources, effectiveness implies the ability to achieve the desired effects.[32]

The two main criteria for measuring efficiency are: Pareto's efficiency[33] and Kaldor[34]-Hicks[35'] efficiency. In the first model, efficiency is achieved when the sum of resources after the transaction is equal or greater than the initial sum, without any of the parties being harmed. If the sum is equal, and there is no other superior situation, we are faced with the Pareto optimum. In turn, if the sum is higher without worsening the situation of others, then we are faced with Pareto superiority.

It should be noted that the Pareto criteria hardly match reality, which produces both winners and losers. Thus, the second criterion states that efficiency can be

---

[30] Ibid, p. 20.

[31] The concept of utility is broader than that of value. While the former is restricted to the monetary issue, the latter refers to satisfaction, happiness, or pleasure, which are consequences of the choices made. The criticism of utilitarianism lies in the difficulty of comparing the preferences of individuals. Sen (2000), p. 77–82.

[32] Zytlberstajn and Sztajn (2006), p. 81.

[33] Pareto (1996).

[34] Kaldor (1939).

[35] Hicks (1939).

verified even if the situation of one of the parties becomes worse, as long as the final result is greater than the loss and it is possible to compensate for it.

This compensation need not actually occur, its possibility is sufficient. In this sense, "[...] potential compensation states that there is no extra income available for distribution - there is no such thing as a free lunch".[36] In view of this, compensation will always involve redistribution of utilities.

As an example, the relocation of a factory from city A to city B will generate losses at first, since people will lose their jobs. According to the Paretian efficiency criterion, these losses should be compensated to the point that the displacement becomes indifferent for losers. In the Kaldor-Hicks criterion, the gains from moving the factory from city A to city B should exceed the losses, that is, the winners should gain more than the losers lose.[37]

For Bergson-Samuelson,[38] efficiency is that which maximizes social welfare, but increased social welfare can lead to injustices.[39] In this sense, Calabresi[40] maintains that the priority of legal systems should be justice and, secondly, wealth maximization and cost reduction. From this, it can be stated that not all efficiency is just, but all inefficiency is certainly unjust.

For Polinsky,[41] efficiency refers to "the size of the pie", while equity corresponds to its apportionment. Thus, increasing the size of the pie will not be feasible if it implies the unequal division of its slices. On the other hand, if it is possible to slice it in the desired way, the increase of the pie will cause the increase of the slices, making efficiency and equity in harmony. Da Silva Neto[42] warns that "redistribution of income has a cost, so there can be a confrontation between efficiency and equity."

For the EAL, legal norms, by being able to allocate economic resources, induce behaviors that may or may not lead to efficiency. Thus, norms can be seen as distortions or as corrective of distortions. In the first case, the standard interferes in an efficient situation, while in the second, the interference occurs in a market failure situation with the aim of correcting it. Added to this is the ability of the norm to guarantee rights and adapt to new realities.[43] In this way, legal norms can increase *the size of the pie.*

It is important to emphasize that economic theories must be interpreted in the light of the values of Law, and efficiency cannot be the only objective of legal norms, under penalty of committing injustices. The interaction between Economics

---

[36] Free translation from: "[...] a potential compensation claims that there is extra income available for distribution—there is such a thing as a free lunch [...]." In: Blaug (1997), p. 574.

[37] See: Cooter and Ulen (2010), p. 65.

[38] Bergson-Samuelson (1979), pp. 73–90.

[39] Dworkin (1999), pp. 345–347.

[40] Calabresi (1970).

[41] Polinsky (1989), pp. 7–8.

[42] Da Silva Neto (2005), p. 30.

[43] Arida In: Zytlberstajn and Sztajn (2006), pp. 63–66.

and Law is necessary, since legal norms can challenge the strict precepts of economic rationality, and it is up to Law to illuminate them.[44]

This implies that Economics is not able to explain Law in a complete way, since it "does not capture the whole underlying reality".[45] For this reason, Economics should be associated with other areas of knowledge.

Amartya Sen[46] He brought philosophy and ethics closer to economics by placing rights and freedoms as the primacy of the Social Sciences and that efficiency is not always consistent with justice. Thus, the less maximizing policy may be more beneficial if it enables freedom than the more maximizing policy but ordered by a central power to the detriment of freedoms. The central concern of the author is to prioritize the general well-being of society, which, for him, presents itself as freedoms.[47]

For Roemer,[48] legal norms must go beyond the principle of efficiency, so that the law can at the same time promote efficiency and justice. This does not mean that there cannot be contradictions between the criteria, but neither do they constitute mutually exclusive criteria.

Thus, an ideal legal system of international trade is one capable of maintaining efficiency between the parties without causing harm to society. "When the norms of International Trade Law do not correspond to social expectations, it is because they derive from an economic model removed from civil society [...]".[49]

Because of this, Gonçalves[50] adds to the concept of efficiency the "principle of economic-social efficiency (PESE)", by which the costs related to the negative externalities suffered by society are considered in the calculation of efficiency, in order to seek the largest possible number of beneficiaries for a more humane, inclusive and less restrictive economy of freedoms.

For PESE, such externalities constitute costs arising from the rights and obligations awarded, so they must be internalized to maximize results, countering social inequalities. Interests must then be optimized, highlighting social interests and compensating for negative externalities. In the words of Gonçalves and Stelzer, PESE:

> It is the elaboration and application of the norm, considering the social reflex, the reciprocity of the actions and the external cost imposed on the present or even future society, in order to be compensated, in full, the losses imposed by the present gain of the parties involved, avoiding the inefficient use of resources, the onerosity caused to the domestic productive process, the diversion of resources and the creation of false market indicators.[51]

---

[44] Ibid, pp. 69–70.

[45] Free translation of: "[...] but not capture all of the underlying reality". In: Cooter (1981), p. 1266.

[46] Sen (2000), pp. 41–42.

[47] For Amartya Sen, development is seen as a "process of eliminating deprivations of freedoms and expanding substantive freedoms of different kinds that people have reason to value". In: Ibid, p. 108.

[48] Roemer (1994), p. 39.

[49] Gonçalvez and Stelzer (2006), p. 42.

[50] Gonçalves (2001).

[51] Gonçalvez and Stelzer (2009), p. 44.

The concept of efficiency adopted is that of Kaldor-Hicks, since that of Pareto does not cover externalities and that of Bergson-Samuelson is too subjective, because in the real world, economic agents are not willing to share their gains.

This does not mean that Law is all about adopting efficiency as the sole criterion of justice. Of course, inefficiency is unfair, since it wastes and reallocates scarce resources, but the criterion of justice must also consider the reality of the market, where not everyone benefits. In this sense, states Gonçalves e Stelzer:

> The Law, revealing choice or adjudication of legal prerogatives, needs to observe the primacy of the PESE, defending the observation of efficiency to obtain the consequent harmonization or balance in the economic action of agents, and should also observe other criteria such as distributiveness, social justice, environmental protection, eradication of unemployment, overcoming nationalism, among others [...].[52]

Considering that selfish and opportunistic behavior is limited by man's need for survival, which in turn depends on society, we seek to discourage inefficiency and encourage alterity.[53] For this reason, the Kaldor-Hicks criterion is adopted together with the PESE, since the former considers the effects of transactions on third parties and the latter takes into account social and temporal variables in its calculation, aiming at greater social inclusion. It is necessary to seek efficiency supported by the PESE so that the apportionment minimally affects society in a negative way.

However, unlike Kaldor-Hicks, who preached compensation for damages:

> Within the pragmatic economist perspective, justice must be achieved not in function of the need for retribution for a damage caused, for example, but of the ideal composition of the parties in order to achieve a superior state of well-being for all involved.[54]

Therefore, it is important that international trade be implemented through rules that "maximize results, minimize losses, internalize costs, and promote social inclusion, according to the PESE"[55] That said, it is possible to understand the importance of the role of the WTO in terms of the efficiency of international trade relations, in order to eliminate transaction costs and promote greater stability, avoiding opportunistic behavior, issues that will be analyzed next.

---

[52] Gonçalvez and Stelzer (2006), p. 58.
[53] Gonçalvez and Stelzer (2009), pp. 46–47.
[54] Gonçalvez and Stelzer (2006), p. 66.
[55] Ibid, p 55.

2.1.2   Transaction Cost

For EAL, cost represents not only the amount to be paid for a given good,[56] but it encompasses all the impediments involved in the exchange, known as transaction costs. The first to recognize them was Ronald Coase,[57] in his article *Nature of the Firm,*[58] by which he demonstrated the important role of firms in reducing market transaction costs.

Transaction costs are all those borne when trading in the market, not restricted to production and transportation costs. They are divided into three types: (a) search costs for the realization of the business; (b) negotiation costs and (c) compliance costs.[59]

In relation to the first, the more specific and peculiar the good or service, the higher the cost of the search and vice versa. In the second type, the costs are more varied since they involve the degree of information available to the parties.[60] In the third, the cost of supervising and punishing is higher according to the length of time it takes to comply with the agreement.

Thus, bounded rationality and asymmetry of information lead to transaction costs. To these are added the costs of strategic behavior that occur due to the asymmetry of information during the execution of the deal and those imposed by the legal rules when imperfect, and those referring to the use of the legal system and its courts at the time of the inspection of negotiated agreements, when these costs are not stable. In this sense, Stephen teaches:

> The law in many cases represents a high or fixed cost that does not affect the efficiency of each bargain. However, in marginal cases, the cost of going to court may represent a considerable roadblock to achieving optimality.[61]

In the absence of transaction costs, the intervention of the courts will not be necessary for the efficient distribution of resources. In his article entitled *The Problem of Social Cost*, Coase[62] established that, "when transaction costs are zero, the distribution of resources is independent of the distribution of property rights".[63] On the other hand, the intervention of the Law is necessary when the transaction costs exceed the benefits that would be obtained in the market.[64]

---

[56] The concept of good also includes those intangibles, such as rights and obligations.

[57] Ronald Coase was a professor at the University of Chicago and winner of the Nobel Prize in Economics in 1991 for the development of the Theory of the Firm.

[58] Coase (1937), pp. 386–405.

[59] Cooter and Ulen (2010), p. 105.

[60] In this case, they are large-scale costs, involving not only knowledge about the deal's goal, production and transportation, as well as matters of political, economic and legal circumstances, such as costs from taxation, the tax incentives and the legal system in general.

[61] Stephen (1993), pp. 38–39.

[62] Coase (1960).

[63] Stephen (1993), p. 31.

[64] Coase (1960).

Therefore, by demonstrating that the main problem of the market was the transaction costs and not the negative externalities, Coase recognized that the Law applied should consider the maximization of the general benefit and not the mere adjudication of duties to the agent that caused the damage.

As an example, we can cite the case of a polluting factory that causes damage to a neighboring condominium. For Law enforcers, the factory should be responsible for the damage caused, that is, the solution to the impasse would be focused on externalities. For the author, the best way to resolve the issue is based on mutual interests, seeking the solution that best prevents the occurrence of the most serious damage. Thus, since the condominium removal costs are greater than the restrictions on polluting activity, the factory will prefer to pay them instead of reducing pollution. In this case, it is possible to verify that, "[…] efficiency requires that the right be allocated to the part that values it most".[65]

Therefore, when transaction costs are zero, the parties' transaction is successful. On the other hand, when such costs are high, the intervention of Law is necessary for the efficient use of resources. In this way, the legal system can contribute to negotiation when it reduces transaction costs, when, for example, rights are defined in a simple and clear way, making the net result of the negotiation positive for both parties.[66]

On the other hand, the legal system can also add new transaction costs when inefficient. The complex and ambiguous definition of subsidies in the WTO, for example, imposes transaction costs between members.

Cooter and Ulen[67] add to the *Coase Theorem* two important normative principles that serve as prescriptive guidance to legislators: (a) minimize the damage caused by private disagreements and (b) minimize obstacles to proven agreements, both in relation to resource allocation. In the first case, the norm must be structured in such a way that it does not constitute an obstacle to private agreements. In the second, in turn, by removing impediments to private agreements, the norm would stimulate cooperation between the parties.

In this way, the Law has the capacity to encourage or discourage the behavior of agents through the creation or removal of transaction costs. To verify whether the norm is fulfilling its role of reducing transaction costs, it is important to study the assumptions of game theory that work with the analysis of possible strategic behaviors to be adopted by economic agents.

---

[65] Cooter and Ulen (2010), p. 102.

[66] Ibid, p. 109.

[67] Ibid, p. 110.

2.1.3 Theory of Games

The theory of games constitutes the study of the decisions made by economic agents in a scenario where there are several opposing interests, the outcome of a decision necessarily depends on the decision of other agents.

It is said that when the decision making of an agent depends on the choice of other agents, the situation resembles games, in which the use of strategies is necessary. In view of this, the theory of games started to be applied to economics to explain the possible strategic behaviors of economic agents, which may be either cooperative or conflictual.

The game is composed of players, their respective strategies and gains obtained with the strategy to be chosen. In addition, it has certain rules and a board. In the specific case, the players are the members of the WTO, who make their decisions according to the rules defined in their agreements, whose loopholes will trigger an opportunistic strategic behavior.[68] The asymmetry of information, for example, allows the adoption of opportunistic strategic behavior by economic agents.

The classic example of this theory is the prisoner's dilemma, according to which the most beneficial situation for all would be reached when players leave antagonistic positions and opt for cooperation. Thus, if both cooperated and kept silent, they would only be imprisoned for 1 year.

However, the structure of the game itself encourages opportunistic behavior, since the one who does not cooperate and confesses will have advantages over the other. Confessing, therefore, is the dominant strategy that will only be changed if the other also changes his behavior, a situation known as *Nash equilibrium*.[69] However, the solution is not pareto-efficient, in which both would do better if they remained silent.

It is noted that the incessant pursuit of internal interests can lead to the situation in which everyone loses, while cooperation can generate better results.

There are variables in this game that must be considered, among them, time and inequalities of economic capacity stand out. In the first case when the games are repeated, the tendency is to adopt cooperative behavior, while single-round games or even fixed rounds stimulate conflictive behavior.

Regarding the second variable, it is stated that cooperation decreases the greater the economic power of the States and their ability to influence prices. States with less economic capacity, in turn, tend to cooperate, because as price takers, conflict imposes even higher costs.[70]

---

[68] Opportunistic behavior is that by which "one of the contractors who, by cunning or force, tries to obtain for himself an advantage in the distribution of the joint gains of the contract, to the detriment of the other contractor". In: Mackaay and Rousseau (2015), p. 422.

[69] *Nash equilibrium* means that no player can do better by changing his behavior without the other players changing theirs.

[70] Hoekman and Kostecki (2009), p. 26.

Therefore, without guarantees that no one will cheat, full cooperation will hardly be achieved. The function of the Law, in this case, will be to discourage such behavior, penalizing uncooperative behavior. In this sense, the States create institutions with powers to monitor their conduct, repressing them when they violate the Law.

2.1.4 Neo-Institutional Economics

New institutional economics has its roots in old American institutionalism, which emerged in the 1880s. First developed by Douglass North in his works *Structure and Change in Economic History* and *Institutions, Institutional Change in Economic History,* respectively of 1981 and 1990, which defined institutions "as the rules of the game in a society or, more formally, are the humanly devised constraints that shape human interactions".[71]

These rules constitute limitations that are presented in two ways: the formal ones, such as the codes, statutes and regulations or the informal ones, which are the rules of conduct of society. When formal limitations are adapted to the information, *institutional balance* is achieved.[72] This means that there will be no violation of the formal limitations.

In short, North's ideas presuppose the existence of uncertainties in the economic and social environment, which generate transaction costs, resolved through institutions, composed of the relationship between formal and informal rules and, from this, the path for the creation of economic, political or social organizations is defined,[73] responsible for the economic development of societies.[74]

In general, economic institutions can be conceptualized as:

> [...] socially and historically constructed regularities of behavior that shape and order interactions between individuals and groups of individuals, producing relatively stable and determined patterns in the operation of the economic system.[75]

In 1937, Coase[76] presented the paper entitled *The Nature of the Firm*, in which he linked the concept of economic efficiency to the limits imposed by institutions, inaugurating what later came to be known as the New Institutional Economics.

---

[71] Free translation of: "Institutions are the rules of the game in a society or, more formally, are the humanly devised constraints that shape human interaction". In: North (1990), p. 3.

[72] Ibid, p. 86.

[73] Organizations are species of institutions made up of individuals or states in pursuit of specific goals.

[74] Gala (2003), p. 103.

[75] Pondé (2005), pp. 119–160.

[76] Coase (1937), pp. 386–405.

Until then, economists were concerned only with exogenous aspects of the market,[77] disregarding its internal arrangement.

As the theory works with the concept of transaction costs, previously explained by Coase, Posner[78] strongly criticizes the lack of novelty for its distinction, since it does not add new elements. Even Coase and Williamson[79] consecrate the new institutional economics, based on transaction costs, however, broadening the neoclassical perspective, considering it incapable of keeping up with the current problems, since, in the real world, transaction costs are greater than zero.

In Coase's study, transaction costs are restricted to those related to the use of market prices, disregarding the costs related to the creation and operation of institutions, which also interfere in decision making. Thus:

> For the neo institutional perspective, the study of the economic analysis of law aims at identifying the instrumental variables and the issues and processes that underlie the operation of legal institutions of economic significance.[80]

In this way, institutions influence behavior to the extent that they determine the *rules of the game* in society. Therefore, institutions are created to optimize the behavior of their members[81] and are therefore important for the study of EAL to promote efficiency.

The postulates adopted by neo institutionalism resemble the neoclassicals: methodological individualism, limited rationality, utility maximization, game theory, and efficiency, including such postulates in the analysis of institutions.

Neo-institutionalist efficiency, therefore, is possible within the framework of organizations, that is, the constraints imposed by them must be considered in order for the analysis to be appropriate.[82] Recognizing the presence of transaction costs in society,[83] institutions have the power to reduce them, contributing to economic efficiency, since the predictability of behavior reduces the chances of adopting opportunistic behavior. In the words of Seabra, Formaggi and Flach:

> Institutions affect economic performance through their impact on production and transaction costs and are also essential in that they reduce uncertainty by creating stable structures for interaction in society.[84]

It must be recognized that individual action is influenced by formal and informal institutions, making it necessary for Law, Economics and Organizations to be analyzed together.

---

[77] Economists were primarily concerned with the influence of the price system on economic resources.

[78] Posner (1993).

[79] Williamson (1985).

[80] Roemer (1994), p. 41.

[81] Roemer (1994), p. 50.

[82] Ibid, p. 53.

[83] Transaction costs in a society are not equal to zero due to imperfect market conditions that lead to negative externalities such as monopolies and information asymmetry.

[84] Seabra et al. (2006) In: Barral and Pimentel (2006), pp. 71–86.

In this sense, institutions can contribute to the economic development of society, which is why they are the central object of the analytical model of neo institutionalism.

On the other hand, North's theory is wrong to link underdevelopment to institutions incapable of creating perfect market conditions.[85] By adopting static and homogeneous assumptions, it disregards historical processes, power relations and the process of exploitation of the colonies and the capitalist model that underlies the creation of institutions.[86] For this reason, North's reductionist neo institutionalism is not sufficient to explain inequalities among states.

The approach must be heterodox, considering the most varied institutional arrangements.[87] It is important to note that institutions, while prescribing behavior to individuals or States, are shaped by them. In this shaping process, the agents bring to the institutions their cultures, structures, values, and interests.[88]

In short, neo institutionalists recognize the dependence of economics on historical, cultural, social, political, and legal contexts, as well as the complexity and diversity of its analysis when concerned with practices and facts applied in the real world.[89]

Therefore, it is considered that the rationality of the agents is limited[90] due to the motivational fragility of human beings and the difficulties of processing information, preventing the completeness of contracts.

Furthermore, it is assumed that "all complex contracts are inevitably incomplete".[91] The incompleteness of contracts makes it impossible to anticipate correct solutions to unpredictable problems, and therefore the presence of strategic behavior is justified.[92]

It can be stated, therefore, that neo institutionalism adopts the contractualist perspective of economic relations, whose contracts are assumed to be imperfect, which generates opportunistic behavior and transaction costs.

Starting from the assumption that institutions are also flawed, one cannot treat them absolutely, nor consider them disorders. Institutions constitute forms of governance whose advantages and disadvantages are analyzed by neo-institutional theory.

According to Roemer, "assuming that individuals act rationally, one might think that the level of costs of any negotiation depends on how the institutional framework is organized".[93]

---

[85] Toyoshima (1999), pp. 95–112.

[86] Cruz (2020), pp. 107–122.

[87] Pondé (2005).

[88] Ibid.

[89] Salama (2008), p. 15.

[90] Simon (1985), p. 293–304.

[91] Williamson (2005) In: Zytlberstajn and Sztajn, p. 22.

[92] Ibid, p. 23.

[93] Free translation from: "Suponiendo que los individuos tratan de actuar racionalmente, puede pensarse que el nivel de los costos de cualquier negociación depende de cómo esté organizado el marco institucional". In: Roemer (1994), p. 52.

The WTO system is a model of institutional organization, and its scope is to regulate the commercial conduct of countries in order to promote free trade and development of these countries.

However, whether the organization is fulfilling its role of reducing transaction costs, preventing the unilateral use of force by ensuring compliance with its norms, to achieve the development of its members in an inclusive manner depends on several factors, mainly on its ability to stimulate the cooperation of its members.[94]

Such capacity is directly related to "jurisdictionalization," which implies the high degree of definition of the rules established in international treaties, the precision of terms, and the delegation of powers. Jackson[95] adds other requirements to be analyzed for the correct allocation of power of the institutions: the rigidity in the amendments of their treaties, governance issues, the decision-making process, in the performance of diplomacy, and in the use of resources for their operation.

Rigidity for treaty change and "jurisdictionalization" contribute to greater predictability of behavior and to avoid subterfuge. On the other hand, flexibility is also important, if it is not exaggerated, because it allows for the composition and not the overlapping of interests.[96]

2.1.5 Rational Choice and Public Choice Theory

For Economic Science, economic agents make their decisions to maximize something: while consumers seek to maximize happiness or satisfaction, businesses seek profits, politicians want votes, and philanthropic organizations aim at social welfare. Maximizing behavior is based on the presumption of rationality of agents.

The scarcity of resources forces agents to make choices. The cost-benefit ratio is an important factor in decision making since individuals tend to choose the alternative of which the benefits exceed the costs. Thus, according to the rational choice theory, when analyzing the available alternatives, individuals tend to seek the option that will provide them with greater utility. The choice is based on each individual's evaluation of the utility of the alternatives.

---

[94] In this sense, Maragno points out that: "In a world with perfect information, full rationality, absence of transaction costs and no uncertainty, the importance of the role of institutions becomes reduced. However, when one of these assumptions is neglected, resources are needed to define and enforce the rules that are indispensable for cooperation. The efficiency of these resources depends, in turn, on the existence of institutional structures that exercise governance capacity at the global level. This governance at the global level gives rise to a proper sphere of international institutions, that is, the effectiveness of the norms, rules, and resolutions issued by the institutions responsible for global governance in international society - in this case the WTO - depends on states that recognize their legitimacy, are willing to obey them, and have the effective governing capacity to make the actors under their jurisdiction comply with them." In: Maragno (2007), p. 31.

[95] Jackson (2002), p. 13–31

[96] Da Silva Neto (2005), p. 244.

From the assumption that the individual is a rational maximizer, three fundamental concepts can be inferred: (a) the inverse relationship between price and quantity; (b) the opportunity cost and (c) the tendency for resources to be allocated to their highest use value.[97]

Due to criticisms regarding the subjectivity of preferences, which makes it difficult to ascertain personal satisfactions, EAL began to adopt as a criterion for measuring utility, people's preferences as data.[98] "Thus, it would be more correct to state that outcome A has more utility to a player than outcome B because he prefers A to B than to state that outcome A is preferred to B by the player because it has greater utility than B".[99]

Similarly, in the face of the restriction on his income, if the individual stops spending one dollar less on product x to spend one dollar more on y, it means that the utility of y has increased. This situation is called the marginal benefit of budget reallocation. The individual will continue with this choice until the benefit of the change (stop buying x in order to buy y) is equivalent to the marginal cost, when the decision reaches its optimal point. From the moment the cost of the change is greater than its benefit, the individual will abandon this choice.

The same applies in relation to the impacts of the agents' conduct on society. As long as the marginal cost, for example, of a certain company investing in technology to reduce pollution is equivalent to the marginal benefits, the investments will remain the same.[100]

To make their choices, it is important that individuals obtain as little information as possible, since the search for additional information cannot generate costs higher than those of the choice itself.[101]

Legal rules are equivalent to prices and, therefore, have the power to stimulate or discourage individuals' choices. Therefore, according to the theory of individual rationality, the effect of rules on the collectivity is explained by the sum of individual choices.

Similarly, the interests that condition government actions, when analyzing the available alternatives, will not always lead governments to elect the option that will best maximize social welfare. The theory that aims to explain this type of situation is known as public choice.

This theory began in the late 1940s, through the debate on welfare economics between Bergson and Samuelson.[102] It gained notoriety in 1966, through the magazine *Papers on Non-Market Decision Making*, name that was changed 2 years later to *Public Choice*. The theory was developed and consolidated with James Buchanan

---

[97] Hirsch (1988), pp. 4–5.

[98] Economists do not have a method for comparing the strength of preferences, but only their order.

[99] Calliari (2003), p. 12.

[100] In this sense, COOTER and ULEN point out that "any extra effort will cost more than it is worth. Any less effort would cause a reduction in the benefits [...]". In: Cooter and Ulen (2010), p. 47.

[101] Posner (1993), p. 19.

[102] Bergson-Samuelson (1979), pp. 73–90.

and Gordon Tullock,[103] that introduced methodological individualism into the analysis of political decision-making, countering the idea that political decision-making seeks the common good. Thus, Buchanan and Tullock defined public choice theory as "politics without romance".[104]

In this way, the theory applies the methods of economics to the analysis of political behavior, being "the economic study of the adoption of decisions that do not belong to market situations, or, simply, the application of economics to political science".[105] Thus, the objective of the theory coincides with that of Political Science, but the methodology adopted belongs to economics, since the individual acts in politics in the same way he participates in the market. For Mueller, "the basic behavior of public choice is the same as that of economics, according to which man is a selfish, rational, utility-maximizing being".[106]

Unlike the neoclassicals, for whom decision making is an exogenous fact, already present in society, the theory of public choice includes the participation of individuals in this process, who seek to increase their welfare. In this sense:

> *Public Choice* is concerned with the behavior of political and bureaucratic entities regarding the decision-making process and its reflection in the real world, where agents maximize interests through policy choices that reveal strategic and optimizing behaviors.[107]

Therefore, the theory analyzes the political decision-making process, its effects on society, voters, and the results obtained by the democratic process, recognizing that the vectors that drive political and economic behavior are different. While the former seek to maintain power, the latter strive for efficiency. In this sense, Sykes states:

> States are supposed to behave as maximizers of economic well-being or to maximize the function of social welfare with greater weight on the electorate. The preferences of the 'state' may be those of its political leaders, who can maximize votes, campaign contributions, or their personal well-being. Countless other variations can be imagined, depending on the context.[108]

The fact that States do not always opt for efficiency does not necessarily imply that their preferences are irrational, but it does mean that the vectors that drive this

---

[103] Buchanan and Tullock (1962). James Buchanan also received a Nobel Prize in Economics for his work on Public Choice Theory in 1986.

[104] Ibid, p. 45.

[105] Free translation from: "Public Choice can be defined as the economic study of non-market decision making, or simply the application of economics to political Science". In: Mueller (2003), p. 1.

[106] Ibid.

[107] Gonçalvez and Stelzer (2009), p. 42.

[108] Free translation from: "States may be assumed to behave as economic welfare maximizers, or to maximize a social welfare function that weighs the welfare of certain constituencies more heavily than others. The preferences of the 'State' may be assumed to be those of its political leaders, who may maximize votes, campaign contributions, or their personal welfare. Innumerable other variations can be imagined depending on the context". In: Sykes (2003), p. 6.

decision process are more complex.[109] In any case, States will opt first for the maximization of their own interests and second for the interests of others.[110]

For this reason, it is necessary to analyze the premises of the *Public Choice Theory*, which has two forms of approach: the positive and the normative. The first seeks to describe political results by studying the conduct of representatives during the campaign and after they are elected, the behavior of voters, and the results resulting from democracy. The second approach, on the other hand, aims to prescribe the institutions that should be adopted.[111]

By adopting the methodological individualism, the theory of public choice is pessimistic in relation to democracy, based on the postulate that elections are determined by interests of individuals or pressure groups. Thus, the expression rent seeking is adopted to designate measures that grant advantages that would not be possible to obtain in the private market and, therefore, are sought by small interest groups through politics.[112]

For Mackaay and Rousseau,[113] "the state is especially concerned with whatever the interest groups can get it to take on; nothing seems to limit the expansion of that agenda." Thus, it is assumed that social values derive from the individual values of society.

These interferences influence the size of the *slice of the pie*. In fact, when governments start caring more about personal interests than general interests, they prevent the size of the pie from increasing.

As an example, one can cite agriculture in the United States and the automotive industry in Brazil. American farmers represent only three percent of the country's total population and benefit from export subsidies that make domestic prices of agricultural products more expensive for the ninety-seven percent of consumers.[114]

Likewise, Brazil has granted subsidies to benefit the national automobile industry through the Inovar-auto program, instituted by Law No. 12.715/2012 and implemented by Decree No. 7.819/2012, which, apparently, aims to encourage technological innovation, benefiting the industry, car sales companies and consumers. However, the incentives are discriminatory and aim to promote the substitution of imports in the country, exclusively benefiting the national automobile industry.[115]

This occurs mainly because small groups organize themselves and pressure the government to adopt policies specific to their interests, while the effects of such policies are disseminated over the majority of the population, which has difficulties in organizing. The logic of public choice theory is that of the visible and invisible,

---

[109] Calliari (2003), p. 77.

[110] Sykes (2003), p. 6.

[111] Roemer (1994), pp. 57–58.

[112] See: Mackaay and Rousseau (2015), pp. 177–179.

[113] Ibid, p. 179.

[114] Ashford   (2012)   http://www.learnliberty.org/videos/
schools-thought-classical-liberalism-part-3-public-choice/.

[115] See: Feriato (2013), pp. 438–459.

whereby "politicians tend to create policies with concentrated advantages and dispersed costs".[116]

Thus, large groups of individuals facilitate opportunistic selfish behavior. In turn, smaller, cohesive groups are hardly dissipated. In addition, small and large groups with specific interests will be more likely to succeed than large groups with general interests.

For this reason, because governments depend on political support from producers, and because producers are more organized than consumers, the interests of producers are privileged. In addition, the costs of these policies of interest to small groups are dissipated among consumers, who feel little pressure to exert any kind of pressure on governments.

In this way, the pessimism of public choice theory breaks down the simple view that the government's interest in using subsidies is restricted to correcting market failures.

International organizations can also influence domestic political decision-making. Congleton[117] He warns of the internationalization of public policies through these organizations, which, in turn, function as an international forum for political decision-making. Concomitantly, this internationalization is determined by domestic politics, "although with an eye on international events and at the request of international interest groups".[118]

In relation to the observance of WTO rules, the reasons that lead a government to cooperate or not, can be either the power, the interest, the knowledge or even the combination of all.[119] Regardless of them, Lucena points out that:

> The reason for acting more cooperatively, in the end, is the cost-benefit analysis he makes, because what one wants, in this specific case, matters more than how one usually acts.[120]

The existence of selfish and opportunistic behavior is assumed here, which in turn is not without its rationality since irrationality leads to the succumbing of humanity. Thus, even the egoist needs to recognize the other for his subsistence.[121]

Given these circumstances, the WTO system must first ascertain this reality, according to which States seek to maximize their interests at the lowest possible cost and benefit. Such recognition is crucial to promote cooperation among members.

Congleton[122] warns about the globalization of public policies:

---

[116] Mackaay and Rousseau (2015), p. 166.

[117] Congleton (2007).

[118] Ibid.

[119] Lucena (2006).

[120] Ibid, p. 218.

[121] Gonçalvez and Stelzer (2009), p. 60.

[122] Congleton (2007).

If new common interests are being identified and advanced, we will all benefit, but if new special and narrow interests are being identified, it is possible that political globalization will leave us worse off.[123]

The responsibility of the WTO, therefore, is to promote the general interests of its members, preventing public policies arising from interests from prevailing. To this end, the organization must be equipped with instruments to control restricted policies, such as specific subsidies, so that individual interests of some do not prevail to the detriment of others.

2.1.6   Economic Contract Theory

Considering that the WTO's institutional support is formed by international treaties, which coordinate transactions among members and, for the EAL, treaties are equivalent to contracts, which is why their breach implies costs, it is necessary to study the economic theory of contract.

Although the more improved analysis of contracts requires contextualized study because of the various types of contracts, there are issues that are common to them and they will be addressed, simultaneously, with the specificities of the WTO agreement.

For Economic Science, contracts are transactions that matter in the exchange of goods and services carried out between two or more parties. Similar to the theories that underpin free trade, contracts are necessary because individuals and States are not self-sufficient. That is, considering that resources are scarce, economic agents value them differently, exchanges move such resources towards the one who values them most.

For economic efficiency, contracts must be fulfilled in full by both parties. When the contract improves the situation of one party without at least worsening the situation of the other, *Paretian* efficiency is realized. Individuals enter into contracts in search of benefits, placing the contracts in a *superior situation* in which all parties win. However, the contracts are incomplete[124] due to the transaction costs imposed for them to be concluded. The transaction costs of contracts are those that operate on the negotiations, drafting and fulfillment of the contract. When such costs outweigh the benefits of contracts, the parties lose interest in contracting. The costs may occur, among others, due to market imperfection, information asymmetry, lim-

---

[123] Free translation of: "If new common interests are being identified and advanced, we all benefit, but if new narrow special interests are being identified, it is possible that we are nearly all are being made worse off by the globalization of politics". In: Ibid.

[124] "A contract will only be complete if the parties can comprehensively specify all present and future contingencies and the anticipated contingencies are symmetrically disclosed to all parties." Free translation of: "A contract can only be called complete, if signatories are able to comprehensively specify all relevant present and future contingencies, and if all anticipated contingencies are symmetrically revealed to all parties". In: Schropp (2009), p. 66.

ited rationality of the parties and market power, generating negative externalities to society.

According to Timm,[125] "the free market tends to produce more than the optimal quantity of these contracts. In other words, not all transactions carried out will have positive economic surplus." In this case, contract Law plays an important role in minimizing transaction costs by offering a secure regulatory framework, providing instruments to curb opportunistic behavior, and providing redress mechanisms.

However, the Law should intervene when the costs of intervention are lower than the costs of externalities, otherwise contracts will cause undesirable costs to society. Thus, the Law may, instead of reducing transaction costs, increase them.

Contracts also cause costs on third parties, causing the private interest of the contractor to differ from the social interest. In the case of international treaties, this occurs when governments act in a way that prioritizes the maintenance of power over the general welfare, as public choice theory explains.

Costs can be before or after the contracting process, as well as exogenous or endogenous. Endogenous costs involve the wills of the parties and imply strategic behavior both in the negotiation and during fulfillment. Exogenous prior costs arise from market failures, information asymmetry, and the limited rationality of the parties[126] that leads to negative externalities and interferes with efficiency. Subsequent exogenous costs, on the other hand, are those that involve the mechanisms to enforce the observance of the contract.[127]

Asymmetry occurs when information is not distributed in an equivalent way to both parties, being a cause for legal concern when it encourages opportunistic behavior.[128] Information asymmetry therefore encourages opportunistic strategic behavior by the more informed party in order to harm the party with restricted information.

Transaction costs related to contracts may occur at three moments: when searching for information, during negotiations and during the execution of the contract. It is also important to emphasize that there will always be a cost for drafting the contract, a moment in which the parties need to foresee and calculate risks and possible occurrences capable of interfering in the efficiency of the contract. In this sense, it is assumed that "contracts will never be complete".[129]

Contract Law aims to "minimize the total of the costs of contract drafting + the costs of interpretation by the courts + the costs of inefficient behavior resulting from

---

[125] Timm (2014), p. 166.

[126] Irrationality occurs if the parties do not have stable preferences or when there is an embarrassment of freedom to contract, such as coercion or state of necessity, for example.

[127] Schropp (2009), p. 63.

[128] Mackaay and Rousseau (2015), p. 411.

[129] Timm (2014), p. 168.

poorly drafted or incomplete contracts".[130] This function is also called *Wittman Function.*[131]

At the time of the Uruguay Round negotiations, the asymmetry of information, the uncertainties about the future, about the actions of the members, the rationality, and the limited resources or even the ambiguity of the texts, made the Marrakech Treaty an incomplete contract.

Market power reduces social welfare by reducing the number of contracts, transferring consumer surplus to the supplier, also allowing the supplier to impose contractual conditions, causing resources to be artificially redistributed.[132]

The risks are allocated in the contract following the same logic of the distribution of property in society: if there are no transaction costs, the rights are allocated to the parties who value them most and the costs related to the risks to those with the ability to bear them in a less onerous way. However, if there are transaction costs, it is necessary to interpose the Law to prevent the negative externalities from materializing.

Due to its incompleteness, the truth is that the biggest problem of contracts is in their non-compliance, also called a *road accident,*[133] that is, eventualities that increase transaction costs to the point of hindering the fulfillment of the contract:

> In this case there is an "accident along the way" in which, in the absence of an express stipulation by the parties - in which respect the effects of the incentives can be examined - it is worth asking who is the cheapest cost avoider, and which signals to send.[134]

By the principle of *cheapest cost avoider,*[135] the duty of reparation will be imposed on the agent who has the best economic conditions to bear it, that is, for whom the duty represents the lowest cost.

Considering that the *accident along the way* creates obstacles to efficiency in the Pareto sense, the intervention of the Law is necessary to discourage the breach of contract, as well as to determine the *cheapest cost avoider*.

It is important to mention that in contracts of immediate fulfilment, that is, concomitant with their conclusion, problems will hardly arise, since, due to the absence of promises, their execution is exhausted instantaneously. However, when there are future promises, fulfilled in the long term, uncertainties and risks appear, causing enforceability to emerge. Thus, "the enforceability of promises encourages exchange and cooperation between people".[136]

---

[130] Free translation from: "In a nutshell, the role of contract law is to minimize the cost of the parties writing contracts + the costs of the courts writing contracts + the cost of inefficient behavior arising from poorly written or incomplete contracts". In: Wittman (2006), p. 194.

[131] Ibid.

[132] Mackaay and Rousseau (2015), p. 412.

[133] Ibid, p. 420.

[134] Ibid, p. 483.

[135] Coase (1960).

[136] Cooter and Ulen (2010), p. 208.

		Cooperate	Taking ownership
First Player (Main or Promissary)	Invest	0,5	1,0
		0,5	-1,0
	Do not invest	0	0
		0	0

Fig. 2.1 Agent and principal game without contract. Second Player (agent or promissor). Source: Cooter and Ulen (2010) (Ibid, p. 209)

Schropp[137] distinguishes *enforcement* and *enforceability*, both of which are necessary to encourage the fulfillment of contracts. While enforceability means the possibility of verifying and quantifying the non-observance of the contract, enforcement is intended for coercive remedies capable of forcing compliance. These issues are extremely relevant at the international level, which lacks the supranational strength to enforce the commitments made.

Similar to repetitive games, it is important that the Law ensures cooperation between the players by enforcing the obligations between the parties rather than repairing damages. In principle, parties are considered to contract with the intention of fulfilling the obligations assumed, but this depends, among other factors, on the feasibility and enforceability. Cooperative behavior varies according to the efficiency of both institutes, which, when weak, encourage opportunistic behavior. Therefore, "the best legal remedy for breach ensures optimal commitment to the contract, which causes efficient drafting, fulfillment and trust".[138]

Considering that the challenge of the parties is to seek the solution closest to efficiency, it is necessary that the Law develops an efficient system of contract execution in a way that is more advantageous to the parties and society. This occurs when the costs of legal intervention are less than the benefits it brings. This system aims to prevent non-compliance with contracts, based on the assumption that, when the costs of disruption are greater than the benefits, agents tend to observe the rules.

Thus, cooperation will occur when the benefits of compliance outweigh the costs of noncompliance. In this context, Law plays a crucial role in transforming non-cooperative games into cooperative ones, according to the enforcement of the contract for both parties.

Suppose a game in which the first player, who can be, for example, an investor, decides whether to place a good under the control of the second player. The second player, in turn, decides whether to cooperate or to appropriate the good, according to the following Figs. 2.1 and 2.2.

Note that in a game where there is no contract or, if there are obstacles, such as corrupt courts, cooperation generates a surplus of 1 and allows the second player to keep the investment without producing wealth. Thus, if the first player chooses to

---

[137] Schropp (2009), p. 32.
[138] Cooter and Ulen (2010), p. 248.

Fig. 2.2 Principal and
agent game with contract.
Source: Cooter and Ulen
(2010) (Ibid, p. 211)

Second Player

First playerad		Comply	Break
	Invest	0,5	-0,5
	(contract)	0,5	0,5
	Do not invest	0	0
	(no contract)	0	0

Offender

Victim	Exercise caution	Does not exercise caution
Exercise caution	-5; -9	-5 -10
Does not exercise caution	0 -15	0 20

Fig. 2.3 Precautionary costs in the absence of liability. Source: Timm (2014), p. 191

invest, it will be more advantageous for the second player to appropriate, that is, to adopt an opportunistic behavior. When anticipating this possibility, the first player therefore chooses not to invest. Therefore, legal rules are crucial for cooperative outcomes.

The scenario changes when there is a judicially enforceable contract, in which investing still brings better results for the first player than not investing. Adding up the figures, one notices that the breach of contract by the second player, by having to compensate the first player for the breach, will cost him 1.5 (1 referring to the first player's investment and 0.5 on the loss of profit). The return that the second player would get if he fulfilled the contract is 1.0, which leads to the conclusion that the enforceability of the contract promotes cooperative behavior.

From the point of view of society, appropriation is the worst solution, since it redistributes wealth, transferring it from the first player to the second. Not investing doesn't change anything, while investing and cooperating brings benefits. In this sense, the main function of the contract is to transform non-cooperative games into cooperative, that is, efficient, solutions.

However, when the costs of performing the contract are high, the Law begins to play a significant role in determining the liability for the default, since the cost of non-compliance with the contract varies according to the legal remedy applicable to its breach.

If liability rules for unlawful acts do not exist, agents tend not to take adequate precautions, as Fig. 2.3 shows.

In the absence of liability imputation, the victim will bear both the cost of precaution and the damage, while the offender has no interest in exercising any precaution. The opposite occurs when the offender's liability is unlimited, making him bear all the costs of precaution and imputation of responsibility, while the victim is not interested in bearing anything, except in situations where the damage is irreversible.

However, when liability exists, both subjective and objective, both will tend to adopt precautionary measures, which, in a first moment, can be said to lead to the efficient result. However, "when we add more complex variables to the problem, we reach the conclusion that there is no rule of civil liability that achieves the optimal result in all cases".[139]

Regarding liability, legal rules may determine either indemnification for damages or specific performance. While the former carries a low cost of noncompliance when compared to the latter, it still allows the choice between compliance or indemnification, since perfect indemnification leaves the victim in a situation of indifference regarding compliance and default.

Note that the EAL recognizes the possibility of efficient breach of contracts, whereby damages are compensated for. Thus, for this theory:

> If the contract can generate a gain by contracting with a third party by breaking the initial contract, even with full compensation to the frustrated contractor, such non-performance is desirable and deserves to be upheld by the courts.[140]

This theory encourages opportunistic behavior, generating uncertainty and destabilizing business relationships, because it allows for the deliberate resilience of contracts. At the international level, this would allow rich countries to violate international agreements because they are better able economically to pay for the illicit conduct.

In this sense, when the costs of compensation for the breach on the part of the promisor are equal to the benefit of compliance for the promissory, those will be internalized by him in the breach. Thus, "the promissory party has efficient incentives for compliance and non-compliance when the civil liability for the breach is equal to the benefit lost by the promissory".[141]

Furthermore, it should be emphasized that it will be difficult for compensation to be efficient, since the costs must be internalized by both the author of the damage and the victim. For this to happen, the former must fully compensate the latter, who, in turn, will not be able to receive full compensation for the damages. This situation is called the *indemnity paradox*[142] which permeates all areas of private Law and which, in contract Law, applies as follows:

> 1) For the promissee party to internalize the benefits of precaution, it must fully indemnify the promissory party for breach of promise; 2) For the promissory party to internalize the costs of trust, it must not receive the compensation for breach; 3) In contract law, the compensation paid by the promissee party for breach of the promise is equivalent to the compensation received by the promissory party; 4) Therefore, contract law cannot internalize the costs to the promissee and the promissory as efficiency requires.[143]

---

[139] Ibid, p. 199.

[140] Mackaay and Rousseau (2015), p. 490.

[141] Cooter and Ulen (2010), p. 214.

[142] Ibid, p. 270.

[143] Ibid, p. 273.

Therefore, it is not possible to internalize both costs at the same time, for this reason, it is said that the indemnity is inefficient. However, the calculation of compensation is complex when it comes to irreplaceable rights, such as the social losses that a State suffers as a result of the default of obligations by another State. Furthermore, in calculating compensation, certain costs, such as those arising from litigation and those imposed on third parties, are not computed. The negative externalities caused to society must be included in the compensation as determined by the PESE, which makes it difficult to repair the damage.

Despite this, the courts make use of the damages, mainly, when the goods are easily replaceable and when the illicit is irreversible, and specific execution is no longer possible. In this case, other alternatives are the specific execution or even the renegotiation of the contract.

In fact, the efficient *pareto* alternative is contract-specific execution. Two principles justify this statement: the principle of bargaining and the principle of indifference. By the former, it is assumed that the parties are best placed to find the solution that most closely matches their interests. The second, in turn, determines that the victim should not feel the difference between the execution and any other remedy, since both generate problems for compensation for losses and damages.[144]

Renegotiation, on the other hand, is only possible if the parties have equivalent bargaining powers, which is not the case when the remedy to be granted is damages. Specific performance, on the other hand, encompasses both principles, being *Pareto* efficient, since it does not admit any other form of solution, except the fulfillment of the obligation as desired in the contractual clauses negotiated by the parties.[145]

Regarding the promisor, the Law should also impose a high cost for misleading proposals since they imply non-cooperative behavior. Therefore, legal rules contribute to the efficiency of contracts by imposing costs on non-cooperation, since economic agents make their decisions based on cost-benefit analysis.

However, in the case of state decision-making, the cost-benefit assessment also considers internal causes. If the domestic benefit decreases or its cost increases due to compliance with an international obligation, the government will come under domestic pressure not to cooperate. Furthermore, the government must also compare the domestic result with the international one; if the former is more beneficial, in case of non-compliance, it will influence the decisions at the international level for non-cooperation.[146]

The politicians in government, on the other hand, are interested in staying in power. For this reason, they will spare no effort to make the effects of their policies visible to their voters.[147] The opposite is also true, politicians will procrastinate as much as possible on the negative effects of their actions so that the next government will bear the consequences.

---

[144] Mackaay and Rousseau (2015), pp. 487–488.

[145] Schropp (2009), pp. 58–59.

[146] Lucena (2006), p. 222.

[147] Mackaay and Rousseau (2015), p. 168.

Given this, it is possible to affirm that particular short-term internal interests can trigger the choice of non-cooperation to the detriment of long-term interests. In the case of subsidy policy, governments tend to keep them for immediate political purposes, to the detriment of SCM rules and DSB decisions, for which the responsibility of the State will be after a long period of time.

Considering that the main function of the Law is to prevent opportunistic behavior, provided that the costs of intervention are lower than the costs of contracts, the EAL will serve as an instrument to analyze, descriptively, the flaws inherent in the WTO treaties, specifically, the SCM and the ESC, capable of encouraging opportunistic behavior due to the low cost of its non-compliance. Therefore, in accordance with the normative dimension of the EAL, it will be proposed to change the system in relation to subsidies in order to encourage cooperative behavior.

References

Arida P (2006) Research in law and economics: around the historicity of the norm. In: Zytlberstajn D, Sztajn R (eds) Direito e Economia: Análise Econômica do Direito e das Organizações. Elsevier, Rio de Janeiro, pp 63–66, 69–70

Ashford N (2012) Schools of thought in classical liberalism, Part. 3: Public Choice. http://www.learnliberty.org/videos/schools-thought-classical-liberalism-part-3-public-choice/

Barral W, Pimentel LO (org) (2006) Teoria Jurídica e Desenvolvimento. Florianópolis, Fundação Boiteux

Bergson-Samuelson (1979) Social welfare functions and the theory of social choice. Q J Econ 93(1):73–90

Blaug M (1997) Economic theory in retrospect, 5th edn. Cambridge University Press, Cambridge, p 574

Buchanan J, Tullock G (1962) The calculus of consent: logical foundations of constitucional decmocracy. Michigan, Ann Arbor, p 45

Calabresi G (1961) Some thoughts on risk, distribution and the law of torts. Yale Law J 68

Calabresi G (1970) The cost of accidents: a legal and economic analysis. Yale University Press, New Haven

Caliendo P (2009) Direito Tributário e Análise Econômica do Direito: uma visão crítica. Elsevier, Rio de Janeiro, p 16

Calliari MP (2003) A Aplicabilidade da Teoria dos Jogos ao Direito Internacional: um estudo exploratório. Thesis (doctorate) - São Paulo Law School Postgraduate Course, São Paulo, p 12, 77

Coase R (1937) The nature of the firm. Econ New Ser 4(16):386–405

Coase R (1960) The problem of social cost. J Law Econ 3:1–44

Coelho CO (2007) A Análise Econômica do Direito enquanto Ciência: uma explicação de seu êxito sob a perspectiva da História do Pensamento Econômico. Berkely Program in Law & Economics

Congleton RD (2007) The globalization of politics: rational choice and the internationalization of public policy. http://ssrn.com/abstract=979459

Cooter R (1981) Law and the imperialism of economics: an introduction to the economic analysis of law and a review of the major books. UCLA Law Rev 29:1260, p 1266

Cooter R, Rubinfield D (1989) Economic analysis of legal disputes and their resolution. J Econ Liter XXVII, Set 1989, pp 1067–1097, p 1068

Cooter R, Ulen T (2010) Direito e Economia. 5ªed. Porto Alegre, Bookman, pp 35, 47, 102, 105, 109–110, 208–209, 211, 214, 248, 270, 273

Cruz SV (2020) Teoria e história: notas críticas sobre o tema da mudança institucional em Douglas North. Revista de Economia Política 23(2) (90), April–June, pp 107–122

Da Silva Neto OC (2005) Análise Econômica do Procedimento de Solução de Controvérsias da OMC: os conflitos entre exceções legítimas de políticas públicas e regras substantivas dos acordos. Thesis (Doctorate in Law)—Graduate Program, Law School of the University of São Paulo, São Paulo, pp 30, 244

Dworkin R (1999) O Império do Direito. Martins Fontes, São Paulo, pp 345–347

Feriato JMF (2013) O Novo Regime Automotivo Brasileiro e o Acordo sobre Subsídios e Medidas Compensatórias da OMC. XXII CONPEDI/UNICURITIBAMENEZES, pp 438–459

Gala P (2003) A Teoria Institucional de Douglass North [Douglass North's Institutional Theory]. Revista de Economia Política 23(90), abril-junho, p 103

Gonçalves EN (2001) A Tomada de Decisões Técnico-Legais para o Mercosul: uma apreciação do dumping sob o enfoque da Análise Econômica do Direito. Thesis (Doctorate)—Postgraduate Course in Law, Federal University of Minas Gerais, Belo Horizonte

Gonçalvez EN, Stelzer J (2006) Law and economics e o Justo Direito do Comércio Internacional. In: Barral W, Pimentel LO (org) (2006) Teoria Jurídica e Desenvolvimento. Florianópolis, Fundação Boiteux, pp 39, 42, 45–55, 58, 66

Gonçalvez EN, Stelzer J (2009) Economic analysis of law: an innovative general theory of law. In: Oliveira AF (coord) (2009) Direito Econômico: Evolução e Institutos. Rio de Janeiro, Forense, pp 38–39, 42, 44, 46–47, 56, 60, 62

Gonçalvez EN, Stelzer J (2013) Law and economics and fair international trade law

Hicks J (1939) The foundations of welfare economics. Econ J 49(196)

Hirsch W (1988) Law and economics: an introductory analysis. Academic, London, pp 4–5

Hoekman B, Kostecki M (2009) The political economy of the world trading system: the WTO and beyond. Oxford University Press, New York, p 26

Jackson J (2002) Sovereignty, subsidiarity, and separation of powers. In: Kennedy DLM, Southwick JD (eds) The political economy of international trade law. Cambridge University Press, Cambridge, pp 13–31

Kaldor N (1939) Welfare propositions. In: Economics and interpersonal comparisons of utility. Econ J 49(195)

Lucena AF (2006) Cooperar ou não cooperar, eis a questão: a Organização Mundial do Comércio, o Brasil e o Contencioso Embraer-Bombardier. Thesis (Doctorate in International Relations)—Doctoral Course in International Relations of the University of Brasilia, p 218, 222

Mackaay E, Rousseau S (2015) Análise Econômica do Direito. Trad. Rachel Sztajn. 2.ed. São Paulo, Atlas, pp 166, 168, 177–179, 411–412, 420, 422, 483, 487–488, 490

Maragno RC (2007) Reflexo das Barreiras Comerciais Europeias sobre as Exportações Brasileiras: uma abordagem utilizando a nova economia institucional. Dissertation (Master's Degree) - Graduate Program in Production Engineering. São Carlos Engineering School of the University of São Paulo, p 31

Mueller DC (2003) Public choice III. Cambridge University Press, Cambridge, p 1

North DC (1990) Institutions, institutional change and economic performance. Cambridge University Press, p 3, 86

Oliveira AF (Coord) (2009) Direito Econômico: Evolução e Institutos. Rio de Janeiro, Forense

Pareto V (1996) Manual de Economia Política. Trad. João Guilherme Vargas Netto. São Paulo, Nova Cultural

Polinsky M (1989) An introduction to law and economics, 2nd edn. Little, Brown & Co., Boston, pp 7–8

Pondé JL (2005) Institutions and Institutional Change: A Schumpeterian Approach. Revista Economia, Brasília (DF) 6(1), jan/jul, pp 119–160

Posner R (1993) The new institutional economics meets law and economics. J Inst Theor Econ 149:73, p 6, 19, 27

Roemer A (1994) Introducción al Análisis Econômico del Derecho. Mexico: Fondo de Cultura Económica, pp 5–6, 13–15, 19–22, 39, 41, 50, 52–53, 57–58

Salama BM (2008) O que é Pesquisa em Direito e Economia? In: GV Law Notebook (in press). São Paulo, FGV/EDESP. http://works.bepress.com/bruno_meyerhof_salama, pp 15–31

Schropp S (2009) Trade policy flexibility and enforcement in the WTO: a law and economics analysis. Cambridge University Press, London, pp 32, 58–59, 63, 66

Seabra F, Formaggi L, Flach L (2006) O Papel das Instituições no Desenvolvimento Econômico. In: Barral W, Pimentel LO (2006) Teoria Jurídica e Desenvolvimento. Florianópolis, Boiteux, pp 71–86

Sen A (2000) Desenvolvimento como Liberdade. São Paulo, Companhia das Letras, pp 41–42, 77–82, 108

Silva Neto OC (2005) Análise Econômica do Procedimento de Solução de Controvérsias da OMC: os conflitos entre exceções legítimas de políticas públicas e regras substantivas dos acordos. Tese (doutorado em Direito)—Programa de Pós-graduação, Faculdade de Direito da Universidade de São Paulo, São Paulo, pp 47–50

Simon H (1985) Human nature in politics: the dialogue of psychology with political science. Am Polit Sci Rev 79:293–304

Stephen FH (1993) Teoria Econômica do Direito. McGraw-Hill, São Paulo, pp 2, 38–39

Sykes AO (2003) The economics of WTO rules on subsidies and countervailing measures. Law and Economics Working Paper, n. 186, The Law School, University of Chicago, p 6

Timm L (2014) Direito e Economia no Brasil.2 ed. São Paulo, Atlas, pp 166, 168, 191, 199

Toyoshima SH (1999) Instituições e Desenvolvimento Econômico—Uma Análise Crítica das Idéias de Douglas North. IPE-USP, Estudos Avançados 29(1):95–112

Williamson O (1985) The economic institutions of capitalism: firms, markets, relational contracting. University of Illinois

Williamson O (2005) Por que Direito, Economia e Organizações. In: Zytlberstajn D, Sztajn R (eds) (2006) Direito e Economia: análise Econômica do Direito e das Organizações. Elsevier, Rio de Janeiro, pp 22–23

Wittman D (2006) Economic foundations of law and organization. Cambridge University Press, p 194

Zytlberstajn D, Sztajn R (2006) Direito e Economia: análise Econômica do Direito e das Organizações. Elsevier, Rio de Janeiro, p 81

Chapter 3
Regulation of Subsidies at the Multilateral Level and in Brazil

Abstract Subsidies are political-economic instruments of States either to protect national industry or to enable export. As their effects, subsidies cause distortions that might be very prejudicial to industries that lack this type of support. Besides, subsidies must be ruled internationally otherwise if all types of subsidies were allowed, stronger countries would be privileged since they have better economic conditions to promote their industries. For this reason, multilateral cooperation must also be encouraged by international law. Specificity is the main criteria for prohibited subsidies by WTO once the more specific they are, greater distortions they cause. In view of that, the study explores the multilateral trade system, its rules, illegal and actionable subsidies, and it also analyzes WTO's unilateral system for countering illegal subsidies, known as countervailing measures. In the end, it shows how subsidies are treated by law under Brazil's structure.

Considering that subsidies are regulated in the international market by the World Trade Organization, it is pertinent to highlight that international organizations contribute to a greater institutionalization of international relations, enabling the opening of discussion forums and the regulation of common interests. The principles, rules and procedures established within its scope contribute to greater "jurisdization" of the system.

In this sense, this chapter aims to study primarily the regulation of subsidies in the WTO framework, to better understand the problem of their ineffectiveness. To this end, first, it is necessary to analyze the role of subsidies on the international economy, and then to present the structure and regulation of subsidies and compensatory measures within the WTO and domestic Law.

J. Marteli Fais Feriato, *Legal, Political and Economic Strategies of Subsidies within the World Trade Organization*, European Yearbook of International Economic Law 40, https://doi.org/10.1007/978-3-031-73869-2_3

3.1 Subsidies in the International Economy

Subsidies are political-economic instruments[1] State intervention in the economy, which, through direct financial aid, tax incentives and the concession of goods and services for production, aims to protect the national industry and/or enable it to compete in international trade.

There are two types of subsidies, those intended to promote export and those called by Sykes[2] of protectives, which, intended for the substitution of imports, serve to protect the national industry.

The influence of subsidies on trade is undeniable, so much so that some authors, such as Fernandez, equate them with tribute, but in reverse. According to the author: "the subsidy can be interpreted as a negative sign tax, so that its effects on market equilibrium are analogous but not equal, mainly by the inverse distortion that it creates [...]³". Thus, subsidies can be granted through tax exemption, suspension, tax refund, as well as for any tax benefit, producing direct effects on the market balance.

The theme resumes the discussion between liberalism and interventionism since subsidies are state instruments to promote exports and protect the national industry through import substitution.

One of the criticisms of liberalism lies in the divergence between the interests of States and private initiative, creating the need for state intervention precisely to guarantee state interests, since companies, especially multinationals, are not concerned with the social issues of States.[4]

On the other hand, liberalism allows for the optimization of production factors and the reduction of costs, which in turn increases consumption and production, providing increased employment and social welfare. Moreover, liberalism generates interdependence among nations and consequent cooperation, as occurs, for example, with the regional blocks.[5]

Protectionist industrial policies therefore trigger a series of negative consequences, such as the accommodation of national industry, which, due to lack of competition, is not obliged to improve its quality, and the formation of monopolies that distort fair competition. On the other hand, protectionist policies result in less vulnerability of the national industry, in the protection of natural resources and in the guarantee of employment, factors that can be harmed by foreign industry, which, with more competitive prices, can undermine the national industry.

Faced with this impasse and the reality of an imperfect market, there is currently talk of neoliberalism, represented by the minimal State: liberal in the sense of reducing trade barriers, but interventionist when it is necessary to counter negative

---

[1] Also considered modalities of State intervention in the economy are tariff and non-tariff barriers (technical and sanitary barriers), import and export licenses, quotas, customs tariffs, among others.

[2] Sykes (2003).

[3] Fernandez (2009), p. 45.

[4] Maia (2011), p. 156.

[5] Ibid, p. 155.

externalities, including unfair trade practices. Moreover, subsidies are not neutral with respect to income distribution and, in the short term, can be beneficial.[6] However, determining the limits for the use of subsidies is a complex issue and, for this reason, has constantly been on the WTO's agenda.[7]

It should be noted that, in a situation of free trade, countries seek to specialize in the production of goods in which they have a comparative advantage based on comparative opportunity cost. That is, considering that resources are scarce, countries seek to optimize the available production factors. However, within the imperfect market scenario, state intervention is necessary to correct market failures. It happens that, many times, the means used to correct them can trigger new failures, causing market inefficiency and reallocation of resources.

Subsidies, therefore, have been used as instruments of intervention for trade policy purposes to achieve market efficiency. This is because of their ability to influence prices, either upward or downward.

Considering that export subsidies are granted through tax incentives, it is verified their close relationship with taxes, urging the need to, first, study the role that taxation plays on international trade.

3.1.1 The Role of Taxation on the International Economy

Taxation is intrinsically linked to the performance of the State: the greater its intervention in the regulation of the economy and its commitment to social development, the greater its need for collection. Thus, the profile of tax rules also changes according to the performance of the State.

In the liberal State, the tax rules served only the fiscal function, that is, they had as their scope the collection of resources to meet the financial needs of the State, which should be minimal. In this way, taxation should be neutral in relation to the economy and social issues.

Considering that at that time few people enjoyed the rights enshrined in the French Revolution due to their privileged economic position, the State was given the task of guaranteeing such rights. To this end, taxation gained a new function, as the State began to be concerned with economic and social issues. In this sense, Bobbio points out:

> The phenomenon of promotional law reveals the passage from the State that, when intervening in the economic sphere, limits itself to protecting this or that productive activity for itself, to the State that also proposes to direct the economic activity of a country, towards

---

[6] Sumner distinguishes between cotton and rice subsidies; while the former benefits little the poor people living in poor countries, such as the African countries, the latter contributes significantly to the poor people who are not producers of agricultural goods, who are able to consume the product due to its lower price. In: Sumner (2006). In: Anderson and Martin (2006), pp. 271–292.

[7] Sykes points out that the major problem lies with protective subsidies, while a general ban on non-agricultural export subsidies has been helpful. Sykes (2003).

this or that objective - the passage from the merely protectionist State to the programmatic State.[8]

Taxation became the instrument for the realization of the new functions of the State. Currently, taxes are not restricted solely to a collection purpose, but have a structuring tax justice functionality, enhancing the production of a sector or a region of the country in favor of the collective interest.

This new function is called extra fiscal, since the main purpose of the tax is no longer the collection, which Schoueri[9] calls it an "inducing tax rule",[10] because it intervenes in the economic domain, to promote certain behaviors. In this way, the economic agent will not be compelled by the norm to perform a certain behavior by means of repression, but rather induced to choose the less onerous option, which can occur by the punctual burdening of certain facts or by the exoneration resulting from tax incentives.

Tax incentives have been the most widely used means today to regulate extra fiscal economic activities.[11] However, it is noteworthy that even taxes with a merely collecting characteristic can exert a certain influence on economic agents, even if indirectly, stimulating less costly activities and discouraging those that suffer greater tax burden.

Taxes, therefore, are considered as costs, which raise the price of goods in the importing country and decrease them in the exporter, while their renunciation generates benefits, relieving prices. Thus, in the importing country, consumers are harmed by higher prices, but producers gain, and, in addition, the State collects more, while in the exporting country, consumers win, but producers lose.[12]

Due to the distortions caused by both taxes and tax incentives, theories arise that oppose the intervention of the State through inducing tax rules. These theories, known as fiscal neutrality theories, preach that taxation should be a means of exceptional economic regulation and not an essential element of inducing economic agents.[13]

Considering that every economy needs institutional organization to operate, and that this, in turn, must be financed by taxation, neutrality is utopian. For this reason, the economic equilibrium must be preserved with the least possible effect of taxation on the price system.

Moreover, the use of the tax for specific non-collection purposes generates insecurity and discourages investment in the activity and its expansion. For this reason, the use of the extra fiscal function of the tax must be eventual, justified, and

---

[8] Bobbio (2007), p. 71.

[9] Schoueri (2005), pp. 43–44.

[10] The Brazilian Federal Constitution of 1981 already foresaw for inducing tax rules in relation to customs taxes, however, it cannot be said that this type of rule was frequent at the time, but an exception.

[11] Pires (2007). In: Martins et al. (2007), pp. 18–19.

[12] Krugman and Obstfeld (2010), pp. 141–142.

[13] Caliendo (2009), pp. 101–117.

Fig. 3.1 Shows the
equilibrium point and the
displacements of the
supply line by taxes and
subsidies. Source: Author

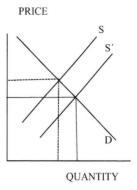

PRICE

QUANTITY

temporary, and the tax cannot be used primarily to intervene in the economy in order to favor some.[14]

Thus, the least possible intervention of the State should be used to avoid inefficiencies and undue allocation of factors of production, but at the same time, taxation is necessary to guarantee fundamental rights and the implementation of policies that promote social welfare.

The problem is the use of social justifications to implement specific subsidy programs designed to promote an industry or sector, distorting trade, that is, disguised distorting subsidies, as one comes to study.

3.1.2   Economic Assessment of Subsidies

Subsidies alter market equilibrium, which is achieved when the "price reaches the level at which the quantity supplied is equal to the quantity demanded",[15] represented by the point of intersection of the supply and demand curves. Thus, "at the equilibrium price, the quantity of the good that buyers desire and can buy is exactly equal to the quantity that sellers desire and can sell".[16]

In the Fig. 3.1, S represents the point of equilibrium between supply and demand, represented by line D. The intersection between S′ and D demonstrates the displacement of the supply line due to the use of subsidies.

Taxation, like compensatory measures, is able to shift the supply line to the left, increasing the price and consequently reducing the quantity of demand. On the other hand, export subsidies shift the supply line to the right (effect represented at the intersection between D and S′), artificially decreasing the production costs of

---

[14] Ibid, p. 121.

[15] Mankiw (2009), p. 75.

[16] Ibid, p. 76.

Table 3.1 Impact of subsidies and tariffs on producers, consumers, government, and national welfare. Source: Bruno (2013)[a]

	Fare		Export subsidies	
	Large country	Small country	Large country	Small country
Producer's gain	Increases	Increases	Increases	Increases
Consumer gain	Decreases	Decreases	Decreases	Decreases
Government gain	Increases	Increases	Decreases (more)	Decreases
National welfare	Ambiguous	Decreases	Decreases (more)	Decreases

[a]Bruno (2013), pp. 300–320

the domestic industry and the final consumer, increasing the price received by producers.

The countervailing measures are justified as measures capable of counterbalancing the effects of subsidies, relocating the S′ line to the point of equilibrium prior to the use of subsidies, where S meets D.

In view of this, it is possible to verify that subsidies have the opposite effects of taxes: while taxes increase the price in the importing country, subsidies cause the price to increase in the exporting country and decrease in the importing country.

Moreover, Krugman points out that "the export subsidy worsens the terms of trade to the extent that it lowers the price of exports in the foreign market [...][17]". At first, this may seem beneficial to consumers in the foreign country, but in the long run, by distorting prices, they reallocate resources and can eliminate competing foreign industry.

Protective subsidies, intended for import substitution, cause the same effects of taxation regarding the reallocation of resources from the external market to the domestic market. This is because subsidies artificially lower the production costs of domestic industry, causing goods and services to no longer be produced at the lowest possible cost, which would be possible with importation.[18]

Therefore, for the economic analysis, subsidies generate perverse effects in relation to the distribution of income, directly in the country that subsidizes and, indirectly, in the other countries of the world. This is why subsidies are justified on political rather than economic grounds. Krugman states that, "export subsidies undoubtedly generate costs that exceed their benefits".[19]

It is true that the impact of subsidies will depend on the share of representation of each economy. This means that subsidies granted by rich countries, such as the United States, will have a greater impact on world trade than those granted by poor countries. Internally, subsidies harm the consumer, reduce government earnings and national welfare, as can be seen in Table 3.1.

---

[17] Krugman and Obstfeld (2010), p. 145.

[18] Sykes (2003).

[19] Krugman and Obstfeld (2010), p. 145.

Note that consumers are the most affected in both cases, because taxes make imported goods more expensive, while subsidies raise, internally, the prices of domestic goods by increasing the supply for the foreign market.[20]

In turn, in the importing country of subsidized goods, subsidies initially benefit consumers by reducing the prices of imported goods, but later the subsidized industry can eliminate competition, obtain a monopoly, and raise prices.

In the subsidizing country, the costs brought about by subsidies financed by taxation, which in turn falls on consumers, reduce social welfare. The effects of subsidies are bad for the subsidizing government, unlike the effects of taxation, which are beneficial to it.

One must also consider the elasticity of the supply line, because the more elastic it is, the greater the absorption of the subsidy by producers and, in turn, the greater the benefits received. Elasticity is an economic concept that refers to the sensitivity of demand and supply functions. Fernandez exemplifies:

1. If the elasticity of demand for a given good or service is less than unity, then the demand curve is said to be inelastic, indicating that the demand function is relatively insensitive to changes in price.
2. If the elasticity of demand for a good or service is greater than unity, the demand curve is said to be elastic, meaning that the demand function is relatively sensitive to changes in price.[21]

Thus, tax neutrality must be achieved, especially in the more inflexible sectors, because the *lower* the elasticity of the good, the greater the distortive effects of subsidies. For Stigler, those who possess more specialized resources are able to make more profit by applying a subsidy, since "they will have no alternative uses for their resources and thus their income will vary directly with the volume of production of the industry".[22]

Stigler[23] confirms the benefits generated by specificity. Thus, when the elasticity of supply is small, the industry will prefer direct subsidies rather than protection by tariff or non-tariff barriers,[24] or by import quotas, and continues:

> We have already outlined the main explanations for the fact that an industry with the power to obtain government favors generally does not use that power to obtain money: unless the list of beneficiaries can be limited, given that any amount of subsidies the industry obtains will be dissipated among an increasing number of rivals.[25]

---

[20] The use of subsidies stimulates the production of the subsidized good and therefore increases its supply in the foreign market.

[21] Fernandez (2009), p. 25.

[22] Stigler (1977). http://web.mit.edu/xaq/Public/Stigler.

[23] Ibid.

[24] Tariff barriers constitute an import burden through taxes, while non-tariff barriers are technical or sanitary barriers, which require that minimum requirements be observed for the imported product to enter the country.

[25] Free translation of: "We have already sketched the main explanations for the fact that an industry with power to obtain governmental favors usually does not use this power to get money: unless the

It is evident that the more specific the subsidies, the greater the distortions caused, which contribute to the reallocation of resources and the discrimination of goods, causing the non-subsidized market to lose competitiveness and increase poverty, reducing world prices. Such a situation is inconsistent with the objectives of the WTO, which are free trade and development.

Added to this problem is the fact that the transnational economy weakens the power of states to control trade, since they are more susceptible to the new, economically powerful, international actors. This is why the specificity of subsidies becomes interesting. Caliendo warns of the possibility of misuse of state mechanisms, so "[...] Behind a discourse in favor of tax incentives beneficial to the whole society can hide an odious privilege for a small economic group [...]".[26]

With regard to fair competition, subsidies specific to some companies or sectors discourage the increase in the level of efficiency of the economy, since they allow the elimination of competitors by practicing predatory prices.

Economic activity must be free, this means that economic agents must decide what, how much and how to produce from the freedom of initiative. The free market depends on free competition, that is, on equal chances among economic agents.

This way, the introduction of a subsidy can create perverse obstacles to international trade, unbalancing economic activity, discriminating against competitors by providing them with different competitive conditions, and restricting freedom of initiative.

Subsidies are only justified as an instrument for correcting social inequalities or market failures, to equalize distorted prices in the face of imperfect market structures. Nevertheless, Sykes points out that specific export-linked subsidies are hardly the best response to market failures. In case a Country opts for a subsidy policy, the most appropriate is that they are not specific.[27]

In this sense, subsidies should be tolerated as rules of intervention in the economic domain, but their use is limited by domestic Tax and Competition Law and by the international rules of the WTO.[28]

The line between the advantages and disadvantages of subsidies on free trade is very thin and difficult to ascertain, because at first, the subsidy may seem interesting as an anti-cyclical measure against economic crises, but in the long run, it can generate harmful consequences on international prices, raising them and causing protectionist reactions by the affected governments. According to the World Bank:

> [...] when a country imposes export barriers or reduces trade and consumption taxes, choosing to insulate its domestic market from international price increases, while at the same time benefiting its domestic market, it cooperates with the exacerbated increase in world prices.[29]

---

list of beneficiaries can be limited by acceptable device, whatever amount of subsidies the industry can obtain will be dissipated among a growing number of rivals." In: Stigler (1977).

[26] Caliendo (2009), p. 34.

[27] Sykes (2003).

[28] Catão (2003), p. 74.

[29] World Bank (2008), p. 16.

Moreover, it must be considered that governments adopt exclusively economic criteria to determine their trade policies, other, non-economic forces (employment, the equitable distribution of income, the profit of companies or of some) exert influence at the moment of decision making, which makes subsidies the means to achieve these ends.

3.2   Economic Foundations of Multilateral Subsidy Regulation

Trade regulation at the multilateral level is necessary to promote cooperation and prevent unfair practices, such as subsidies, from occurring. Faced with the fact that, for greater fluidity of trade, there can be no discrimination, multilateralism presents itself as the cornerstone of free trade.

Now, when considering that free trade can serve as an instrument for development, its deviation can lead to totally different and perverse effects. In this sense, Jacob Viner[30] examines the paradox of free trade areas and customs unions, which both create trade through *intra*-bloc liberalization and divert it by imposing *extra*-bloc barriers, which he calls "trade creation and trade detour".

In free trade zones, the member countries reduce or eliminate tax and non-tariff barriers to trade within them. For example, in Mercosur, the importation of a Brazilian product by Argentina would not be subject to taxes such as import duty. In customs unions, besides having a free trade area, the member countries adopt a common external tariff, that is, the import of products from countries that are not part of the block is subject to the same taxation, regardless of the country through which they enter.

In trade detour, factors of production are diverted from optimal uses to inefficient uses in order to ensure national production, while trade creation, by not admitting discrimination, allows factors of production to be used efficiently, ensuring better reallocation of resources.

In this sense, according to Viner, multilateral trade agreements that adopt the clause that does not allow discrimination between imported and domestic products guarantee a better reallocation of resources to the country that is efficient, creating trade, while preferential agreements, tariff or non-tariff barriers and subsidies cause trade detour because they allow non-efficient countries to gain an advantage in the price of their products.[31]

As an example, Mercosur can create intra-bloc trade, but at the expense of diverting other trade, and may produce negative net results in the end. As an example, Krugman[32] cites the case of Brazil's automotive industry, protected and inefficient,

---

[30] Viner (2014).

[31] Ibid.

[32] Krugman (2008), p. 182.

but which benefited from the bloc's tariff reduction and conquered the Argentinian market to the detriment of imports from elsewhere, outside the bloc.

Viner[33] emphasizes the advantages of multilateralism, since regional agreements concomitantly create and divert trade, therefore, for them to be beneficial, trade creation must surpass detour. In turn, agreements made at the multilateral level would have a greater capacity to create trade.

It is essential that the regulation of subsidies be resolved at the multilateral level, as it follows the logic of the prisoner's dilemma,[34] whereby cooperation would be the best solution. This means that in the case of export subsidies:

> [...] where industries from multiple countries compete for the same export markets. Each country would fare better, according to its own perception, if all other countries eliminated their export subsidies except itself. If everyone continued to subsidize, everyone would fare worse than if they didn't, because they would spend money, but they would not gain any more markets than if everyone eliminated their subsidies or reduced them to the same level.[35]

Therefore, for the proper functioning of international trade, so that everyone wins from it, it is essential that trade policies are coordinated. If a country A makes a bilateral concession to country B, reducing the tariffs on product x, exported by B, and the latter, in turn, grants the same benefit to product y, exported by A, both will obtain gains. However, these gains can reach country C, exporter of product x, without it having to make concessions.

Concerning subsidies, Reich[36] reinforces the need for its multilateral regulation and greater effectiveness, because it is a subject that, if not addressed through the

---

[33] Viner (2014).

[34] The Prisoners' Dilemma is a very famous game that represents well the dilemma between cooperating and betraying Briefly, the story is as follows. Two suspects, A and B, are arrested by police. The police does not have enough evidence to convict them, so they separate the prisoners into different rooms and offer them both the same deal: (a) If one of the prisoners confesses (betrays the other) and the other remains silent, the one who confessed goes free while the silent accomplice serves 10 years.

(b) If both remain silent (collaborate with each other), the police sentences 1 year each. (c) If both confess (betray the accomplice), each takes 5 years in jail. The big problem in the Prisoners' Dilemma is that balance (Betray-Betray) is not the best outcome because there is another possible and better: if both choose to Collaborate (stay silent) each would be left with only 1 year in prison. Thus, the Prisoners' Dilemma is an abstraction of ordinary situations in which the choice of the best individual leads to mutual betrayal, while collaboration would provide better results. The Science of Strategy. http://www.teoriadosjogos.net/teoriadosjogos/list-trechos.asp?id=.

[35] Free adaptation of: "where the industries of several countries compete for the same export markets. Each country would be best off, according to its own perception, if the other countries all eliminated export subsidies, except for itself. If everybody continues to subsidize, they are all worse off than if they didn't, because they spend money but don't gain more markets than what they would have if everybody stopped subsidizing, or brought down subsidies to the same levels." In: Reich (2009). http://ec.europa.eu/education/jean-monnet/doc/confglobal06/contribution_reich.pdf.

[36] Ibid.

cooperation of all countries, those not participating will have some advantage over the others.

The regulation of international trade on a multilateral basis is important to ensure the stability and predictability of trade relations. However, some economists thought that economic regulation was sufficient to correct possible market failures and predatory competition. With his economic theory of regulation, Stigler changes this view and warns about the power of the State to compel the reallocation of resources, inducing the choices of economic agents without their consent.[37]

From this, he analyzes the theory of regulation, concluding that, most of the time, it serves the interests of specific sectors of the economy instead of the public interest in general, which are usually diverse, thus occurring the replacement of the economic decision-making process by the political decision, whose result is economic inefficiency.[38]

It turns out that the regulation of subsidies has been lenient with States, with respect to their application, allowing political decisions and promoting harmful subsidy competition due to the lack of efficiency in the WTO's countering mechanisms, depriving the weakest countries of challenging them and, consequently, of the developmental advantages promised by free trade.

The issue is difficult to converge between governments due to the difficulty of finding common values when it comes to subsidies, but it cannot be said that the issue will be resolved at the regional or bilateral level. On the contrary, an effective solution can only be achieved on the basis of cooperation among all WTO member States.

Given the above, it was possible to verify in this chapter that some neoliberal ideas, as well as contradictory interests of governments, were transferred to the World Trade Organization, which, at the time of its formation, continued to prioritize the reduction of import restrictions, allowing the promotion of exports, still under the auspices of Classic International Law.

However, subsidies, by serving as an instrument of economic intervention by the State to promote exports and protect the domestic industry, cause distortions in the international market. And although the subject has already been regulated at the multilateral level, it still generates impasses in the WTO. For this reason, the next chapter will present the Economic Analysis of Law theory, which will serve as a basis for understanding the rationality of governments in making use of subsidy programs in the face of the spaces found in the multilateral trade system, making it ineffective for developing and least developed countries.

---

[37] Fiani (2004), p. 83.
[38] Ibid, p. 85.

3.3   The WTO Multilateral Trading System

The economic collapse resulting from World War II caused states to seek cooperation to ensure the stabilization of the economy, concluding that the elimination of
barriers on the international market was indispensable. In light of this, an agreement
was created to reduce trade tariffs, known as GATT/47.

After seven rounds of negotiations, the WTO was founded in 1994 with the rati-
fication of the Marrakech Agreement by 123 countries,[39] which, besides having
absorbed GATT/47, brought important innovations. When it comes to reducing
taxes on foreign trade in industrial goods, developed countries have reduced them
by an average of 60%, more specifically, from 6.3% to 3.8%,[40] while for developing
countries, the reduction, although variable, was significant (an average of 50% for
India, Singapore and South Korea). The overall average of taxes levied on trade in
goods fell from 40% to 5%.[41]

In addition, the countries also committed to significantly reduce export subsidies
on agricultural goods, as well as those aimed at providing domestic support to producers, amounting to $18 trillion.[42]

The WTO is an independent international organization, with legal personality
under public international law, endowed with a legal system and its dispute settlement system of a jurisdictional nature, in the sense that it renders decisions based on
law, final and binding, although not res judicata.[43] In this sense, Sanchez asserts that
"[…] the international trade system, in this sense, is recognized as one of the most
"jurisdictional" of the global economic system".[44]

The WTO has gone beyond mere tax reduction, as Stichele points out, the organization […] "covers a wide range of sectors, with implications for most aspects of
life, for example in the area of intellectual property rights (biotechnology), agriculture (food), the service sector (transport) and telecommunications".[45]

A myriad of multilateral agreements stand out, obligatory by the principle of
single undertaking, for all acceding states, on the following subjects: agriculture,
sanitary and phytosanitary measures, textiles and clothing, technical barriers to

---

[39] WTO (1994) Constitutive Agreement, internalized in Brazil by Decree no. 1.355, December 30.

[40] GATT Secretariat (1994) The Results of the Uruguay Round of Multilateral Trade Negotations:
Market Access for Goods and Services: overview of the results. http://www.ub.edu/prometheus21/
articulos/archivos/gatt.PDF.

[41] Ibid.

[42] Ibid.

[43] It is said that the decisions of the Dispute Settlement Body do not become res judicata because
the parties may, at any time, conclude agreements.

[44] Sanchez (2004), p. 63.

[45] Free translation from: "This pattern persists despite the WTO having developed its jurisdiction
well beyond the area of tariff reduction. The WTO now covers a wide range of sectors with implications for most aspects of life, for example, in the area of intellectual property rights (biotechnology), agriculture (food), the services industry (transport) and telecommunications". In:
Stichele (1998) http://www.tni.org/archives/reports_wto_wto3.

trade, investment, rules of origin, subsidies and countervailing measures, safe-guards, trade in services, intellectual property, agreement *antidumping*, import licensing, customs valuation, and the Dispute Settlement Understanding (DSU), as well as the Trade Policy Review Mechanism.

Regarding barriers to trade and the possibility of using unilateral measures to eliminate trade disparities, GATT/47 was more flexible, admitting interventions for "public morals, human, animal and plant life and health, trade in precious metals, national artistic, historic and archaeological heritage, etc."[46] In the WTO, although the organization has maintained the principles of GATT/47, Gonçalves continues, "there are distinct codes for eliminating trade disparities and barriers to free trade - quantitative, tariff, and non-tariff restrictions in general".[47]

Moreover, by obliging member states to adhere to all multilateral agreements,[48] the rule of *single undertaking* reinforces the primacy of rules in the WTO, which, unlike the GATT, known as *a la carte,* allowed the free choice of agreements by the States according to their interests. This principle raises the degree of "jurisdictionality" of the multilateral trading system, since "[...] the more rigid the agreement, the more security is given to commitments and thus the more credibility to the system is guaranteed".[49]

It is also worth noting that although the GATT/47 mandated that states seek to settle their disputes, it did not have the means to guarantee such a solution. Moreover, any decision in its scope could be rendered innocuous by the simple refusal to comply with it, regardless of justifications, and it can be said that the aggrieved State tended to fail to comply with it.

The WTO, in turn, has a structure that provides a jurisdictional function, represented by the Dispute Settlement Body (DSB), whose methods and procedures are provided for in the agreement known as the Dispute Settlement Understanding (ESC),[50] establishing a coercive mechanism for the settlement of disputes, with a double degree of jurisdiction. In addition, the rule for the adoption of its decisions is that of negative consensus, which means that it can only be rendered innocuous by the consensus of all members of the organization. In this way, the adoption of decisions is practically automatic since the winning member will always accept it.

Thorstensen highlights the differences between GATT/47 and the WTO, stating that:

---

[46] Gonçalves and Stelzer (2010). http://www.conpedi.org.br/manaus/arquivos/anais/fortaleza/3755.pdf, p. 2409.

[47] Ibid.

[48] The WTO differentiates multilateral from plurilateral agreements in terms of mandatory adoption. While the former are binding on all members by the principle of *single undertaking*, the latter are optional and are restricted to only four agreements: aircraft trade, public tendering, dairy products and beef.

[49] Sanchez (2004), p. 62.

[50] World Trade Organization. Understanding on Rules and Procedures Governing the Settlement of Disputes. http://www.wto.org/english/docs_e/legal_e/28-dsu.pdf.

> [...]one of the main problems of the old GATT was that parties losing the panel could block its adoption, since the practice was to adopt decisions by consensus. However, despite not having the strength of a court, the GATT exerted strong political pressure on the parties to the agreement to comply with the pre-established rules. This situation only changed with the WTO.[51]

Considering this, it can be said that the multilateral trading system is no longer exclusively, *power oriented* and became *rule oriented*, which implies strengthening the primacy of rules in international trade.[52] It is worth noting Jackson's remark about the term *rule oriented*, which, he said, contrasts with the terms "rule of law" or "rule-based system"[53]:

> *Rule oriented* implies a less rigid adherence to the 'rule' and denotes some fluidity in legal approaches that seems to accord with reality (especially mattering in bargaining or negotiation). Phrases that emphasize, too strongly, the strict application of rules sometimes frighten decision-makers, although in reality they may achieve the same goal. Any legal system must accommodate the ambiguities inherent in the rules and the constantly changing needs of society. The key point is that rule enforcement procedures, which often focus on a dispute resolution procedure, should be designed in such a way as to promote, as much as possible, the stability and predictability of the rules. To this end, the procedure must be respectable, "legitimate", and reasonably efficient (difficult criteria).[54]

The fact that the multilateral trade system is institutionalized in an international organization extends and strengthens its "jurisdiction" by establishing clearer and more precise rules and procedures, and therefore guarantees greater predictability. On the other hand, Member States may, by agreement, make changes to the system. According to Sanchez:

> On the one hand, the organizations present themselves as forums for the concentration of converging interests, which regulate interests in maintaining the system in force; and, on the other hand, they are arenas for the contribution of elements that alter the very system on which they were founded.[55]

Regarding the delegation of powers to the organization, the multilateral trade system has a medium-high level of jurisdiction, due to the institutionalization of its trade policy review and dispute settlement mechanisms, which are still directed by the States that may converge in opposite ways, which is the reason why jurisdiction

---

[51] Thorstensen (1999), p. 31.

[52] Goyos (1994), pp. 13–14.

[53] Jackson (2000), p. 8.

[54] Free adaptation from: "Rule orientation implies a less rigid adherence to 'rule' and connotes some fluidity in the rule approaches which seems to accord with reality (especially since it accommodates some bargaining or negotiation). Phrases that emphazise too strongly the sctrict application of rules sometimes scare policy-makers, although in reality they may amount to the same thing. Any legal system must accommodate the inherent ambiguities of rules and the constant changes in the pratical needs of human society. The key point is that the procedures of rule application, which often center on a dispute settlement procedures, should be designed so as to promote as much as possible the stability and predictability of the rule system. For this purpose the procedure must be creditable, 'legitimate' and reasonably efficient (not easy criteria). In: Ibid, pp. 8–9.

[55] Sanchez (2004), p. 71.

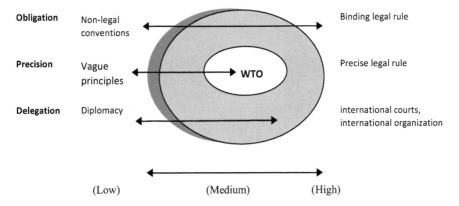

Fig. 3.2 Degree of "WTO Jurisdiction". Source: Sanchez (2004) (Ibid, p. 87.)

has not reached its highest level. However, the level is medium-low when it comes to the precision of the principles and delegation, due to the many ambiguous concepts found in the agreements and the permission to take market-distorting measures.[56] This analysis is made by Sanchez, who summarizes it in Fig. 3.2.

The weakness of the "jurisdictional" system derives from the GATT/47 model, absorbed by the WTO. It should also be noted that WTO rules can be limited by member States, which have the power to negotiate or modify them, in some cases by bilateral agreement[57] or, even if negotiated multilaterally, can be contested by interested parties when they are not complied with.[58]

Although the WTO system has flaws, there has been an increased degree of "jurisdictionalization" in multilateral trade relations, which have been partly transferred to the organization, while still retaining certain powers for member States.

For a better understanding of the "jurisdictionalization" of the WTO, it is necessary to know its structure, as well as its basic principles, which will have repercussions on the regulation, interpretation and application of the rules concerning subsidies, which will be studied next.

3.3.1 Functions and Principles

The WTO plays an important role in the development of trade relations among its members, with the main function of facilitating and managing the functioning of the agreements that make up the multilateral trading system, serving as a forum for international trade negotiations while overseeing the implementation of trade

---

[56] Ibid, p. 88.

[57] Members can, for example, enter into settlement agreements after the final decision rendered by the Dispute Settlement Body.

[58] See: Sanchez (2004), pp. 88–89.

policies.[59] The WTO is also responsible for administering the dispute settlement system and cooperating with other governmental and non-governmental organizations.

Another important function of the organization is the provision of technical assistance to developing and least developed countries to better integrate them into the multilateral trading system. When the Doha Round was launched, members recognized the essentiality of technical cooperation and capacity building for system development.[60]

According to the preamble of the WTO, international economic relations are to be conducted based on rising living standards, full employment, increasing real incomes and demand, expanding production and trade in goods and services, and the sustainable use of resources for the protection and preservation of the environment.

Moreover, the means to this end must be compatible with the needs and interests of countries at different levels of development. In this regard, the instrument recognizes the need to make efforts to integrate developing and least developed countries into international trade in proportion to their development needs.[61]

To achieve these objectives, still according to its preamble, the WTO has two instruments: the reduction of tariff and non-tariff barriers and the elimination of discriminatory treatment. Although these instruments were determined as recently as GATT/47, the WTO agreement provides the basis for a more integrated, viable and durable system.[62]

For Hoekman,[63] The WTO's main function is to serve as a forum for international trade policy cooperation, a space that functions as a marketplace where member States exchange trade agreements that result in codes of conduct. It is precisely in this function that lies the greatest difficulty of the organization, since the States exchange commitments instead of buying them, as occurs with the relations between suppliers and consumers.

It should be noted that, currently, the WTO has 164 members, with different economic realities, and should reach consensus on the rules to be adopted. In practice, States form coalitions that, on the one hand, alter the balance of power in negotiations, but on the other, in view of the large number of members, facilitate the construction of consensus and strengthen the legitimacy of the results.[64]

---

[59] The so-called WTO agreements encompass the GATT 1947 and the results of the Uruguay Round, and have 29 individual legal texts and 25 ministerial understandings, decisions, and declarations, in which additional commitments and obligations of its members are specified. Source: World Trade Organization. http://www.wto.org/english/docs_e/legal_e/legal_e.htm#schedules.

[60] WTO (2001) Doha Ministerial Declaration. http://www.wto.org/english/thewto_e/minist_e/min01_e/mindecl_e.htm.

[61] Ibid. Agreement Establishing the World Trade Organization. http://www.wto.org/english/docs_e/legal_e/legal_e.htm#wtoagreement.

[62] See: Bossche and Zdouc (2013), p. 83.

[63] Hoekman (2014), pp. 41–42.

[64] Sella (2010), p. 19.

This arduous task of negotiating treaties must respect some guiding principles of the organization, which should also be observed in its interpretation and application in furtherance of the WTO's objectives as set out in the Marrakech Agreement, as follows:

> Recognizing that their trade and economic relations should be conducted with the aim of raising living standards, full employment and a large and constant volume of real incomes and effective demand, and expanding the production and trade of goods and services, while allowing the optimal use of the world's resources, in accordance with the objective of sustainable development, seeking to protect and preserve the environment and improve the means to do so in a manner consistent with the respective needs and concerns at different levels of economic development.[65]

For the equal achievement of these objectives, it is noted that the Member States have established the following principles: non-discrimination, free trade, predictability, competitiveness, special treatment to the least developed and developing countries and the safety valve, principles that will be studied shortly thereafter.

3.3.1.1 The Principle of Non-Discrimination

The principle of non-discrimination, established since GATT/47 and now expressed in the preamble of the WTO's constitutive agreement, constitutes the fundamental pillar for achieving the Organization's objectives, determining that any discriminatory protectionist attitude must be avoided so that there is parity of treatment between foreign goods and between foreign and domestic goods. Thus, this principle is subdivided into two, both provided for in GATT/47 in its Articles I and III, which were absorbed by the WTO, namely: the most favored nation (*MFN*) principle and the national treatment principle.

For the first, a good produced in a member country cannot be treated less favorably in comparison with a similar good produced in another member country. This, if good X produced in a member country enjoys a better rate applied to imports in the amount of 5%, this benefit must be extended to the others.[66] As already decided by the WTO Appellate Body in the WT/DS246 case, the most-favored-nation clause is "[…] the cornerstone of the GATT and one of the pillars of the WTO trading system".[67]

---

[65] Free adaptation from: "Recognizing that their relations in the field of trade and economic endeavour should be conducted with a view to raising standards of living, ensuring full employment and a large and steadily growing volume of real income and effective demand, and expanding the production of and trade in goods and services, while allowing for the optimal use of the world's resources in accordance with the objective of sustainable development, seeking both to protect and preserve the environment and to enhance the means for doing so in a manner consistent with their respective needs and concerns at different levels of economic development". In: World Trade Organization. http://www.wto.org/english/docs_e/legal_e/legal_e.htm.

[66] Hoekman (2014), p. 42.

[67] WTO Introducción a los princípios y normas básicos de la OMC. http://ecampus.wto.org/admin/files/Course_273/Module_1110/ModuleDocuments/TBT-M2-S.pdf, p. 3.

It is important to emphasize that the application of this principle is not restricted to tariff issues, but to any advantage, whether fiscal, customs, financial, regulations or formalities of any kind, capable of benefiting imports or exports, applied even if the goods have already been nationalized.[68]

To ascertain the similarity between products, four criteria were adopted by WTO jurisprudence: (a) their physical characteristics; (b) purpose of use; (c) consumer preferences and (d) customs classification.[69]

According to Hoekman,[70] One of the advantages of the most-favoured-nation principle that deserves to be highlighted is its unconditional and automatic application, since the first ensures that the least developed countries are not exploited by the market power of developed countries, which cannot burden imports from a country or a group of countries. This prevents less developed countries from suffering protectionist measures in times of economic crisis. The automatic application of the principle reduces the cost of negotiations since the result of a bilateral tariff reduction negotiation will be automatically extended to all WTO members. Thus, countries with less bargaining power can benefit from bilaterally negotiated tariff reductions.

Regarding the principle of national treatment, it can be said that its main function is to ensure that trade liberalization agreements are not undermined by domestic measures, thus preventing domestic products from benefiting to the detriment of imports, once they enter the national territory of member countries, placing them on equal competitive conditions. As decided in the case *Alcoholic Beverages II,*[71] "[…] The principle of national treatment obliges countries to provide a level playing field for imported products relative to domestic products".[72]

The principle of national treatment applies to customs duties and taxes, as well as to regulations and formalities, provided they are internal and affect in any way the sale, purchase, transport and distribution on the internal market, as provided for in Article III of GATT 1947:

> The contracting parties recognize that taxes and other internal charges, as well as laws, regulations and prescriptions affecting the sale, offering for sale, purchase, transport, distribution or use of products in the domestic market and internal quantitative regulations prescribing the mixing, processing or daring of certain products in specified quantities or proportions, they should not apply to imported or domestic products in a manner that protects domestic production. Products within the territory of any Contracting Party, imported by another Contracting Party, shall not be subject, directly or indirectly, to internal taxes or other internal charges of any kind in excess of those imposed, directly or indirectly, on domestic products. Moreover, no Contracting Party shall otherwise apply internal taxes or

---

[68] It is said that the merchandise was nationalized when it entered the national territory for customs purposes, that is, after the occurrence of customs clearance through the payment of customs and tax duties.

[69] Brazil. Decree No. 1355 of December 30, 1994.

[70] Hoekman (2014), p. 42.

[71] Appellate Body Understanding in the case Japan—Alcoholic Beverage II.

[72] Ibid.

other internal charges to domestic imported products, contrary to the principals set out in paragraph 1.[73]

Once it enters the territory for customs purposes, upon completion of the customs clearance process, the imported product is nationalized and, therefore, cannot suffer less favorable treatment than the national one, that is, it must be treated, internally, in the same way in which the products produced in the national territory are treated. Thus, except for the import tax, all internal taxes or tax incentives must be levied equally on domestic and nationalized products.

It is important to emphasize that, for the WTO, the commercial effects of the principle are irrelevant for its violation to occur, even if the difference applied on the imported and domestic goods is minimal, or if the tax difference is non-existent, since the violation of the principle is not linked to the occurrence of damage.

The principle of non-discrimination must be observed by all member States in all agreements, except for the exceptions governed by paragraphs 2 to 4 of Article I and paragraph 3 of Article XXIV (border trade in customs unions and free trade areas), both of GATT/94.[74] The recognition of such exceptions demonstrates their importance in preparing the countries for future liberalization in the multilateral ambit, since the regional ambit has lower social-economic costs for the States.[75]

3.3.1.2   The Principle of Free Trade

The principle of free trade, the foundation of the entire World Trade Organization, implies the reduction of obstacles, such as tariffs and non-tariff trade barriers, gradually and through negotiation. These reductions have been taking place since the time of the GATT/47, through rounds of negotiations and continue until the present moment in the Doha Round.

For the WTO, based on David Ricardo's theory of comparative advantage, market opening is seen as advantageous for all countries, considering that the pursuit of particular interests triggers general welfare.[76] In the words of Gonçalves:

> Within the neo-liberal political-economic model, GATT/94 and the WTO are organized in an international market perspective in which the individualistic and rational methodology seeks the individual satisfaction of the needs of the agents; but, which, by consequence, leads to a general welfare—economistic utilitarianism.[77]

---

[73] GATT 1947. General Agreement on Tariffs and Trade 1947. http://www.mdic.gov.br/arquivo/secex/omc/acordos/gatt47port.pdf.

[74] GATT/94 is one of the integrated agreements of the WTO, comprising provisions from GATT/47, the Uruguay Round and the Marrakech Agreement, exclusively concerning trade in goods.

[75] See: Gonçalves and Stelzer (2010), http://www.conpedi.org.br/manaus/arquivos/anais/fortaleza/3755.pdf, p. 2409.

[76] WTO Argumentos a favor de um comércio aberto. http://www.wto.org/spanish/thewto_s/whatis_s/tif_s/fact3_s.htm.

[77] Gonçalves and Stelzer (2010). http://www.conpedi.org.br/manaus/arquivos/anais/fortaleza/3755.pdf, p. 2410.

However, the individualistic and rational methodology cannot generate the general welfare when countries are at different levels of economic and social development, urging the need to make some adaptations in the WTO agreements.

It is important to mention that, in addition to being free, trade must be fairly competitive, avoiding distorting measures such as unfair trade practices, such as the practice of *dumping* and some subsidies. In the words of the Ministry of Development, Industry and Foreign Trade (MDIC):

> The WTO tries to guarantee not only a more open trade, but also a fairer one, by preventing unfair commercial practices such as dumping and subsidies, which distort the trade conditions between countries. The GATT already dealt with these principles in Articles VI and XVI, but these mechanisms could only really be implemented after the Anti-dumping and Subsidies Agreements had defined dumping and subsidy practices and provided for appropriate measures to counter the damage arising from these practices.[78]

In this context, fair and unfair trade is differentiated based on the imposition of restrictions, which contribute to the inefficiency of local industry, to monopolies, as well as to damages to local consumers, since they make prices more expensive due to the lack of substitute products and the lack of competitiveness resulting from the imposition of barriers to prevent the entry of competitors.[79]

Subsidies are an example of trade-restrictive measures, as they create artificial conditions of competition through financial or fiscal aid from the government granted to specific sectors, generating an increase in cost, since "[…] Producers in a situation of subsidized production, are unaware or do not operate subject to the real costs of the process, which leads to waste and misallocation of scarce productive factors".[80] However, as we have already seen, the WTO recognizes that subsidies can be useful in the face of failures caused by the free market.

In this sense, it can be said that the WTO principle of free trade is not and cannot be absolute, since it admits, even if eventually, restrictions, often necessary to counter crises, distortions or even to force compliance with its agreements, as will be seen in the following items. Therefore, the WTO can be seen as a system in favor of open and fair competition.[81]

3.3.1.3 The Principle of the Safety Valves

According to countries 'peculiarities, the WTO has two principles to fulfill this function: *safety valves* and special treatment for the least developed and developing countries. While the former can be triggered by all member states, provided that the

---

[78] Ministério do Desenvolvimento, Indústria e Comércio Exterior. Princípios da OMC. http://www.mdic.gov.br/sitio/interna/interna.php?area=5&menu=368&refr=366.

[79] See: Gonçalves and Stelzer (2010). http://www.conpedi.org.br/manaus/arquivos/anais/fortaleza/3755.pdf.

[80] Ibid.

[81] Reis et al. http://www.anpec.org.br/sul/2013/submissao/files_I/i5-f863ffba99f341d2f0f1f52c344169ae.pdf.

requirements set out in the agreements are met, the latter benefits only a few, considered by the WTO to be developing or less developed.

The safety valve makes the commitments undertaken more flexible, allowing States to restrict trade in certain circumstances: (a) in cases of protection of public health, national security, or even national industry seriously damaged by international competition; (b) in cases of balance of payments[82] or to assist nascent industries of countries; and (c) to ensure fair competition, such as countervailing measures against subsidies or *anti-dumping* measures.[83]

The justification for recognizing these exceptions is that "a set of uniform multilateral rules creating identical obligations for all participants in the multilateral trading system, regardless of their level of development, independent of its degree of development, it brings more harm than good".[84]

3.3.1.4 The Principle of Special and Differential Treatment for Developing and Least Developed Countries

Whereas, of 164 signatories, three quarters are from developing countries and one fifth from least developed countries,[85] GATT/94 recognizes, in Part IV, Articles XXXVI, XXXVII and XXXVIII, a special and differential treatment to these countries to be better integrated into the system, essential to achieve the fundamental objective of the WTO, that is, the "raising of living standards and the progressive development of the economy".[86]

Article XXXVI establishes the principle of non-reciprocity in trade negotiations between developed and developing countries, that is, the latter are not obliged to make concessions incompatible with their developmental needs. Another aspect that deserves to be highlighted in this device is the recognition of the continued

---

[82] Chapter B of Article XVIII allows restrictions on imports to prevent a serious decline in monetary reserves or, if reserves are inadequate, to achieve a reasonable rate of increase in reserves.

[83] Hoekman (2014), p. 44.

[84] Saldanha (2012), pp. 298–299.

[85] Until 1979, GATT only mentioned the least developed countries, when, through the Enabling Clause, provisions were created to increase the trade opportunities of developing countries. However, in the WTO, it is the countries that define themselves as less developed or developing and will only be considered as such, when the condition is accepted by the other members. This way, the status of developed, developing and least developed country is determined by a unilateral declaration by the governments of the Member States, which can be contested. It is based on the criteria established by the UN. Of the total of 48 least developed countries, 34 are WTO members: Angola, Bangladesh, Benin, Burkina Faso, Burundi, Cambodia, Central African Republic, Chad, Democratic Republic of the Congo, Djibouti, Gambia, Guinea, Guinea-Bissau, Haiti, Lao People's Democratic Republic, Lesotho, Madagascar, Malawi, Mali, Mauritania, Mozambique, Myanmar, Nepal, Niger, Rwanda, Senegal, Sierra Leone, Solomon Islands, Tanzania, Togo, Uganda, Vanuatu, Yemen, Zambia. Developing countries are all those found on the UN list. In this sense, see: http://www.un.org/en/development/desa/policy/wesp/wesp_current/2012country_class.pdf.

[86] Brazil Decree No. 1355 of December 30, 1994.

dependence of these countries on exports and, therefore, developed countries should grant more favorable conditions for the access of primary and industrialized products to the world market.

The enabling clause is added, by which developed countries can grant benefits to developing countries without having to extend them to others, as imposed by the most-favored-nation clause.

Article XXXVII states that developed countries should avoid imposing tariff and non-tariff barriers on exports by developing countries. In this way, developed countries must take special consideration of the interests of developing countries, and the latter must also consider the interests of other developing countries.

Article XXXVIII, in turn, obliges all members to cooperate in order to achieve the objectives of the previous articles, especially with regard to access to world markets for primary products.

Throughout the WTO agreements are also found provisions on special and differential treatment, which are classified into: (a) for the increase of trade opportunities; (b) to safeguard the interests of developing and least developed countries; (c) to provide flexibility in commitments, measures and the use of policies; (d) the transitional period; (e) technical assistance; and (f) specific provisions for least developed countries.[87]

In this sense, the above-mentioned articles provide that the contracting parties shall spare no efforts to ensure the equitable participation of the least developed and developing countries in international trade and shall pay special attention to the interests of these countries when applying measures authorized by the agreement that may significantly affect them.

These provisions are subject to criticism, since the lack of specificity of these norms makes their applicability and legal enforceability difficult, generating moral obligations and opening spaces for political discussions. In this sense:

> It is feasible that devices that simply camp agreements of "good intentions" lead to the opening of a more political space for debate, which ends up creating difficulty for a merely analytical vision regarding the evaluation of the real needs of development.[88]

This way, the rules on the principle of special and differential treatment need to be restructured in order to fill the gaps by determining specific obligations. To this end, it is necessary to reconcile the political desire of the Member States.

Meanwhile, gaps are filled in the dispute settlement procedure. Despite the criticism, the provisions establishing special and differential treatment for developing countries are still obligations that may be required in the DSB. In the case *European Communities—Refunds on Exports of Sugar*, Brazil, as complainant, claimed that the continuation of the European Union's sugar subsidy program constituted

---

[87] Conferência das Nações Unidas para Comércio e Desenvolvimento (2012) Assegurando ganhos de Desenvolvimento a partir do Sistema Comercial Internacional e das Negociações de Comércio. http://unctad.org/pt/docs/td397_pt.pdf.

[88] Saldanha (2012), p. 303.

conduct incompatible with Article XXXVIII. *Panel* followed Brazil's argument and concluded that:

> The increase in sugar exports through the use of subsidies in the particular market situation of 1978 and 1979, and where developing Member Countries took steps within the framework of the EIA to improve conditions on the world sugar market, inevitably reduced the effects of the efforts made by these countries. For this period of time and for this particular field, the European Community has therefore not collaborated with the other [Members] to carry out the principles and objectives set out in Article XXXVI, in accordance with the general lines in Article XXXVIII.[89]

It should be noted, therefore, that the rights arising from the aforementioned provisions can be implemented through the WTO dispute settlement procedure. In addition, detailed situations are regulated in specific agreements. Regarding the agreement on subsidies, for example, the developing country will not suffer compensatory measures if the subsidies applied do not exceed 2% of the unit value of the exported product, while the limit for developed countries is 1%. In addition, they will also not be susceptible to countervailing measures when the developing country's exports are less than 4% of its international market or, considering the total market of all developing countries, do not exceed 9%.[90]

The difficulty of distinguishing the categories of countries in the WTO lies in the fact that, while the least developed countries are those so considered by the UN, developing countries are free to define themselves as such. This situation has repercussions on the special and differential treatment granted to developing countries about the use of subsidies, because when poorly framed, the benefits can generate distorting effects.

As an example, one can cite China, which, despite calling itself a developing country, in fact, presents itself as a strong world economic power, with a high performance in both negotiations and dispute settlement in the WTO, whether as complainant or defendant. In 2014, China overtook the United States, which until then was considered the world's largest economy.[91]

Future changes in order to effectively apply special and differential treatment to the countries that need it most, transparency is key. Without knowing the rules and trade policies adopted by the member States, one cannot negotiate treaties, adopt

---

[89] Free adaptatation from: "The Panel recognized the efforts made by the European Communities in complying with the provisions of Articles XXXVI and XXXVIII. It nevertheless felt that increased Community exports of sugar through the use of subsidies in the particular market situation in 1978 and 1979, and where developing contracting parties had taken steps within the framework of the ISA to improve the conditions in the world sugar market, inevitably reduced the effects of the efforts made by these countries. For this time-period and for this particular field, the European Communities had therefore not collaborated jointly with other contracting parties to further the principles and objectives set forth in Article XXXVI, in conformity with the guidelines given in Article XXXVIII." In: *Panel Report* on *EC – Sugar Exports (Brazil)*, 30 at conclusions.

[90] See: Hoekman (2014), p. 169.

[91] See: Stiglitz. http://www.vanityfair.com/news/2015/01/china-worlds-largest-economy.

trade policies or change them, or even comply with existing agreements or demand that they be complied with, nor enforce the other principles.

3.3.1.5 Principle of Transparency

According to the WTO glossary, transparency means the "degree of openness and predictability of trade policies and practices, as well as the process by which they are established".[92] Provided for in Article X of the GATT, the principle of transparency obliges Member States to inform and provide clarification on any regulation or commercial policy adopted.

Transparency is the essential principle for the good functioning of the organization. According to Prazeres,[93] its importance lies "in the process of building the reciprocal trust necessary to strengthen the multilateral trade system". There are several benefits: reduction of uncertainties, possibility to verify eventual violations, among others, thus guaranteeing justice in decision making.

Transparency presents itself as the driving force of global cohesion, which holds States accountable for their trade practices: its objective is to reduce the asymmetries of information between States, enabling the supervision of their commercial practices.

It can be seen that the principle of transparency operates in three different ways, which have been separated by Wolfe,[94] in generations: the first, already regulated in GATT/47, refers to the right of access to information, the second, originating in the Tokyo Round, concerns the monitoring of the trade policies of the member States, while the third has the scope not only to allow access to information, but the possibility of its use.

Access to information also makes it possible to monitor the external community, which is very important for citizens and private economic agents, who can put pressure on member States to fulfill, as expected, the commitments they have undertaken.[95]

At this point, it is important to make clear the relationship of the transparency principle with the legitimacy of the organization, since it will not be possible to apply its rules and principles without access to information, its monitoring, and the possibility of its effective use.

For the proper functioning of the organization and for its objectives to be realized, the WTO has a complex structure, with more than sixty organs, distributed between permanent and *ad hoc*, which will be studied below.

---

[92] In the original: "degree to which trade policies and practices, and the process by which they are established, are open and predictable". In: WTO Glossary. http://www.wto.org/english/thewto_e/glossary_e/glossary_e.htm.

[93] Prazeres (2003), p. 43.

[94] Wolfe . http://www.wto.org/english/res_e/reser_e/ersd201303_e.pdf, pp. 8–13.

[95] Hoekman (2014), p. 44.

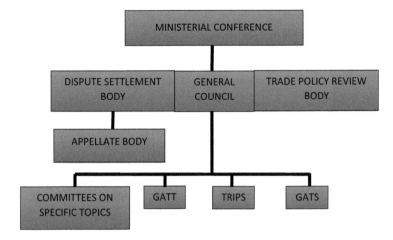

Fig. 3.3 Simplified organizational chart of the WTO structure. Source: Author

3.3.2 *Structure and Bodies*

As for the structure and organs of the WTO, those who work with decision-making, monitoring, and dispute settlement, specifically related to the subject under study, will be highlighted.

The WTO has 35 permanent and about 30 *ad hoc* bodies that meet regularly and are divided into four organizational levels as follows in Fig. 3.3.

At the first level is the Ministerial Conference, the WTO's most important decision-making body. It is composed of the Ministers of Foreign Affairs or Trade of each member State, who meet at least every 2 years to set the agenda for the rounds of negotiations.[96]

It is important to emphasize that this body has decision-making power on any issues related to WTO multilateral agreements, to which all members of the organization will be bound. Specific powers include adopting interpretations of the agreements, granting exemptions, adopting amendments, deliberating on the accession of new members and also the election of the Director General of the organization, as well as staff regulations.

The second is represented by three bodies: the General Council, the Dispute Settlement Body (DSB), and the Trade Policy Review Body. In fact, they all belong to the General Council, which meets to deal with different issues. Responsible for implementing the decisions of the Ministerial Conferences, the General Council is the WTO's most significant body, whose function is to oversee and administer the

---

[96] In total there were nine rounds after the Uruguay Round, which created the WTO: Singapore (1996), Geneva (1998), Seattle (1999), Doha (2001), Cancun (2003), Hong Kong (2005), Geneva (2009 and 2011) and Bali (2013).

organization's agreements and day-to-day activities, including the monitoring of trade policies and dispute settlement.

At the third level are the Councils for major areas of trade, including the Council for Trade in Goods, Council for Trade in Services, and the Council on Intellectual Property Rights. Each must submit reports on its activities to the General Council, informing it regularly.

In addition to these, other small committees should keep the General Council informed: Committee on Trade and Development, environment, regional trade agreements, and administrative issues. The following committees were created in Singapore (1996): investment and competition, transparency in public procurement, and trade facilitation. The Doha Development Agenda Trade Negotiations Committee is also added.

Each Council at this level has small committees, which are located at the fourth level. The Council for Trade in Goods, for example, has 11 committees, among them the Committee on Agriculture and the Committee on Subsidies, whose functions are linked to the application of specific agreements.

These committees receive notifications of the trade policies adopted by member States and submit their reports to the Council. They may be consulted by members at any time concerning the progress of the agreement and its objectives. Exceptionally, the Subsidies Committee may determine whether the transitional subsidy policy adopted by a developing country can be extended.[97]

In addition, the Subsidies Committee created a group of five experts in this area with the power to suggest solutions to disputes on the matter, to provide consultations to the Committee or, confidentially, to the members of the organization upon request.

Finally, it is important to point out that all members are integrated in these Councils and Committees, but since they deal with specialized topics, different levels of expertise are required and, therefore, the people who participate in them are different.[98]

These reports are intended to inform the organization about the commercial policies of its members, which may be questioned within the scope of the Dispute Settlement Body.

To support all this work, the WTO also has a secretariat headed by the Director-General. Currently, the secretariat has 629 employees of 76 different nationalities, including 8 Brazilians.[99]

Its main functions are (a) to provide technical support for councils and committees; (b) to provide technical assistance to developing countries; (c) to monitor the development of international trade in order to publish information; (d) to organize ministerial conferences; and (e) to assist in the dispute settlement process.

---

[97] Bossche and Zdouc (2013), p. 126.

[98] See: World Trade Organization Understanding the WTO. http://www.wto.org/english/thewto_e/whatis_e/tif_e/utw_chap7_e.pdf.

[99] Ibid.

It should be noted that both do not have the competence to initiate any decision-making procedure within the organization, whether of a legal or political nature. Its functions are restricted to facilitating such processes, since the WTO is led by its members.

3.4   The Regulation of Subsidies and Countervailing Measures in the WTO

Until the Tokyo Round, which took place between 1973 and 1979, the GATT agreements were restricted to the mere reduction of tariffs on trade, and little was said about subsidies. There were only four articles, which only tangentially touched on the subject, basically recommending that States avoid their use and check their effects when applied.

The Subsidies Code that emerged in that round expanded its regulation and restricted its use to exports, admitting the opening of the procedure for the application of countervailing measures. Only twenty-five states have ratified it, which was permissible in GATT times. It should be noted that at no time did the agreement address the definition of subsidies.

The Uruguay Round, which created the WTO, besides being more ambitious than the previous ones in terms of the range of agreements, also reinforced the primacy of the rule, bringing some innovations relevant to the issue of subsidies, such as: the creation of the Committee on Subsidies and Countervailing Measures, the subsidy notification system, the gradual reduction of subsidies within a predetermined period of time, the establishment of standards for investigation of countervailing measures and, mainly, the definition of subsidies. In this way:

> [...] the negotiation of a definition for the term subsidies during the Uruguay Round can be considered a major breakthrough in GATT/WTO history, as the absence of such a definition was giving rise to serious trade disputes.[100]

Despite the achievement, the WTO's Agreement on Subsidies and Countervailing Measures (SCM) still has ambiguities, causing repeated deadlocks among the organization's members, which can be seen from the high rate of cases involving the agreement.

The number of cases submitted to the DSB that deal with the subject makes this agreement one of the most relevant in the organization. The SCM is the third most discussed agreement in the field of dispute settlement, representing a little more than 10 percent of the demand by the year 2021, behind only GATT 1994 and the *Antidumping* Agreement.[101]

---

[100] Thorstensen (1999), p. 123.

[101] WTO. Dispute Settlement Activity—some figures. https://www.wto.org/english/tratop_e/dispu_e/dispustats_e.htm.

It is important to remember that agricultural subsidies are dealt with in a specific agreement—Agreement on Agriculture—and represent 8% of DSB cases. However, compensatory measures applied against agricultural subsidies should comply with the provisions of the SCM.

The theme also demonstrates relevance for Latin American countries, since it is among the five most cited in demands initiated by them before the DSB.[102]

It can be noted that the SCM is also among the five most cited agreements against Latin American countries.[103]

The relevance of subsidies to the WTO member States can be seen, since import restrictions as well as tariff barriers were already significantly reduced back in the days of GATT/47. In this way, countries seek other ways to protect their domestic market, among them, subsidies can be highlighted. According to Pascal Lamy, former WTO Director, "[...] in the world of value chains, it is export restrictions that impose the greatest problem [...]".[104]

Subsidies constitute trade barriers, since they are able to restrict exports from other countries, by the diversion they cause to international trade, while protecting domestic industry when destined to import substitution. Due to the difficulties of identifying them according to the criteria established in the SCM, subsidies are also disguised ways of protecting trade. It is necessary, therefore, to study the categories of subsidies disciplined by the WTO, in order to understand the difficulties in determining such practices.

3.4.1   The Agreement on Subsidies and Countervailing Measures

The SCM is divided into 11 parts. In the general part, it brings the definition of subsidies and conceptualizes its key element, which is specificity. The following three parts classify subsidies into prohibited, actionable, and non-actionable. Part V regulates the application of countervailing measures, while Part VI establishes the Committee on Subsidies and Countervailing Measures.

Subsequently, the agreement establishes important notification and monitoring procedures and, in Part VIII, ensures special and differential treatment for developing countries. Part IX refers to WTO accessions and transitional economies, while Part X sets out the rules applicable to dispute settlement, and finally the final provisions, in addition to including the definition of serious injury, present the list of non-actionable subsidies. In annex, the agreement also presents: I—illustrative list

---

[102] ICTSD. Latin America and the WTO Dispute Settlement System. http://www.ictsd.org/downloads/2013/12/latin-america-and-the-wto-dispute-settlement-system-ready-for-print.pdf, p. 13.

[103] Ibid, p. 14.

[104] Free translation of: "Mais dans le monde des chaînes de valeur, c'est la restriction à l'exportation qui pose davantage problème". In: Lamy P. L'Organisation mondiale du commerce. http://entempsreel.com/wp-content/uploads/2014/07/Pascal-Lamy-En-temps-r%C3%A9el.pdf, p. 17.

of export subsidies; II—guidelines on the inputs consumed in the production process: III—Guidelines for determining whether *drawback* systems constitute export subsidies in cases of substitution; IV—calculation of the total *ad valorem* subsidy for the purposes of Article 6.1(a) (serious harm caused by actionable subsidies); V—procedures for obtaining information concerning serious damage (Annex V); VI—procedures for *on-site* verifications of Article 12.6 (application of compensatory measures) e VII—coverage of developing and least developed member countries.

For now, the present item aims only to understand the discipline of subsidies, its definitions and classification. In the following items, we will address the countervailing measures, the main subsidies applied, the subsidies applied during the 2008 economic crisis and the regulation of subsidies and countervailing measures in Brazil.

3.4.1.1 Subsidies: Concept, Definition and Classification

In order to fill in the gaps in GATT, the WTO, for the first time, defines the concept of subsidies. Despite this advance, the concept continues to generate discussions due to the vagueness, imprecision, and ambiguity of its terms.

In this sense, subsidies can be defined and applied in countless ways and for different purposes, which makes it even more difficult to ascertain. The subject is sensitive to members' trade policies since the regulation of subsidies limits these policies when considered prohibited by the WTO.

To better understand its concept, we should keep in mind that, "the general policy of the Gatt/WTO system is to prevent, or at least minimize, distortions in international trade".[105] In the same sense is consolidated the understanding of the DSB, when affirming that "the object and purpose of the SCM Agreement is to impose multilateral disciplines on subsidies that distort international trade".[106]

This means that not all subsidies are prohibited by the WTO, leaving some leeway to be applied when necessary for the promotion of economic and social objectives. For this reason, it is necessary to study them in order to understand the mechanisms offered by the system that legitimize or prohibit government trade policies.

First, to constitute a subsidy, according to Article 1 of the ASCM, it is necessary that "there is a financial contribution by a government or public body within the territory of a Member (hereafter referred to as the 'government')".[107]

It can be noted that the basic definition of SCM subsidies itself is complex and, therefore, needs to be studied in more detail. Firstly, a governmental practice is not

---

[105] Martins (2007), p. 44.
[106] Bossche and Zdouc (2013), p. 747.
[107] Free adaptation from: "SCM Article 1 [...] (a)(1) there is a financial contribution by a government or any public body within the territory of a Member (referred to in this Agreement as "government")".

only those performed by the direct or indirect public administration, but also those resulting from private entities, whose powers have been delegated by any governmental body.

According to the *Panel* Report in the case *United States—Measures Treating Export Restraints as Subsidies (Canada)*, to configure the delegation, it is indispensable that an affirmative action of command or delegation occurs directed to a specific entity, whose object is a task or duty.[108]

The crux of the matter is whether the body "exercises governmental authority; it is not enough that it is controlled by the government".[109] Thus, even if it is private, if the entity is exercising public function, that is, under the command of the government,[110] when it grants subsidies, government aid is considered to be characterized.

Regarding financial contribution, for subsidy purposes, Article 1 of the SCM brings in its body an enumerative list of modalities that configure the existence of a subsidy when:

(a) 1. there is a financial contribution by a government or public body within the territory of a Member (hereafter referred to as "government"), i.e..:

(i) where the government practice involves direct transfers of funds (e.g. grants, loans and capital contributions), potential direct transfers of funds or obligations (e.g. loan guarantees);

(ii)   when government revenues due are forgiven or go uncollected (for example, tax incentives such as tax bonuses);

(iii)   when the government provides goods or services in addition to those intended for general infrastructure or when it acquires goods;

(iv)   when the Government makes payments to a system of funds or entrusts or instructs a private body to perform one or more of the functions described in subparagraphs (i) to (iii) above, which would normally be incumbent upon the Government and whose practice does not differ in any significant way from the practice normally followed by governments;

or (b) (2) there is any form of revenue or price support within the meaning of Article XVI of GATT 1994;
    and
    (c) this confers an advantage.[111]

---

[108] Panel Report in case United States—Measures Treating Export Restraints as Subsidies (Canada), par 155.

[109] Thorstensen and Oliveira (2013), pp. 22–23.

[110] The Appellate Body manifested itself in the case *US—Antidumping and Countervailing Duties,* in the sense of admitting the actual exercise of governmental functions in order to characterize the "governmental authority" element, no formal instrument of delegation being required. In: Appelate Body Report, US—Antidumping and Countervailing Duties (China), par 318.

[111] Free adaptation from: "Article 1.1 SCM Agreement: [...] (1) there is a financial contribution by a government or any public body within the territory of a Member (referred to in this Agreement as "government"), i.e. where: (i) a government practice involves a direct transfer of funds (e.g. grants, loans, and equity infusion), potential direct transfers of funds or liabilities (e.g. loan guar-

The hypotheses cited above are not exhaustive, as understood by the Appellate Body in the case *US—Large Civil Aircraft*, but only indicate possible transactions that the agreement seeks to cover, not excluding others.

Regarding the tax incentives provided for in item (ii), the WTO understands that members are sovereign and may choose not to tax any type of revenue, as long as they observe the rules of the organization. The term "due" or "*otherwise due*" in English implies a comparison of what would normally be due under the members' internal rules if it were not for the subsidy. By interpreting items (i) and (iv) jointly, it is possible to conclude that transfers should be made by the government, not necessarily in a direct way, and that such power may be granted to private entities. Item (iii), in turn, is concerned with the supply of goods and services by the government, which goes beyond the supply of general infrastructure,[112] as well as the acquisition of goods from companies.[113] Such activities are of concern because the former has the ability to artificially decrease production costs and the latter can artificially increase revenues from the sale of goods.[114]

The price support of Article XVI of GATT 1994 does not imply any government policy that can influence prices indirectly, such as taxes or quantitative restrictions, but rather policies whose purpose is to fix prices through direct government intervention.[115]

All the practices listed must configure a benefit to characterize the existence of a subsidy, and all forms of government contribution must be linked to a benefit. For this reason, the Appellate Body understands that the analysis of the contribution should not focus on the cost of the government, but on the existence of the benefit, which can only be ascertained by comparison, based on market conditions.[116] In this case *Canada—Aircraft*, the OPA disciplined as follows:

> We are also of the opinion that the word "benefit" as used in paragraph 1 b) of Article 1 implies some kind of comparison. This is because there can be no "benefit" to the recipient unless the "financial contribution" puts him in a better situation than that in the absence of such a contribution. In our opinion, the market provides an appropriate basis of comparison for determining whether a "benefit" has been granted, because the possible trade-distorting effects of a "financial contribution" can be identified by verifying whether the recipient has

---

antees); (ii) government revenue that is otherwise due is foregone or not collected (e.g. fiscal incentives such as tax credits);(iii) a government provides goods or services other than general infrastructure, or purchases goods; (iv) a government makes payments to a funding mechanism, or entrusts or directs a private body to carry out one or more of the type of functions illustrated in (i) to (iii) above which would normally be vested in the government and the practice, in no real sense, differs from practices normally followed by governments; or (a) (2) there is any form of income or price support in the sense of Article XVI of GATT 1994; and (b) a benefit is thereby conferred".

[112] General infrastructure means, according to the DSB, that it is available to all or nearly all and not just to a single entity or a limited group. In: Bossche and Zdouc (2013), p. 755.

[113] Note that the acquisition of services was excluded from the second part of the item (iii).

[114] Appellate Body's understanding of the case US—softwood Lumber IV.

[115] Appellate Body's understanding of the case China—GOES.

[116] Appellate Body's understanding of the case Canada—Aircraft, par 154.

received a "financial contribution" on terms more favorable than those available to the recipient in the market.[117]

Therefore, the benefit translates into economic advantage, which would not be possible to obtain under normal market conditions. The analysis of the benefit considers its recipient, when comparing the advantages obtained by it in relation to the contributions available, in general, in the market.

Article 14 of the SCM regulates the calculation of the earned benefit and ratifies the understanding that the analysis should be based on the recipient rather than the government cost and always considering the market conditions, as will be noted in the following transcription of excerpts from that article:

> For the purposes of PART V, any method used by the investigating authority to calculate the benefit realized by the recipient in accordance with Article 1, paragraph 1, shall be provided for in national legislation or supplementary regulations of the Member concerned and its application to any particular case shall be transparent and clearly explained. In addition, any such method shall be consistent with the following guidelines:

(a) [...] (b) A government loan shall not be considered to constitute an advantage unless there is a difference between the amount that the borrowing enterprise must pay for the loan and the amount that the borrowing enterprise would otherwise pay for an equivalent commercial loan that it could normally obtain on the market. In this case, the advantage will be the difference between these two amounts.

(b) (c) A credit guarantee by the government will not be considered to confer a benefit, unless there is a difference between the amount that the firm receiving the guarantee pays for the loan so guaranteed and the amount that the firm would pay for a commercial loan without a government guarantee. In this case, the difference between these two amounts, calculated to take account of any differences in fees or commissions, will constitute benefit.

(d) The provision of goods or services or purchase of goods by the government shall not be considered to confer a benefit unless the provision is made for less than adequate remuneration or the purchase is made for more than adequate remuneration. The adequacy of remuneration shall be determined by reference to prevailing market conditions for the relevant goods

---

[117] Free adaptation from: "We also believe that the word "benefit", as used in Article 1.1(b), implies some kind of comparison. This must be so, for there can be no "benefit" to the recipient unless the "financial contribution" makes the recipient "better off" than it would otherwise have been, absent that contribution. In our view, the marketplace provides an appropriate basis for comparison in determining whether a "benefit" has been "conferred", because the trade-distorting potential of a "financial contribution" can be identified by determining whether the recipient has received a "financial contribution" on terms more favorable than those available to the recipient in the market". In: Appellate Body Report on the case Canada-Measures Affecting the Export of Civilian Aircraft, par 157.

or service in the country of provision or purchase (included therein). [...][118]
(griffon added)

The article makes it clear that the configuration of the benefit is directly related to the distortions it may cause in the market. It can be noted that the above understanding is consistent with the pillars of the WTO seen in this work, such as free and fair trade, since it pays attention to the distorting effect of the benefit.

To cause distortions, the benefit must be granted in a specific way "to a company or industry, group and industries or companies or to a sector that are within the grantor's jurisdiction".[119] According to Article 2 of the SCM, the subsidy defined in Article 1 must be specific in the following terms:

2.1 [...] the subsidy will be deemed specific if the granting authority, or the legislation by which that authority is to be governed, explicitly limits access to the subsidy to certain enterprises only;

(b) specificity will not occur where the granting authority, or the legislation by which that authority is to be governed, establishes objective conditions or criteria governing the access right and the amount to be granted, provided that the right is automatic and that the conditions and criteria are strictly respected. The conditions and criteria must be clearly stipulated in law, regulation or any other official document, in such a way that verification can be made;

(c) if there is an appearance of non-specificity resulting from the application of the principles set out in subparagraphs (a) and (b), there are reasons to believe that the subsidy under consideration is in fact specific, other factors may be considered such as: predominant use of a subsidy program by a limited number of enterprises, the granting of a disproportionately large share of the subsidy to certain enterprises only, and the manner in which the

---

[118] Free adaptation from: "Article 14 SCM Agreement. For the purpose of Part V, any method used by the investigating authority to calculate the benefit to the recipient conferred pursuant to paragraph 1 of Article 1 shall be provided for in the national legislation or implementing regulations of the Member concerned and its application to each particular case shall be transparent and adequately explained. Furthermore, any such method shall be consistent with the following guidelines: (a) government provision of equity capital shall not be considered as conferring a benefit, unless the investment decision can be regarded as inconsistent with the usual investment practice (including for the provision of risk capital) of private investors in the territory of that Member; (b) a loan by a government shall not be considered as conferring a benefit, unless there is a difference between the amount that the firm receiving the loan pays on the government loan and the amount the firm would pay on a comparable commercial loan which the firm could actually obtain on the market. In this case the benefit shall be the difference between these two amounts; (c) a loan guarantee by a government shall not be considered as conferring a benefit, unless there is a difference between the amount that the firm receiving the guarantee pays on a loan guaranteed by the government and the amount that the firm would pay on a comparable commercial loan absent the government guarantee. In this case the benefit shall be the difference between these two amounts adjusted for any differences in fees; (d) the provision of goods or services or purchase of goods by a government shall not be considered as conferring a benefit unless the provision is made for less than adequate remuneration, or the purchase is made for more than adequate remuneration. The adequacy remuneration shall be determined in relation to prevailing market conditions for the good or service in question in the country of provision or purchase (including price, quality, availability, marketability, transportation and other conditions of purchase or sale)".

[119] Panel Report, United States—Export Subsidies on Upland Cotton, par 7.1139.

granting authority exercised its discretion in deciding to grant a subsidy. In applying this subparagraph the diversity of economic activities within the jurisdiction of the granting authority, as well as the length of time during which the subsidy program has been in effect, will be taken into account.

2.2 Subsidy that is limited to certain enterprises located within a geographical region within the jurisdiction of the granting authority shall be considered specific. It is understood that the establishment or change of generally applicable rates by any and all levels of government having the authority to do so shall not be considered a specific subsidy for purposes of this Agreement.

2.3 Any subsidies included in the provisions of Article 3 shall be considered specific.

2.4 Any determination of specificity under the provisions of this Article shall be clearly based on positive evidence.[120]

Preliminarily, it should be noted that article 2 refers to the principles that must be observed for the characterization of specificity, which implies that its subparagraphs can be applied together, being analyzed on a case-by-case basis.[121] It is also important to note that the concept of specificity applies to all WTO regulations, including the Agreement on Agriculture.

Thus, the concept of specificity is extremely important not only for the interpretation of the SCM, but for the entire WTO, since only subsidies considered specific

---

[120] Free adaptation of: "Article 2 SCM Agreement: 2.1In order to determine whether a subsidy, as defined in paragraph 1 of Article 1, is specific to an enterprise or industry or group of enterprises or industries (referred to in this Agreement as "certain enterprises") within the jurisdiction of the granting authority, the following principles shall apply: (a)Where the granting authority, or the legislation pursuant to which the granting authority operates, explicitly limits access to a subsidy to certain enterprises, such subsidy shall be specific. (b)Where the granting authority, or the legislation pursuant to which the granting authority operates, establishes objective criteria or conditions governing the eligibility for, and the amount of, a subsidy, specificity shall not exist, provided that the eligibility is automatic and that such criteria and conditions are strictly adhered to. The criteria or conditions must be clearly spelled out in law, regulation, or other official document, so as to be capable of verification.(c)If, notwithstanding any appearance of non-specificity resulting from the application of the principles laid down in subparagraphs (a) and (b), there are reasons to believe that the subsidy may in fact be specific, other factors may be considered. Such factors are: use of a subsidy programme by a limited number of certain enterprises, predominant use by certain enterprises, the granting of disproportionately large amounts of subsidy to certain enterprises, and the manner in which discretion has been exercised by the granting authority in the decision to grant a subsidy. In applying this subparagraph, account shall be taken of the extent of diversification of economic activities within the jurisdiction of the granting authority, as well as of the length of time during which the subsidy programme has been in operation. 2.2 A subsidy which is limited to certain enterprises located within a designated geographical region within the jurisdiction of the granting authority shall be specific. It is understood that the setting or change of generally applicable tax rates by all levels of government entitled to do so shall not be deemed to be a specific subsidy for the purposes of this Agreement. 2.3 Any subsidy falling under the provisions of Article 3 shall be deemed to be specific. 2.4 Any determination of specificity under the provisions of this Article shall be clearly substantiated on the basis of positive evidence."

[121] See: Appellate Body Report, United States—Definitive Antidumping and Countervailing Duties on Certain Products from China, par 364.

can be challenged. In this sense, Bliacheriene points out that specificity is not part of the concept of subsidies, but:

> The "specificity test" serves exactly to trace, in practice, the outline of the tenuous boundary that separates permitted and therefore non-actionable government activities from those that are not. Subsidies can be considered specific a priori, as in the case of the prohibited subsidy, or a posteriori, after passing the sieve of the specificity test.[122]

Thus, according to article 2 of the SCM, subsidies are specific when the government aid is intended to benefit: (a) a company or an industry[123]; (b) an economic sector; (c) companies/industries located in a specific region[124]; and (d) the subsidies prohibited in the dictates of article 3, which are those linked to export or intended for import substitution.

Note that, in the first three criteria, specificity must be proved, while in the last one, it is presumed, as can be inferred from Article 2.3. Therefore, when granted based on general and horizontal criteria, they will not be subsidies to the WTO. As an example of horizontal application of these criteria, one can cite the size of the industry, the number of employees and the automatic eligibility. In this sense, explains Martins:

> It should be noted that when the granting body or the legislation through which said body operates define clear criteria or requirements, that is, that do not impose favoritism on given companies and that have an economic nature and horizontal application, such as number of employees or size of the company, which stipulate about the right to obtain and the amount to be offered, since this right is automatic and the criteria and requirements are fully respected, there will be no such specificity.[125]

However, objective criteria do not prevent the concealment of subsidy concessions when, for example, only a single industry or sector fits the established criteria.

Therefore, it is necessary to pay attention to the possibility of the specificity being granted by law or in fact. The former is easy to verify, since its terms are expressed in law. In fact, specificity is more difficult to verify, since it can only be verified at the time of application of the measure.

In any case, the analysis of specificity is complex and therefore must be case by case. Thorstensen and Oliveira point out that in the *Panel US—Upland Cotton*, it was stated that "[…] the specificity of a subsidy is subject to rigid quantification",[126] It is not possible to determine it previous manner.

---

[122] Bliacheriene (2006), p. 84.

[123] The Appellate Body defines industry as a form or branch of productive work, a trade or manufacture. In: Appellate Body Report: United States—Antiduping and Countervailing Duties on Certain Products from China, par. 366. In turn, a group of industries or sector is ascertained according to the type of product produced. In: Panel Report, United States—Upland Cotton, par 7.1142.

[124] The Panel Report in the caso European Union and certain member States—Large Civil Aircraft, par 7.1223, understood that the regional subsidy is specific even when available to all companies located in the designated region.

[125] Martins (2007), p. 68.

[126] Thorstensen and Oliveira (2013), p. 38.

To verify specificity, one must analyze whether access to subsidies is limited, not from the point of view of the recipients, but rather, by the wishes of the conceding authority. Therefore, the fact that only one company opts to receive the benefit does not mean that its access has been limited and, therefore, the measure does not constitute a subsidy.[127]

The possibility of choice by the economic agent is common when the government uses "inductive tax rules"[128] to induce behavior, since they are not penalized for not complying with the norms. However, when the subsidy program aims to consciously induce a company or a sector through tax incentives, adapting to its particular needs, the criterion of specificity is realized.

Therefore, the focus for the verification of specificity is on the eligibility criteria found in the legislative program or in the act of the granting authority and not on the choice of the economic agent, nor on whether the agents actually received the benefit.[129] Thus, there can be no discrimination with regard to access to the subsidy.

There is no doubt about the importance of the criterion of specificity in the concept of subsidies and its condemnation by the WTO. The reason for this is its ability to promote the benefit of some to the detriment of the public interest, leading to trade detour, as demonstrated in chapter one. Therefore, the more specific the subsidy, the greater its distortive capacity.

---

[127] See Appellate body report in the case United States—Anti-dumping and Countervailing Duties, par 372.

[128] Schoueri (2005), p. 43.

[129] In this sense, see the Panel Report in the case Japan—DRAMs, par. 7.374. "[...]If an investigating authority were to focus on an individual transaction and it arose from a generally available support program, the normal operation of which would generally result in financial contributions on predetermined terms (which are not tailored to the recipient company), this individual transaction would not, in our view, be specific within the meaning of Article 2.1 simply because it was provided to a specific company. An individual transaction would be specific, however, if it resulted in a molded program whose normal operation (1) would generally not result in financial contributions, and (2) would not pre-determine the conditions under which financial contributions would be provided, but rather, would require (a) conscious decisions as to whether or not to provide financial contributions (to one applicant or another), and (b) conscious decisions as to how the terms of the financial contribution should be tailored to the needs of the recipient". Free adaptation from: "[...] if an investigating authority were to focus on an individual transaction, and that transaction flowed from a generally available support programme whose normal operation would generally result in financial contributions on pre-determined terms (that are therefor not tailored to the recipient company), that individual transaction would not, in our view, become specific in the meaning of article 2.1 simply because it was provided to a specific company. An individual transaction would be specific, though, if it resulted from a framework programme whose normal operation (1) does not generally result in financial contributions, and (2)does not pre-determin the terms on which any resultante financial contributions might be provided, but rather requires (a) conscious decisions as to wheter or not to provide financial contribution (to one applicant or another), and (b) conscious decisions as to how the terms of the financial contribution should be tailored to the needs of the recipient company".

In short, WTO subsidies are government financial contributions, which will necessarily give a specific economic advantage to a particular industry or sector, which, under normal market conditions, would not be possible to obtain.

In view of its constituent elements, it is necessary to study the modalities of subsidies according to the WTO, which will differ according to the level of government intervention. Such modalities are a novelty brought by the Uruguay Round, which classifies subsidies into: prohibited, actionable and non-actionable, or green, yellow and red, as they are known by the traffic light system. These categories follow their own disciplines, still under the auspices of the SCM, which will be studied below, but it is necessary to emphasize that the general concept of subsidies in Article 1 applies to all of them.

Prohibited Subsidies

The prohibited subsidies are considered specific *per se,* because they are linked to export performance or are designed for import substitution. They are prohibited because they affect trade adversely, causing adverse effects on other members. They are regulated in Article 3 of the ASCM, in the following terms:

> Except as provided in the Agreement on Agriculture, the following subsidies as defined in Article 1 shall be prohibited subsidies linked in law or in fact to export performance, either individually or as part of a set of conditions, including those indicated by way of example in Annex I;
>
> (b) subsidies linked in fact or right to the preferential use of domestic products to the detriment of foreign products, either individually or as part of a set of conditions
>
> 3.2 A Member of this Agreement shall not provide or maintain the subsidies mentioned in paragraph 1.[130]

In a footnote to Article 3, the ASCM clarifies that export subsidies must be linked to actual or anticipated export earnings. Thus, the fact that a subsidy is granted to exporting companies does not automatically imply a prohibition.

In this sense, for a subsidy to be considered prohibited under Article 3 of the SCM, it is indispensable that its benefit be conditional on legal devices (*de jure*) or, in fact to export performance, independent of its results. The intention of the members in prohibiting subsidies, in fact, is to avoid subterfuge to circumvent the SCM rules.

---

[130] Free adaptation from: "Article 3 SMC Agreement: 3.1 Except as provided in the Agreement on Agriculture, the following subsidies, within the meaning of Article 1, shall be prohibited:(a) subsidies contingent, in law or in fact, whether solely or as one of several other conditions, upon export performance, including those illustrated in Annex I; (b) subsidies contingent, whether solely or as one of several other conditions, upon the use of domestic over imported goods. 3.2 A Member shall neither grant nor maintain subsidies referred to in paragraph 1".

Subsidies of law are those whose conditions are expressed in legal devices, sub-sidies are not in fact found in norms, but the facts demonstrate their existence in the terms of footnote 4 of the SCM.[131]

For the Appellate Body, both factual and legal subsidies are disciplined by the same rule, what changes is the way in which they must be proven.[132] While *de jure* subsidies can be proven from their text, de facto subsidies require a thorough analy-sis of all the circumstances surrounding their concession, as hardly a single fact would be enough to determine their existence.[133]

As for Annex I, mentioned in that article, it presents a list of eleven prohibited subsidies, both direct and indirect, that is, granted through direct financial aid or through tax incentives. The *Panel Canada—Autos* confirmed the exemplificative character of Annex I, opening the possibility of other prohibited subsidies not men-tioned in the list.[134]

Developing countries often argue that subsidies should not be prohibited when they serve to compensate for disadvantages faced by exporters due to the low level of development of the State. However, the *Panel* in the case *Brazil-Aircraft* deter-mined that:

> In items (e), (f), (g), (h) and (i) of the Illustrative List, which refer to exemptions, remissions or deferrals of taxes or import charges, there is no indication that a tax advantage would not constitute an export subsidy simply because it reduced the tax burden on the exporter to a level comparable to that borne foreign competitors.[135]

The referred list enumerates some exceptions, allowing the use of subsidies, in the same way that practices not included therein will be considered allowed. It must be emphasized that, even if permitted *prima facie*, subsidies can be contested when they produce adverse effects on trade.

According to item (e) of the Illustrative List, "[...] the total or partial exemption, remission or deferment, specifically related to exports, of direct taxes or social

---

[131] Footnote to Article 4: "This standard shall be satisfied when the facts demonstrate that the grant-ing of a subsidy, even if it is not legally linked to export performance, is in fact linked to exports or gains from actual or anticipated exports. The mere fact that subsidies are granted to exporting enterprises shall not, in itself, be regarded as an export subsidy in the sense defined in this Article." Free adaptation from: "This standard is met when the facts demonstrate that the granting of a sub-sidy, without having been made legally contingent upon export performance, is in fact tied to actual or anticipated exportation or export earnings. The mere fact that a subsidy is granted to enterprises which export shall not for that reason alone be considered to be an export subsidy within the meaning of this provision". In: SCM.

[132] See: Panel report on the case European Communities—Large Civil Aircraft.

[133] See: Panel report on the case Australia—Automotive Leather II, par 9.67, which considered that the fact that the domestic market was too small to absorb all subsidized production indicated the link of the subsidy to export performance.

[134] Panel Report on the case Canada—Certain Measures Affecting the Automotive Industry, par 167.

[135] Panel Report on the case Brazil—Export Financing Programme for Aircraft, par 7.25.

contributions due by industries or companies"[136] are prohibited subsidies. However, the mentioned tax incentives, when applied on indirect taxes,[137] will only be prohibited if excessive in comparison to the amount that would be collected in the domestic market.[138]

In the practice of international trade, exports are not taxed, that is, indirect taxes should not be passed on to consumers in another country, since the imported products will be onerous for the taxation of the receiving country. For this reason, the WTO admits the refund of indirect taxes, if it does not exceed the charges paid by the exporter.

The same line of rationale applies to the operations of *drawback*, which consists of tax exemption on the importation of inputs, parts, pieces, and raw materials in general for the manufacturing of products that will be exported. For the operation not to configure a prohibited subsidy, the raw material must necessarily be used in the finished product, which is often difficult to ascertain. If the national raw material is used with a tax incentive, there is a prohibition of subsidization within the meaning of Article 3(b), known as import substitution.

Subsidies aimed at import substitution are also prohibited, since they are conditioned to the requirements of employment of national products in detriment of imported ones.

The practice of import substitution was widely used in the 50s and 60s as a means of State intervention in the economy in order to foster industrialization for development. However, when verifying the distortive effects of this practice, economists began to doubt the adequacy of these trade policies. For this reason, WTO member states have agreed on the presumption of specificity and harm caused by import substitutions.

As an example, the Appellate Body condemned the following measures: (a) payments made by the Brazilian government linked to the export of aircraft, which were intended to ensure credit advantages under item (K) of the Illustrative List, by covering the difference between the interest contracted with the importer and the lender's cost of raising funds[139]; (b) the exemption of direct taxes granted by the US government to companies FSC (Foreign Sales Corporations), who, being outside the US territory, should, under US law, pay taxes on income earned in the place where they were located and in the United States[140]; (c) the donation of 30 million

---

[136] Free adaptation from: SCM, Annex I, and: "The full or partial exemption remission, or deferral specifically related to exports, of direct taxes or social welfare charges paid or payable by industrial or commercial enterprises".

[137] Indirect taxes are those levied on sales, consumption, added value, inventory, equipment, borne by third parties, while the direct taxes are levied on income and are borne by the taxpayer of the tax obligation.

[138] Granados (2003), p. 12.

[139] See: Appellate Body Report in the case Brazil—Export Financing Program for Aircraft, par 196.

[140] See: Appellate Body Report in the case United States—Foreign Sales Corporations, par 275: "As a whole, the benefits granted to FSCs represent a systematic effort by the United States to exempt certain types of income, which, in the absence of the program, would be taxed." Free

Australian dollars and a loan of 25 million granted to a single company producing and exporting automotive leather.[141]

Finally, it is emphasized that the rules regarding subsidies of the Agreement on Agriculture and the SCM must be interpreted harmoniously, since both are part of the WTO Constitutive Agreement. Thus, if there are no caveats in the Agreement on Agriculture, the SCM rules should be applied. In addition, under Article 27, Article 3 subsidies will be considered actionable for least developed countries.

Actionable Subsidies

Government contributions that do not fall into the category of prohibited subsidies can still be contested when they produce adverse effects on trade. Article 5 of the ASCM provides that "no member shall, through the application of any subsidy referred to in paragraphs 1 and 2 of Article 1, cause adverse effects on the interests of other members [...]".[142]

Therefore, actionable subsidies are those that are not prohibited but that cause damage to international trade. They are specific, but their specificity is not presumed as is the case with prohibited ones. As they are not specific and reprehensible *per se,* it is necessary to prove the causal link between the benefit and the damage. If this cannot be proven, the subsidy will be allowed. In Magalhães' words, such subsidies "[...]is prohibited from using it upon proof that it has harmful effects on the interests of another member country or, exceptionally, when there is an imminent and clear threat of damage".[143]

These effects are presented in paragraphs of Article 5 of the SCM:

(a) damage to the domestic industry of another Member11;
(b) nullification or impairment of advantages accruing to other Members, directly or indirectly, of the GATT 1994, in particular the advantages of concessions bound under Article II of the GATT 199412;
(c) serious damage to the interests of another Member[144];

---

adaptation from: "Viewed as an integrated whole, the exemptions provided by the FSC scheme represent a systematic effort by the United States to exempt certain types of income which would be taxable in the absence of the FSC scheme".

[141] In this sense, see: Appellate Body Report in the case Australia—Automotive Leather II.

[142] Free adaptation from: "SCM Agreement, article 5 [...] No Member should cause, through the use of any subsidy referred to in paragraphs 1 and 2 of Article 1, adverse effects to the interests of other Members [...]".

[143] Magalhães (2007), p. 127.

[144] Free adaptation from: "SCM Agreement, article 5 [...](a) injury to the domestic industry of another Member (192); (b) nullification or impairment of benefits accruing directly or indirectly to other Members under GATT 1994 in particular the benefits of concessions bound under Article II of GATT 1994 (193); (c) serious prejudice to the interests of another Member".

Note that subsidies are actionable when subsidized imports cause or threaten to cause damage to the domestic industry[145] that manufactures a similar product,[146] or when the damage is suffered by another member.

To determine the occurrence or the imminence of damage, it is necessary to determine the volume of subsidized imports and their effects on prices in the domestic market and, furthermore, if there was a significant increase in imports to the point of causing impacts to the domestic industry.[147]

Note that the adverse effects caused by subsidies constitute an important element in the analysis of their existence. Thus, even when granted before the creation of the WTO, if its effects remain over time, they can be questioned based on Article 5.[148]

In the case of threatened damage, Article 15.7 of the SCM requires that the determination must be based on clearly foreseeable and imminent facts, and that mere allegations, conjectures, or remote possibilities are not sufficient. To this end, the referred article establishes elements that must be analyzed together: (a) the nature of subsidies and their effects; (b) significant increase in subsidized imports in the domestic market; (c) significant increase in subsidized exports; (d) depressing or suppressing effect[149] of domestic prices, increasing the demand for subsidized imported goods; d) the stocks of the subsidized product.[150]

In both cases, whether the damage occurs or is imminent, for the subsidy to be considered actionable, it is essential that the subsidy caused the damage the causal

---

[145] The definition of domestic industry is disciplined in Article 16.1 of the ASCM: For the purposes of this Agreement, except as provided in paragraph 2, the term 'domestic industry' shall be interpreted as referring to the domestic producers as a whole of the like product or to those of them whose collective output of the products constitutes a major proportion of the total domestic production of such products, except where producers are related to exporters or importers or are themselves importers of the allegedly subsidized product or of the like product from other countries, in which case the term 'domestic industry' may be interpreted as referring to such other producers. Free adaptation from: "SCM Agreement, article 16.1:For the purposes of this Agreement, the term "domestic industry" shall, except as provided in paragraph 2, be interpreted as referring to the domestic producers as a whole of the like products or to those of them whose collective output of the products constitutes a major proportion of the total domestic production of those products, except that when producers are related to the exporters or importers or are themselves importers of the allegedly subsidized product or a like product from other countries, the term "domestic industry" may be interpreted as referring to the rest of the producers".

[146] To verify the similarity of the products, the following elements are considered: physical characteristics, purposes of use, consumer habits and preferences, and customs classification. See: Bossche and Zdouc (2013), p. 780.

[147] Ibid, pp. 781–782.

[148] This understanding is shared by the Appellate Body in the case EC and Certain Member States—Large Civil Aircraft (2011), par 686.

[149] While price depression is easier to verify and is realized with the reduction of prices, suppression implies situations that prevent prices from rising, for this reason, they can only be ascertained by comparing current prices with the prices that could occur in the absence of the subsidies. In this sense, see the Appellate Body Report in the case US—Upland Cotton (2008), par 351.

[150] Article 15.7 SCM.

link between the subsidy and the respective damage must be proven. Any damage caused by other factors cannot be challenged under the auspices of the SCM.[151]

When article 5 mentions the term "effect," it is intended to focus on the results produced by the subsidies. This way, there needs to be a link between the subsidy and the adverse effects. The Appellate Body has already ruled that: "The effect - price suppression - must result from a chain of causation that must be linked to the impugned subsidy".[152]

This effect may continue even if the subsidy is no longer in effect, which does not prevent it from being impugned. The Appellate Body has already determined that it is natural for there to be an interval between the benefit and its effects.[153]

However, the treatment should be differentiated regarding the remedies granted to counter serious damage that has already occurred or exists, which may pertain over time, from the threat of future damage.[154]

Finally, under Article 5(b), subsidies are also actionable when they nullify or reduce advantages obtained by members, such as tariff concessions bound under Article II:1 of GATT 1994.

Non-Actionable Subsidies

Non-actionable subsidies cannot be impugned because they lack the criterion of specificity. Until the end of 1999, this category still had some specific types of subsidies, determined in Article 8 of the ASCM, which, however, were extinguished by virtue of Article 31.

It was basically assistance for research and development activities, for adaptation to the new environmental legislations, as well as for promoting regional development.

This category was to be in force for only 5 years, after which it would be revised. Given that this review did not take place, there is a consensus that the category has expired. However, there is still much discussion on the subject in the WTO due to the relevance of these subsidies for the development of less favored countries.

In any case, it is important to point out that the extinction of the category does not prevent such subsidies from being considered permitted, if they are granted in a non-specific way, since, once the specificity is ascertained, the subsidy may be considered actionable if it causes the damages provided for in Article 5 of the SCM.

---

[151] Appellate Body Report in the Case Japan—DRAMs (2007), par 267.

[152] Free adaptation of: "The effect – price suppresion – must result from a chain of causation that is linked to the impugned subsidy". In: Appellate Body Report in the Case United States– Subsidies on Upland Cotton, par 372.

[153] Panel's report on the case United States—Subsidies on Upland Cotton, par 477.

[154] Panel's report on the case United States—Subsidies on Upland Cotton, par 244.

Thus, it can be stated that subsidies are allowed by the WTO, as long as they are not specific and are not linked to export performance or intended for import substitution, modalities whose specificity is presumed.

3.4.1.2   Compensatory Measures

To counter all types of subsidies, prohibited or actionable, the WTO authorizes its members to initiate an investigation to apply countervailing measures, a form of countermeasures,[155] whose purpose is to eliminate the harmful effects caused to the domestic industry of the importing country.

The imposition of countervailing measures depends on the wishes of the importing State, as long as it proves the following requirements (a) a finding by the investigating authority that the imports are subsidized; (b) injury to the domestic industry and (c) causal link between the subsidized imports and the damage.

If the subsidy is not proven, the compensatory measure will be considered illegal, by administrative decision, whose investigative procedure must be conducted in accordance with articles 10 to 23 of the ASCM, which must be observed by the internal legislation of the States, under penalty of complaint to the DSB.

This procedure may be initiated by the domestic industry or on its behalf,[156] or yet, by the state authority,[157] upon written petition accompanied by sufficient evidence of subsidy, injury and causal nexus, describing the subsidized product, its origin and the respective exporters.

Once initiated, the investigating authority should, previously, make consultations with members that export the product under investigation for clarifications and, if possible, the resolution of the problem by agreement, opportunities that will also be granted during the entire procedure.

The investigation period will be 1 year and in special circumstances may be extended to 18 months. During this period, measures may be applied provisionally in order to prevent damage during the procedure of the investigation.

The method used to calculate the benefit from the subsidy depends on each member's domestic legislation, provided that the general guidelines in Article 14 of the ASCM are observed. Thus, the compensatory measures must be sufficient to eliminate the damage to the domestic industry for as long as necessary, not exceeding a limit of 5 years. From this, two conclusions can be reached: (a) the amount of the measures cannot exceed the value of the subsidies and (b) the measures may have a value lower than the subsidy, if this is sufficient to remove the damage.

---

[155] Also, countermeasures in the WTO are: *antidumping* and safeguards.

[156] According to Article 11.4, the domestic industry is the one whose production represents more than 50% of the total production of the similar product, expressing both its support and rejection of the measure. The investigation will not be initiated when the supporting producers represent less than 25% of the domestic production.

[157] The State can initiate the investigative procedure as long as it has enough proof about the existence of the subsidy.

3.5   Main Subsidies and Compensatory Measures Applied

Data on major applied subsidies can only be obtained through the submission of notifications by members regarding subsidies granted, cases brought to the DSB, and notifications of countervailing measures adopted.[158]

It must be considered that not all members fulfill the obligation to notify annually the adopted subsidies.[159] Until October 28, 2014, for example, only 40 members had notified the Committee about applied subsidies, while 22 members notified informing that they had not adopted practices subject to notifications in the year 2013.[160]

Furthermore, it cannot be said that reported subsidies are prohibited, actionable, or permissible, since members must report any contribution that generates economic benefits to a specific industry, independent of the category it falls into. Moreover, it is not for the Committee to conduct this type of analysis, but rather to provide transparency of such practices.

The deadline for notifications is every June 30th of each year, but unfortunately the number of delays and omissions is quite significant. Generally, members tend to omit specific subsidies on the most sensitive sectors. For example, Brazil has been assiduous in notifying its agricultural subsidies, which are considered legal, but, on the other hand, it omits tax benefits in sectors such as the automotive sector, a sector that could be questioned by the developed countries.

Nonetheless, countries may also find it difficult to notify their subsidy programs due to the complexity of the SCM and the very concept of subsidies, the language that may prejudice the interpretation of the agreements, especially by countries that do not adopt the WTO official languages as their mother tongue, or due to the lack of internal transparency that makes it difficult to put the data together.

The last *World Trade Report* compiled by the WTO on the subject was in 2006 and revealed that Canada, the United States, Australia, Japan, Switzerland, India and South Africa significantly omitted their subsidy policies between 1998 and 2002, while the European Union, the Republic of Korea and Brazil had a high rate of notifications, as Table 3.2 shows.

The last annual report of the Grants Committee, dated November 3, 2014, testified that only forty members submitted subsidy notifications and twenty members notified that they did not maintain subsidy programs subject to the notification requirement.

---

[158] Countervailing measures are unilateral measures imposed by members to counteract the adverse effects of subsidies and will be studied in detail in chapter 3.

[159] The obligation to notify subsidy practices is determined in paragraph 1 of Article 25 of the SCM, which will be further analyzed in chapter 3.

[160] WTO (2014) Informe (2014) del Comité de Subvenciones y Medidas Compensatórias. N°. del doc. 14.6352.

Table 3.2 Average subsidy expenditure by different sources in billions of dollars, 1998–2002. Source: World Trade Report 2006[a]

States	National accounts data	Notifications
Canada	7.7	0.9
United States	43.5	16.3
Australia	4.7	0.3
Japan	34.3	4.2
Switzerland	10.8	0.7
India	12.2	–
South Africa	0.9	–
European Union	109	96.3
Korea	1.0	1.3
Brazil	2.0	1.7

[a]WTO (2006) World Trade Report 2006: exploring the links between subsidies, trade and the WTO. Geneva, WTO http://www.wto.org/english/res_e/booksp_e/anrep_e/world_trade_report06_e.pdf

More current data shows that, notifications have dropped from 75% to 35% from 1995 to 2021. This prevents data analysis and enforcement of the Committee's subsidy policies.[161]

Regarding the dispute settlement, by December 2021, the SCM was cited in 130 cases. Of that number, almost half involved prohibited subsidies disciplined by Article 3. Interestingly, all the cases that mentioned Article 3.1, which deals with subsidies linked to export performance, also involved Article 3.2, which refers to import substitution. The actionable subsidies in Article 5, on the other hand, were questioned in 18 cases.[162]

As for the sector, the most cited was the automotive sector, with 17 cases, followed by aircraft trade with 8 cases, tax benefits linked to exports with 7 and 3 cases of tax benefits in general, including case DS 472, initiated by the European Union against Brazil, referring to tax benefits granted by the country to the automotive sector, technology and electronics, goods produced in free trade areas and also to exporters.[163]

On the other hand, notifications of countervailing measures are made by advance and the Annual Report of the Subsidies Committee showed that from January 1, 1995, to June 30, 2014, 193 measures were adopted out of 355 initiated, and the hardest hit sector was base metals and their manufactures.

During the economic crisis that began in 2008, culminating in 2009, compensatory measures increased significantly from 2 to 11, again hitting the metals sector to

---

[161]WTO (2022) Subsidies, Trade and International Cooperation. https://www.wto.org/english/res_e/booksp_e/repintcoosub22_e.pdf, p. 13.

[162]WTO. Índice de Diferencias por Acuerdo. http://www.wto.org/spanish/tratop_s/dispu_s/dispu_agreements_index_s.htm?id=A20#selected_agreement.

[163]WTO. Índice de Assuntos. http://www.wto.org/spanish/tratop_s/dispu_s/dispu_subjects_index_s.htm.

a greater degree. Chinese exports suffered the most compensatory measures, imposed mainly by the United States, the European Union and Canada, amounting to 85% of the measures applied since 1995.[164]

The cited report also shows that Brazil, China, India, and Turkey started to initiate more anti-dumping and countervailing measures from 2017 onwards.[165] The pandemic crisis caused by COVID triggered new state interventions, among them, only 3 subsidies were notified to the WTO, all applied by the Australian government.[166]

Given this scenario, it is necessary to study the WTO's guidelines to its members on subsidy policies to contain global economic crises. However, little is known about the subsidies applied in the pandemic because of the inexpressive number of notifications.

3.5.1 The Subsidy Package After the 2008 Crisis

At the beginning of the GATT era, world exports of goods reached $59 billion a year. In 2011, after the effects of the 2008 crisis, world exports reached almost US$ 18 trillion. The 2008 crisis caused a 12% drop in world exports, the largest since World War II.[167]

While the 2008 volume was around $16 trillion, in 2009 it dropped to $12 trillion, increasing again to $15.3 trillion in 2010. From that year on, the increases were not as significant: in 2011, the increase was 5%, with the value of $18.4 trillion, and went up to $18.8 in 2013.[168]

The crisis of 2008 began in the United States in the real estate sector, in the face of the excess in the granting of loans without sufficient guarantees. In addition, due to U.S. war spending throughout the 2000s, the Central Bank raised interest rates, causing debts to increase, making it difficult to repay them and thus causing the devaluation of real estate and the bankruptcy of banks.

Given the globalization of the economy and the economic importance of the United States, holder of one of the most influential economies in the world, the

---

[164] WTO. Subsidies, Trade and International Cooperation. https://www.wto.org/english/res_e/booksp_e/repintcoosub22_e.pdf, p. 9.

[165] Ibid.

[166] WTO. COVID Support Measures. https://www.wto.org/english/tratop_e/covid19_e/trade_related_support_measures_e.htm.

[167] WTO. International Trade and Market Access Data. http://www.wto.org/english/res_e/statis_e/statis_bis_e.htm?solution=WTO&path=/Dashboards/MAPS&file=Map.wcdf&bookmarkState={%22impl%22:%22client%22,%22params%22:{%22langParam%22:%22en%22}}.

[168] Ibid.

paralysis of its financial market has impacted all of its trading partners,[169] resulting in a significant decrease in international trade.

Trade reduction is a matter of concern for the WTO, especially with regard to the protectionist measures that may be adopted by members in order to counter the damaging effects of economic crises.

Among the possible providences that can be adopted in these moments, *anti-dumping* measures stand out, safeguards, import barriers, as well as subsidies and countervailing measures. However, these measures do not cease to have their detrimental side to trade and may prolong or even intensify the effects of crises. In this sense, the World Bank pronounced itself in its work entitled *Lessons from World Bank Research on Financial Crises*:

> [...] when a country imposes export barriers or reduces trade and consumption taxes, choosing to insulate its domestic market from international price increases, while at the same time benefiting its domestic market, it cooperates with the exacerbated increase in world prices.[170]

Thus, the 2009 WTO Annual Report, whose main objective was to pronounce itself on the crisis contingency measures, recognized the necessity of adopting these measures, nevertheless, there was a warning about its consequences: "the fact that contingency measures are necessary to ensure future trade liberalization does not mean that there are no negative consequences".[171] Pascal Lamy, WTO Director-General at the time, emphasized that "protectionism is not the answer".[172]

As consequences of the application of such measures, more specifically, the practice of subsidies and the imposition of countervailing measures, it is necessary to warn about the danger of these practices becoming permanent. Furthermore, it is difficult to distinguish lawful from unlawful contingency measures, which brings the discussion to the DSB.

---

[169] According to 2013 data obtained by the Brazilian Ministry of Foreign Affairs, the United States has a GDP of $16.8 trillion and its main partners to which its exports are directed are: Canada, Mexico, China, Japan, the United Kingdom, Germany, Brazil, the Netherlands, Hong Kong and South Korea. American imports come from the following countries, in order of importance: China, Canada, Mexico, Japan, Germany, South Korea, the United Kingdom, Saudi Arabia, France, and India. In: Ministry of Foreign Relations. Estados Unidos: Comércio Exterior. http://www.brasil-globalnet.gov.br/ARQUIVOS/IndicadoresEconomicos/INDEstadosUnidos.pdf.

[170] Free adaptlation from: "A similar collective-action problem emerged during the recent sharp rise in food prices whereby a number of countries decided to insulate their domestic markets from food price increases by imposing export barriers or reducing trade and consumption taxes. While these policy responses made sense from the point of view of each individual country, the collective effect was to exacerbate the increases in world prices". In: World Bank (2008), p. 16.

[171] Free adaptation from: "[...] the fact that trade contingency measures are necessary to ensure further trade opening does not mean that there are no negative consequences". In: World Trade Organization (2009) World Trade Report 2009: trade policy commitments and contingency measures. Geneva: WTO, 2009. http://www.wto.org/english/res_e/publications_e/wtr09_e.htm.

[172] Free translation from: Proteccionism is not the answer. In: World Trade Organization (2009) Global Crisis Requires Global Solutions. http://www.wto.org/english/news_e/news09_e/tpr_13jul09_e.htm.

Considering that subsidies artificially reallocate economic resources, the WTO considers that their use continues to be harmful to the importing country due to their impact on world prices, reducing them.[173] Another concern of the WTO in relation to the issue concerns the *lobbies* formed internally in the States to maintain the subsidies, which may prolong their concession even after the crisis.

Countervailing measures, in turn, are seen as detrimental to consumers in the importing State under perfect market conditions, although they can also be useful in neutralizing and discouraging subsidies.

From this report, it can be inferred that the WTO was more flexible with the measures to counter the economic crisis of 2008, although there was the fear of its prolongation, leading to endless protectionism. It happens that the last WTO report, published in 2014, referring to the year 2013, showed that the scenario of 2008 was different from that in which the previous crises occurred, and, for this reason, its effects were different from those expected in the 2009 Report.

The 2014 report aimed to analyze the transformations that have occurred in the relationship between trade and development since the beginning of the millennium. It identified four trends that have changed the way trade affects development.

The first refers to the link between increased trade flows and rapid economic growth in developing countries. The second deals with global value chains and their contribution to development, while the third involves rising agricultural commodity prices and the importance of agriculture.[174] Finally, the fourth trend concerns the increasingly global nature of economic crises, as occurred in 2008-2009. In this sense, the organization's current CEO, Roberto Azevedo, pointed out in the 2014 report that:

> The strong reduction in trade and investment flows, exacerbated by the fall in aggregate demand and the drying up of trade in finance, helped transmit the economic shocks to producers and traders in developing economies. However, the fact that we have not seen a protectionist surge on a scale that occurred in previous crises means that a substantially worse drop in international trade has been avoided.[175]

One must consider that the greater the economic volatility of the country, the greater the incidence of the effects of the crisis, which is to say that the effects can be mitigated by decreasing volatility. In this sense, the 2014 report points out that the more

---

[173] See: WTO (2009) World Trade Report 2009: trade policy commitments and contingency measures. Geneva: WTO, 2009. http://www.wto.org/english/res_e/publications_e/wtr09_e.htm, p. 101.

[174] See: WTO (2014) World Trade Report 2014: Trade ande development: recent trends and the role of the WTO. See: http://www.wto.org/english/res_e/booksp_e/world_trade_report14_e.pdf, p. 4.

[175] Free adaptation from: "A sharp reduction in trade and investment flows, exacerbated bya fall in aggregate demand and the drying up of trade finance, helped transmit the economic shocks to producers and traders in developing economies. However, the fact that we did not see an outbreak of protectionism on the scale experienced in previous crises meant that a significantly worse fall in international trade was averted". In: WTO (2014) World Trade Report 2014, p. 4.

open and diversified the market and its trading partners are, the less economic volatility.[176]

However, unlike previous crises, for example, the Great Depression of 1929, the crisis of 2008 occurred in a more open market scenario that was under the auspices of multilateral trade rules, which restricted countercyclical practices of a protectionist nature, making their effects less devastating.

Another factor that contributed to the reduction of the impacts caused by the 2008/2009 crisis and the use of protectionist practices was the expansion of global value chains, which cooperated for a greater dissemination of trade and common interests.[177]

A study conducted by Andrew Rose[178] contributed to this conclusion, breaking the paradigm, according to which protectionist measures are, essentially, countercyclical. The author proved that protectionism, currently, is a cyclical, that is, it no longer serves as a countercyclical instrument, and this is due to the efforts of governments to reduce protectionism in the face of crises.

Obviously, there are variables in this study, which Rose himself recognizes, such as the country's level of development, the degree of trade openness, non-tariff barriers, among others, that may generate different results. In this specific case, Rose's main focus was on trade between the United States and the European Union.

However, studies have proven that when it comes to developing countries, such as Argentina, Brazil, India and others, there is a countercyclical pattern in the use of protectionist measures, such as compensatory measures.[179]

The situation is even more peculiar when it comes to agricultural subsidies, a sector where subsidies are more frequent, especially in developed countries, which in turn continue to significantly affect developing countries.[180]

3.5.2   Subsidies in Doha

Initiated 2 months after the terrorist attacks of September 11, 2001, by consensus of the members, the Doha Agenda, also known as the Development Round, aimed to promote further trade liberalization, paying attention to the particular needs of developing countries.

It is true that trade liberalization has brought gains for developing countries. WTO data stipulate that the Uruguay Round resulted in an increase of between $109 billion and $510 billion in annual world income, with the average annual increase in income for developing countries being $116 billion. The increase in trade was

---

[176] Ibid, p. 12.

[177] Ibid, p. 171.

[178] See: Rose (2012) http://www.nber.org/papers/w18062.pdf.

[179] See: WTO (2014) World Trade Report 2014, p. 179.

[180] Ibid, p. 10.

estimated to be between 9 and 24 percent, and for developing countries, the increase was estimated to be 50 percent more than the world average.[181]

However, it is also true that trade liberalization has still occurred gradually, leaving aside the most sensitive sectors, which became part of the Doha agenda. In this sense, Krugman points out that:

> Most of the potential gains from freer trade would result from reduced tariffs and export subsidies, which represents the last sector to be liberalized because it is the most politically sensitive. It is estimated that the liberalization of agricultural trade would produce 63 percent of the total global gains from free trade as a whole. Hard-won gains, since farmers in rich countries are highly efficient when it comes to exerting political pressure to obtain favors.[182]

Import rates had already been sufficiently reduced by the start of the Doha Round. Manufactured goods represented the largest volume of trade between the States,[183] since most of them were free of barriers. Thus, few issues remained to be negotiated, but these were the most complex on the agenda: trade in services, the issue of subsidies, agriculture, whose trade represented only 10% of world trade[184] and, furthermore, access to manufacturing trade, as well as increased space for maneuvers to foment industrialization.

Among the topics discussed, the elimination of subsidies is not of interest to developed countries, but rather the liberalization of the services sector, while for developing countries, the elimination of rich countries' subsidies, especially in the agricultural sector, is important. As for trade in services, developing countries fear opening it up due to the difficulties in competing in the sector.

In relation to market access for non-agricultural goods, known as NAMA—*Non-Agricultural Market Access*—there was a consensus on the non-linear reduction of tax barriers, known as the Swiss formula, but no agreement was reached on the coefficients. The United States wanted developing countries to adopt a very low coefficient—8%—and that by 2015, it would reach zero. By way of comparison, the European Union has an average tariff of 4% on manufacturing imports, while the U.S. average is 3%.[185]

Due to the impasse, the United States and the European Union were stricter in negotiations on agricultural subsidies, making the agreement conditional on concessions from developing countries in the areas of intellectual property, services, and market access for non-agricultural goods. A maximum tax rate of 15% would be acceptable for developing countries, although insufficient for the European Union to have access to the markets of emerging countries such as Brazil and India.

---

[181] Gatt Secretariat The Results of the Uruguay Round of Multilateral Trade Negotiations. http://www.ub.edu/prometheus21/articulos/archivos/gatt.PDF.

[182] Krugman (2008), p. 177.

[183] In 2005, manufacturing trade reached more than 73% of world trade in goods. In: Presser (2006), p. 63.

[184] See: Hoekman and Kostecki (2009), position 2306.

[185] Presser (2006), p. 66.

On the other hand, still about NAMA, developing countries wanted more space for the implementation of industrial promotion policies. Moreover, these countries demanded that the coefficients be distributed into new categories beyond the division between developed and developing countries, with the justification that some sectors are more sensitive than others.

In Brazil's case, the most sensitive sectors are the automotive, textile, and machinery and equipment sectors, which have average tariff rates of 35%, coincidentally, the maximum allowed by the tariff reduction commitment assumed by the country in the WTO.

In other sectors, developing countries pleaded for clearer and more specific rules in the procedure for imposing countervailing measures, while developed countries were in favor of greater rigidity in the granting of subsidies.

The difficulties in Doha were partly due to the combination of interests of developing countries, which began to act more incisively in the negotiations. China's accession to the WTO, a strong developing country, has contributed to the increase of this power, counterbalancing the interests between strong and weak countries. Because of this strength, such countries were unwilling to accept any agreement.

The 2008 crisis aggravated the situation even more, by increasing the prices of agricultural goods, corroborating in the sense of justifying the State intervention in the economy, as an instrument for the protection of the national industry.

In this scenario, the Director-General of the WTO, at the time, recognized such difficulties, synthesizing them:

> The history of the Doha Round shows precisely how difficult it is for its different actors to converge on a new agenda that corresponds to the new balances, notably among agricultural disciplines, industrial tariff reductions and services market opening. The negotiations of the round were mainly confronted with the delicate subject of agriculture until 2008. For various reasons – primarily, the national objectives of the negotiators – the round cannot be implemented despite the real progress throughout 2008, which at the same time marked the beginning of the global economic crisis.[186]

Many of the topics that were initially to be discussed in Doha were abandoned due to lack of convergence among members.[187] Like all rounds, Doha followed the rule

---

[186] Free translation from: "L'histoire du round de Doha tient précisément à la difficulté que rencontrent ces différents acteurs pour converger sur un nouvel agenda qui corresponde aux nouveaux équilibres, notamment entre disciplines agricoles, réduction des droits de douane en matière industrielle et ouverture du marché des services. Les négociations du round se sont principalement heurtées au sujet délicat de l'agriculture jusqu'en 2008. Pour des raisons diverses—au premier rang desquelles les objectifs nationaux des négociateurs—le round n'a pu aboutir malgré de nets progrès au cours de l'année 2008 qui, au même moment, marquait le début de la crise économique mondiale. In: Lamy. http://entempsreel.com/wp-content/uploads/2014/07/Pascal-Lamy-Entemps-r%C3%A9el.pdf, p. 20.

[187] Initially, the agenda was aimed at continuing the themes from the 1996 Singapore Ministerial Conference, which are: insertion of the social clause, trade in services, environment, regras antitruste, investment and trade facilitation, as well as subsidies, intellectual property, market access, agriculture, and development.

that agreement would only occur if the whole package was agreed.[188] Proposals on changes to the SCM were also a cause of imbroglio and, as a result, were forgotten or negotiated in parallel at the bilateral and regional levels.

The main proposal from developing and least developed countries was to bring Article 8 subsidies, allowed until 1999 but actionable as of that date, back into the category.

Brazil recognized the anachronism of the ASCM, mainly regarding the asymmetry of export credits in items (j) and (k) of Annex I for developing countries, which would hardly be able to obtain the same rate of credit capture in the international market. As an alternative, the country asked that only the variation in the macroeconomic reality of the States be considered in a unique way.[189]

Another problem highlighted was that the gaps in the SCM are only filled by DSB decisions. Meanwhile, difficulties in the investigation of subsidies for the purpose of imposing countervailing measures remain.

The impasses between the members regarding subsidies and, in particular, those of agriculture, as well as the vagueness of the terms of the proposals, held back the round for approximately 10 years. The Bali Ministerial Conference in late 2013 resumed the negotiations and, for the first time, members reached consensus on more specific rules on trade facilitation and subsidy reduction.

The new WTO Director-General, Roberto Azevedo, who took office in September 2013, made a commitment to reactivate Doha and, in part, he succeeded. The Brazilian diplomat working with the WTO, during the period he was representing Brazil, obtained achievements of great significance for developing countries with regard to subsidies.[190] Most important for the return to the round was the recognition of the heterogeneity of the members. In an interview with the German newspaper *Deutsche Welle*, Azevedo declared that:

> We need to recognize that countries are always in different economic cycles, and that to negotiate one should not expect homogeneity, because it is very difficult for this to happen, that is, in a negotiation between almost 160 countries, one cannot expect that all are living the same moment in terms of trade opening.[191]

Considering the economic and social heterogeneity of States was a big step in the WTO negotiations, but at the same time, it raised the complexity of trade relations. Despite this, the WTO Director-General affirmed that taking into account the diversity of interests cooperates to make the organization more inclusive.

Nevertheless, interests have changed during the 13 years of Doha. The classic division of WTO members into developed and developing does not match reality. In

---

[188] The rule is that *"Nothing is agreed upon until everrything is agreed upon"*. In: Hoekman and Kostecki (2009), position 2499.

[189] See: Bliacheriene (2006), pp. 27–28.

[190] Azevedo acted in the emblematic Cotton case between Brazil and the United States, which forced the latter to remove its subsidies in 2008. In 2005, through his work, the European Union also had to remove its subsidies on sugar.

[191] Walter. http://dw.de/p/1AVWq.

fact, "...the inability of the structure and dynamics of the Doha negotiations to reflect this evolution has cooperated with their fall".[192]

Considering countries such as India, Brazil and China as developing countries for the purposes of special and differential treatment has caused great impasse in the negotiations. The opening of trade in these countries is extremely important not only for the developed countries but also for the other developing countries, and the protection they plead on agriculture to be granted, indistinctively, for all the less developed and developing countries, has been blocking the round.

In addition, the long period of the agenda contributed to its failure in view of the changing political scenarios in the member countries. Brazil, for example, began to adopt a more defensive trade position from 2009, while in 2012, China no longer wanted to take risks.[193]

Almost 14 years of Doha in more than 20 years of the WTO's existence have passed. The dynamism of international trade relations depends on institutions that can keep up with these changes under penalty of becoming anachronistic. Schwab pointed out in *World Trade Forum* of WTO, on September 30, 2015 that: "... at least and until we went beyond Doha (...) we will never be able to discuss these problems".[194] The issues she was referring to are new trade issues such as regionalism, the environment, investment, competition, transparency in international bidding, trade facilitation, as well as issues such as e-commerce and global value chains.

3.6   The Regulation of Subsidies and Countervailing Measures in Brazil

Brazil's integration into international trade was consolidated in the 1990s through its submission to the multilateral norms of the WTO. This scenario forced the country to reorganize itself, adapting its internal legislation and administrative organization.

In this sense, Faria points out that "national law acquires, in an expanded way, the form of international law".[195] For this reason, it is necessary to study the adaptations made by the country regarding both its political-administrative structure and its legal instruments for the control and surveillance of subsidies and the application of compensatory measures.

---

[192] Free adaptation from: "The inability of Doha's structure and negotiating dynamic to reflect this evolution has helped ensure its downfall". In: Schwab (2011) https://www.foreignaffairs.com/articles/2011-04-09/after-doha.

[193] Ibid.

[194] Free adaptation from: "... unless and until we get beyond the Doha Round framework [...] we'll never be able to discuss those problems". In: ITCSD (2015) Trade Inclusiveness, Potential in Focus as WTO Public Forum Kicks Off. Bridges. vol 19 - No 32, Oct.

[195] Faria (2010), p. 21.

3.6.1 Internal Legislation

About legislation on the concession of subsidies, Brazil has internalized, through Decree 1.355 of 12/30/1994, all the multilateral agreements of the WTO, following, in general, its determinations. More specific aspects on the control and inspection of subsidies were little explored by internal legislation, except for the procedure for the investigation and application of countervailing measures, which, in addition to the mentioned Decree, is regulated by Decree No. 1.751 of December 19, 1995, which regulates the rules governing administrative procedures. SECEX Circular No. 20 of April 2, 1996, provides a script for the elaboration of a petition concerning the investigation of subsidy practices. CAMEX Resolution no. 63 of August 17, 2010, and SECEX Ordinances no. 21 of October 18, 2010 and no. 14 of May 13, 2011 also address the topic. In 2021, the Brazilian government updated its legislation on subsidies and countervailing measures with Decree no. 10.839 of October 18, 2021.

Within Mercosur, unlike the European Union, there are no rules governing subsidies or the concession of tax incentives. However, from the analysis of the decisions of the Common Market Council, it is possible to verify that the body follows the SCM premises to conceptualize subsidies.[196]

The Brazilian Legal System did not define or regulate subsidies, thus adopting the concept and definitions of the SCM. In fact, control is exercised over the concession of tax incentives, which may constitute subsidies, according to the precepts of the SCM.

Tax incentives are conceded, in Brazil, in the exercise of the tax competences determined by the Federal Constitution of 1988. Tax competence is understood as "[...] the authorization for public law entities to create other rules about taxes, respecting the pre-established material and formal limits".[197]

Note that the limitations on the power to be taxed are inserted in the concept of competence, as well as the negative limitations (the one not to tax), such as constitutional principles and immunities.[198]

The Federal Constitution of 1988, in respect for the federative pact,[199] divided the tax competence among the Union, the States, the Municipalities and the Federal District, a model that, according to Leonetti "[...] helped to make the national tax system more rigid".[200]

The constitutional tax competence rules, besides specifying the competent entities for the creation and administration of taxes, also determine the procedure for its

---

[196] See: Bliacheriene (2006), pp. 86–87.

[197] Bonfim (2011), p. 118.

[198] See: Ibid.

[199] The Brazilian federation model conceded autonomy at the same hierarchical level to the Union, the Member States, the Municipalities and the Federal District; however, the State's sovereignty is restricted to the Union, which, as holder of international legal personality, can enter into international treaties that will be obligatory on all entities.

[200] Leonetti (1998), p. 62.

institution, its content, and the purpose of the norm that these entities will have to observe.

The tax competence must be interpreted in a broad way, encompassing the powers to create, administer and exonerate tributes, both through the exercise of legislative and administrative competence.[201] In this way, the entity competent to institute the tribute may also concede tax incentives concerning it, as long as the constitutional principles are respected.

As an example, one can cite the Union's competence to institute tax on income by law, whose exemption must also be conceded by law, as determined by article 176[202] of the National Tributary Code in consonance with the constitutional principle of legality,[203] which states that:

> Art. 150 - Without prejudice to other guarantees assured to the contributor, it is forbidden to the Union, the States, the Federal District and the Municipalities:
>
> I – to demand or increase tribute without a law establishing it; [...]
>
> § 6.° Any subsidy or exemption, reduction of the calculation basis, concession of presumed credit, amnesty or remission, related to taxes, fees or contributions, can only be granted by means of a specific federal, state or municipal law, that exclusively regulates the issues listed above or the corresponding tax or contribution, without prejudice to the provisions in article 155, § 2.°, XII, g.[204]

It is emphasized that the Constitution, differently from the SCM, does not include exemption as a modality of subsidy, nor does it clarify their differences, but makes it clear that such tax benefits must be conceded by specific law. In this sense, the exemption constitutes a fiscal incentive within the scope of public revenue, since "it presupposes a normative meeting, in which the exemption rule operates as an expedient to reduce the scope of the criteria of the hypothesis or consequence of the tax matrix rule.[205]

Catão adds that tax incentives "are guided by the possibility of State intervention in the economic domain and by the use of the tax as a regulatory instrument".[206]

It should be noted that not all tax incentives are tributary: the former are a genus of which the latter are a species. Therefore, the concept of tax benefit is more

---

[201] See: Bonfim (2011), pp. 116–119.

[202] Art. 176. The exemption, even when provided for in the contract, is always due to a law that specifies the conditions and requirements required for its concession, the tributes to which it applies and, if applicable, the term of its duration. In: Brasil, Código Tributário Nacional. http://www.planalto.gov.br/ccivil_03/leis/l5172.htm.

[203] "[...]the exemption acts on another level, namely that of the exercise of the power to tax: when the competent political person exercises this power by issuing the law that institutes the tax, this law may, using the exemption technique, exclude certain situations which, were it not for the exemption, would be within the incidence field of the tax law, but, by virtue of the exemption rule, remain outside this field". In: Amaro (2010) Direito Tributário Brasileiro. 11ª ed. Rio de Janeiro, Forensic, p. 135.

[204] Brazil, Constituição da República Federativa do Brasil. Brasília, DF, Federal Senate, 1988.

[205] Carvalho (2007), p. 198.

[206] Catão (2003), pp. 215–216.

comprehensive, since it involves both issues related to revenue and expenditure, such as, for example, expenses with subsidies.[207]

However, independent of the nature of the incentives, as well as whether they are direct or indirect taxation, for the WTO, if they are granted specifically, aimed at import substitution or linked to export performance, will be considered prohibited, and if they do not have such purposes, but are specific and in some way injurious to other members' trade, they can be contested as actionable subsidies.

Direct taxes are those borne by the taxable person of the obligation, as with income tax, while indirect taxes are borne by third parties, such as consumers.[208] For the WTO, the difference is relevant in the following terms: The tax incentives that involve direct taxation are expressly forbidden, while the indirect ones will only be considered when excessive, since the practice is not to export taxes, because they will be paid in the importing country. In this sense, the illustrative list of subsidies found in ANNEX I of the SCM, provides the following examples:

(e) The exemption, remission or total or partial deferral specifically linked to export, of **direct taxes** or social contributions due by industries or companies.

(h) The exemption, remission or deferral of indirect taxes on earlier stages of goods or services used in the manufacture of exporting products, in addition to the exemption, remission or postponement of equivalent indirect taxes on earlier stages of goods or services used in the manufacture of a like product intended for the domestic Market **since, however, prior-stage cumulative indirect taxes may be exempted, remitted or deferred on products destined for export even when this does not apply to similar products destined for domestic consumption, if the prior-stage cumulative indirect taxes are applied to inputs that are consumed in the production of the export product (due account being taken of waste)** (...)[209]

Therefore, when intervening in the economy, governments should consider the aforementioned list associated with the criterion of specificity, inherent to the concept of subsidy, since domestic legislation is silent on the matter. Regarding the State's intervention in the economic domain, the Federal Constitution regulates the subject in its article 149[210] and, more specifically, in Title VII, Chapter I, Article 174:

---

[207] See: Almeida (2000).

[208] See: Machado (2008), p. 137.

[209] In the original: ANNEX I. (e) The full or partial exemption remission, or deferral specifically related to exports, of direct taxes or social welfare charges paid or payable by industrial or commercial enterprises. (h)The exemption, remission or deferral of prior-stage cumulative indirect taxes58 on goods or services used in the production of exported products in excess of the exemption, remission or deferral of like prior-stage cumulative indirect taxes on goods or services used in the production of like products when sold for domestic consumption; provided, however, that prior-stage cumulative indirect taxes may be exempted, remitted or deferred on exported products even when not exempted, remitted or deferred on like products when sold for domestic consumption, if the prior-stage cumulative indirect taxes are levied on inputs that are consumed in the production of the exported product (making normal allowance for waste). This item shall be interpreted in accordance with the guidelines on consumption of inputs in the production process contained in Annex II.

[210] Art. 149: The Union is exclusively responsible for instituting social contributions, of intervention in the economic domain, and of interest to professional or economic categories, as an instru-

> As a normative and regulatory agent of the economic activity, the State will exercise, as provided for by law, the functions of fiscalization, incentive and planning, the latter being determinant for the public sector and indicative for the private sector.[211]

It is evident in this article that tax incentives, arising from inductive tax norms, constitute a means by which the State performs the function of a normative agent of the economy.

However, in the CF/88 only two specific hypotheses are admitted that justify the concession of tax incentives: (a) when destined to promote the balance of socioeconomic development in the less favored regions of the country[212] and (b) for public policies for sheltering orphaned or abandoned children and adolescents.[213]

Besides, CF/88 established, by means of programmatic norms,[214] policies to promote productive sectors and reduce inequalities. For Pires: "[…] the main reason for the concession of tax incentives lies in the purpose of economic development, enshrined as a constitutional principle by art. 3, II of the CF".[215]

At the federal infra-constitutional level,[216] the Fiscal Responsibility Law—LRF—has as its main scope to fight bad management of public resources and, therefore, to regulate fiscal incentives. In addition, it has the scope of improving the means of collection and limiting the concession of tax incentives that were being granted in a disorderly manner.[217]

For purposes of the LRF, tax incentives are any measure that implies a discriminated reduction of tributes. Thus, while the creation of taxes is limited by the Federal

---

ment for its actions in the respective areas, observing the provisions in articles 146, III, and 150, I and III, and without detriment to the provisions in art. 195, § 6, regarding the contributions alluded to in the article. In: BRAZIL. *Constituição da República Federativa do Brasil*. Brasília, DF: Federal Senate, 1988.

[211] BRAZIL. Constituição da República Federativa do Brasil. Brasília, DF: Federal Senate, 1988.

[212] Art. 151. It is forbidden to the Union: I—to institute a tax that is not uniform throughout the national territory or that implies distinction or preference in relation to the State, the Federal District or the Municipality, to the detriment of another, admitted the granting of tax incentives aimed at promoting the balance of socio-economic development between the different regions of the Country. In: BRAZIL. *Constituição da República Federativa do Brasil*. Brasília, DF: Federal Senate, 1988.

[213] Art. 227. It is the duty of the family, the society, and the State to ensure to the child, the adolescent, and the youth, with absolute priority, the right to life, health, food, education, leisure, professionalization, culture, dignity, respect, freedom, and family and community life, in addition to protecting them from all forms of neglect, discrimination, exploitation, violence, cruelty, and oppression. § 3—The right to special protection will encompass the following aspects: VI—encouragement by the Public Power, through legal assistance, tax incentives and subsidies, under the terms of the law, to the reception, in the form of guardianship, of orphaned or abandoned children or adolescents. In: Constituição da República Federativa do Brasil (1988) Brasília, DF: Federal Senate.

[214] As an example, one can cite the articles: 145§1°;146;150; 151; 153§1° and 215 of CF/88.

[215] Pires (2007) In: Martins (2007), p. 27.

[216] There are countless laws at the state, municipal, and district scope that have been omitted in this work so as not to make it excessively prolix.

[217] See: Harada (2011).

Constitution, their renunciation is conditioned to the provisions of infra-constitutional law.[218] In an attempt to prevent tax incentives from being conceded according to public interests that are distorted from collective interests, article 14 of the LRF[219] makes the concession of fiscal incentives conditional on the demonstration of impacts in the Budget Guidelines Law (LDO).[220]

Thus, tax incentives must be granted by law and be based on the interests of the community, in line with the constitutional principles, fulfilling the purpose for which they were granted.

From this, it is stated that, in the internal scope, subsidies constitute all governmental aid whose objective is to promote the social development of less favored regions. They are justified when used as an instrument to correct distortions or social inequalities of collective interest, situations in which the State's intervention in the economy via inductive tax norms is admissible.

The only exception to this rule is federal taxes of a regulatory nature that, due to their extra fiscal nature, are subject to the principle of mitigated tax legality, applied to the alteration of tax rates, as determined in article 153 §1° of the Federal Constitution. These are taxes with the purpose of regulating foreign trade, namely: the import tax, the export tax, the tax on industrialized products (IPI) and the tax on credit operations, exchange, insurance, and operations with marketable titles (IOF).

It is highlighted that the national legislation is concerned with the effects provoked by the concession of tax incentives that do not meet social interests and cause a decrease in the tax burden for some and an increase for others. Similarly, the

---

[218] It is important to note that tax incentives can still be creditworthy, such as low interest on loans and direct financial resources, which are not subject to constitutional tax principles but to Financial or Administrative Law, called by Bliacheriene credit subsidy, which implies an action of giving, unlike the so-called tax subsidies. See: Bliacheriene (2006), p. 125.

[219] Art. 14. The concession or expansion of an incentive or benefit of a tax nature from which revenue is waived must be accompanied by an estimate of the budgetary-financial impact in the year in which it is to begin its validity and in the following two, comply with the provisions of the law of budgetary guidelines and at least one of the following conditions: I - demonstration by the proponent that the renunciation was considered in the revenue estimate of the budget law, as per art. 12, and that it will not affect the fiscal result targets foreseen in the proper annex of the budget guidelines law; II - be accompanied by compensatory measures, in the period mentioned in the caput, by means of an increase in revenue, resulting from an increase in rates, expansion of the calculation basis, increase or creation of a tax or contribution.§ 1o The renunciation comprises amnesty, remission, subsidy, presumed credit, concession of exemption in a non-general character, alteration in the tax rate or modification of the calculation basis that implies a discriminated reduction of taxes or contributions, and other benefits that correspond to differentiated treatment.§ 2o If the act of concession or extension of the incentive or benefit dealt with in the caput of this article derives from the condition contained in item II, the benefit will only become effective when the measures referred to in the mentioned item are implemented. §3o The provisions of this article do not apply to: I - alterations in the tax rates of the taxes provided for in items I, II, IV and V of art. 153 of the Constitution, pursuant to its § 1o; II - the cancellation of a debit whose amount is less than the respective collection costs. In: BRASIL. Complementary Law no. 101 of May 04, 2000.

[220] Pires warns that the Law of Fiscal Responsibility "covers only the cases of fiscal incentives that retain a certain degree of discretion by the legislator/administrator". In: Pires (2007) In: Martins (2007), p. 30.

effects of subsidies operate which, due to their specificity, privatize the benefit to some to the detriment of others.

It is also worth highlighting that the baseline national legislation is less restrictive than the international one regarding the application of subsidies. Thus, a tax incentive may be legal according to domestic normative criteria, when granted without affecting public expenditure, but this does not prevent it from being considered a prohibited subsidy or actionable according to the dictates of the WTO.

3.6.2   Political-Administrative Framework of Subsidies and Compensatory Measures

Regarding the political-administrative structure of Brazilian foreign trade, it should be noted that its development has varied according to "[…] the momentary conjunctural politics and international contingencies".[221]

The first reforms of the 1990s began in the Foreign Trade Department, linked to the Ministry of Economy, Finance and Planning, later replaced by the Foreign Trade Secretariat in 1992, which in 1999 was transferred to the Ministry of Industry, Trade and Tourism, now the Ministry of Development, Industry and Foreign Trade—MDIC, responsible for the formulation, implementation and evaluation of public policies aimed at promoting competitiveness, foreign trade, investment and innovation.[222]

The main MDIC bodies are the Chamber of Foreign Trade—CAMEX and the Secretariat of Foreign Trade—SECEX and their respective departments: Department of International Negotiations—DEINT, Department of Foreign Trade Operations—DECEX, Department of Commercial Defense—DECOM and Department of Statistics and Export Support—DEAX, former Department of Planning and Development of Foreign Trade—DEPLA, Department of Competitiveness in Foreign Trade—DECOE.

The last SECEX reform was implemented in 2013 and, besides changing DEPLA's nomenclature to DEAX, it created DECOE, divided DEINT into two coordinations (Multilateral Issues and Regimes of Origin), restructured DECOM into three general coordinations (*Antidumping*, Safeguards and Exporter Support; *Antidumping* and Dispute Resolution; *Antidumping* e Compensatory measures) and also added to DECEX two new coordinations (Import and Export /*Drawback*). The Fig. 3.4 shows this structure.

The new CAMEX was instituted by Decree n°. 3.756 of 21/01/2001, which continues to serve as a forum for discussion, and can also make decisions and deliberate

---

[221] Gonçalves (2001), p. 123.

[222] See: Ministério do Desenvolvimento, Indústria e Comércio Exterior. Estrutura do Comércio Exterior (2018). http://www.mdic.gov.br/arquivos/dwnl_1251143349.pdf.

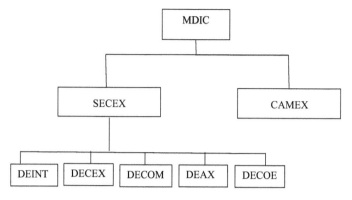

Fig. 3.4 Structure of the Brazilian Ministry of Development and Foreign Trade. Source: Author

on matters of foreign trade. It is an inter-ministerial body, composed by the MDIC, the Chief of Staff, Foreign Affairs, Finance, Agriculture and Planning.

SECEX, in turn, has the function of formulating proposals for foreign trade policies and programs, and may propose exchange and fiscal measures, such as changes in import tax rates, as well as coordinating trade defense actions, among others.[223]

The DEINT has the scope of coordinating the work of Brazilian international negotiations. DECEX, in turn, is responsible for the operationalization of SECEX policies in order to facilitate and avoid bureaucratizing foreign trade operations. DEPLA is responsible for the elaboration of the Brazilian foreign trade statistics.

DECOM, on its turn, coordinates the activities to counter unfair trade practices, acting in three areas: (a) investigation of unfair trade practices; (b) support to the exporter in defenses in investigative procedures initiated in other States and (c) in international negotiations, through the preparation of opinions.[224]

Basically, the opening of the investigative procedure occurs upon petition of the national industry to SECEX, which should contain the requirements of SECEX Circular No. 20, which are: (a) Qualification of the petitioner; (b) identification of the subsidized product, through detailed description; (c) the volume and estimated value of the domestic production of the like product as well as the production of the petitioner; (d) information about the subsidy, such as: subsidized product, country of origin, country of provenance, producers in the country of origin and exporters to Brazil, subsidy program, granting authority, legislation, export price, etc.; (e) evidence of damage and impacts on domestic production; (f) elements proving the causality between the subsidy and the damage to the domestic industry.

---

[223] For more details about CAMEX and SECEX, see: Ministério do Desenvolvimento, Indústria e Comércio Exterior. Estrutura do Comércio Exterior. http://www.mdic.gov.br/arquivos/dwnl_1251143349.pdf.

[224] See: Kolosky (2014), p. 68.

It is important to note that the administrative authority can also initiate the procedure when it has evidence regarding the existence of the subsidy, the damages, and the causal nexus.

Before proceeding with the investigation, an analysis of specificity will be made: if it is verified, the DSB will be notified to authorize the proceeding. Once authorized, the procedure will be processed in DECOM, which will investigate the existence, the degree and the effect of the subsidy. The respective conclusive opinion will be remitted to CAMEX for the adoption of countermeasures, provisional or definitive.[225]

The procedure is similar to the one foreseen in the SCM and must respect the principle of due legal process, transparency, contradictory and ample defense, in order to guarantee the participation of all involved. Thus, if the request for investigation is accepted, the governments concerned will be notified to manifest themselves in relation to the consultations. Foreign producers can also make an undertaking to SECEX to stop the damage to the domestic industry by revising prices or ceasing exports.

When authorized, the compensatory measures must observe the norms of Law no. 9.019 of March 30, 1995, which prescribes, according to its article 1, that the importation of products and services originating from a country that granted a specific subsidy will be charged, independently of any tax obligations, through cash payment.

The countervailing measures are applied by means of an addition to the import tax on the subsidized product. Its value will be proportional to the amount of the subsidies ascertained in the administrative process. It will be calculated per unit of subsidized product exported to Brazil according to the subsidy value.

The revenue collected from these measures is intended for the Ministry of Development, Industry and Foreign Trade and will be used in favor of Brazilian foreign trade. Currently, Brazil has no countervailing measures in force.

In practice, the countervailing measures work like a tribute by raising the import tax.[226] However, they are not tributes, in fact, Decree No. 1.751/95 emphasizes that the countervailing duties will be collected independently of any tax obligations. Nor are they considered tariff barriers for the internationalist doctrine,[227] because they are intended to counterbalance the effects of subsidies, nor are they of a tax nature.[228]

In analyzing *antidumping* and countervailing measures, Barral[229] qualifies them as a type of State intervention in the economic domain by negative induction, while

---

[225] It is also up to CAMEX to review countermeasures in order to suspend, extend, or modify them.

[226] See: Fiatkoski (2009), p. 5.

[227] See: Bliacheriene (2006), p. 142.

[228] Among the arguments for their non-tax nature, one can cite: the countervailing measures are not instituted by law, they are due independently of immunity or exemption from import tax, the practice of subsidies does not generate the compulsory incidence of the measures, etc. See: Ibid, pp. 136–148.

[229] Barral (2000), p. 63.

Lobo[230] states that they are sanctions and therefore cannot be used as a means of inducing behavior.

The SCM qualifies them as a "special right",[231] however, gives no further details about this right, other than its purpose to counterbalance the effects of subsidies. For Bliecheriene:

> [...] the WTO has introduced in trade defense a sanctioning system that moves away from strict legality to the principle of composition and effectiveness of the acts practiced in the protection of the international market. To this new type of sanction, he gave the name of measures *antidumping*, compensatory or retaliatory, whose innovative legal nature is that of a special right.[232]

In this sense, it is affirmed that the compensatory measures constitute a right based on the provisions of GATT/1994 and the SCM, both norms internalized in the Brazilian legal system, classified as international sanctions and, therefore, not subject to the domestic tax system.

In a way, Bliacheriene agrees with Barral in the inducing function of compensatory measures, which can induce the rearrangement of the parties, at any time, by agreement with the objective of suspending them, constituting, therefore, compensatory credits of an optional order for the State importing subsidized product.

The problems related to countervailing measures will be studied in the following chapter. For now, it was necessary to understand their concept, legal nature, as well as the relevant international and domestic legislation in order to discuss the objective of subsidy regulation in the WTO.

Regarding its purpose, the *Panel* has already had the opportunity to express itself several times. In the case *Brazil-Aircraft*, it was found that the objective of the SCM is to impose multilateral rules on distorting subsidies. This understanding was confirmed in the case *Canada-Aircraft*, when the Appellate Body stated that the purpose of the SCM is based on the premise that some government interventions distort or are capable of distorting trade.[233]

It should be noted that, at no time, the provisions of the SCM nor the jurisprudence show concern with the intention of the government or with the purpose of the subsidies, which are justified in domestic law as an instrument of promotion of the public interest, such as social, environmental, technological, and economic development. After all, it is in the collective interest to maintain fair trade between States. In Bliacheriene's words:

---

[230] Lobo (2004), p. 186.

[231] Footnote 36 of the SCM: The term "countervailing measure" shall be understood as a special right perceived for the purpose of counterbalancing any subsidy granted directly or indirectly to the manufacture, production or export of any good, as provided for in paragraph 3 of Article VI of GATT 1994. Translation of: Vera Thorstensen and Luciana Maria de Oliveira. In: Thorstensen and Oliveira (2013), p. 101.

[232] Bliacheriene (2006), p. 159.

[233] See: Bossche and Zdouc (2013), p. 747.

A peculiarity of the WTO system is that the internal reasons that lead a State to decide to grant a subsidy (whether economic, social, environmental, etc.) have no greater significance than its specificity and the effects it causes in the national or international market.[234]

In the WTO system, only specificity matters, that is, subsidies can only be subject to countermeasures or be condemned by the DSB when specific. The specificity is justified, in the dictates of the SCM, by the occurrence of damage to the industry of a State caused by the subsidies,[235] not being legitimized by their social reach.

The Tokyo Subsidies Code allowed developing countries to maintain export subsidies as needed, but the SCM extends the prohibition to all members, using only one objective criterion, that of specificity, without taking into consideration the particular needs of its members.[236]

It is noted that, apart from specific subsidies, there is a wide margin of possibilities for the use of permitted subsidies. However, the anachronism in the WTO rules persists when, on the one hand, in the preamble of its constitutive agreement, a commitment is made to economic and social development and, on the other hand, it prohibits the use of specific subsidies, with no importance given to social interests.

Thus, countries that adopt subsidy programs to realize specific interests can trigger trade detour and inefficiency in competing markets. For this reason, the multilateral trade system must seek economic and social efficiency, for which affirmative actions must be implemented. The use of countervailing measures against unfair trade practices, such as subsidies, protects commercial interests and enables efficiency, as will be explained in the next chapter.

References

Almeida FCR (2000) Uma abordagem estruturada da renúncia de receita pública federal. Revista do Tribunal de Contas da União, Brasília, DF 31(84):19–62

Amaro L (2010) Direito Tributário Brasileiro, 11ª edn. Forensic, Rio de Janeiro, p 135

Barral W (2000) Dumping e Comércio Internacional: a regulamentação antidumping após a Rodada Uruguai. Forensic, Rio de Janeiro, p 63

Bliacheriene AC (2006) Emprego dos Subsídios e Medidas Compensatórias na Defesa Comercial: análise do regime jurídico brasileiro e aplicação dos acordos da OMC. Thesis (Doctorate in Law) – Post-graduation course in Law, Pontifícia Universidade Católica de São Paulo, São Paulo, pp 27–28, 84, 86–87, 91–92, 125, 142, 159

Bobbio N (2007) Da Estrutura à Função: novos estudos de teoria do direito. Manole, São Paulo, p 71

Bonfim D (2011) Tributação e Livre Concorrência. Saraiva, São Paulo, p 85, 116–119

Bossche PV, Zdouc W (2013) The law and policy of the World Trade Organization, 3rd edn. Cambridge University Press, pp 83, 126, 747, 780–782

---

[234] Bliacheriene (2006), pp. 91–92.

[235] See: WTO (2009) World Trade Report 2009: trade policy commitments and contingency measures. http://www.wto.org/english/res_e/publications_e/wtr09_e.htm, p. 101.

[236] See: IPEA. Como colocar o comércio a serviço da população? http://hdl.handle.net/11058/3095, p. 294.

Bruno FMR (2013) Análise Econômica do Direito Aplicada à Concessão de Subsídios e a Imposição de Tarifas no Comércio Internacional. Revista de Direito Brasileira 5(3):300–320

Caliendo P (2009) Direito Tributário e Análise Econômica do Direito: uma visão crítica. Elsevier, Rio de Janeiro, pp 34, 101–117, 121

Carvalho PB (2007) Curso de Direito Tributário. 18. ed. Saraiva, São Paulo, p 198

Catão MAV (2003) Regime Jurídico dos Incentivos Fiscais. Renovar, São Paulo, pp 74, 215–216

Faria JE (2010) Direito e Globalização Econômica: implicações e perspectivas. Malheiros, São Paulo, p 21

Fernandez JC (2009) Curso Básico de Microeconomia. Salvador, EDUFBA, p 25, 45

Fiani R (2004) After all, what interests does regulation serve? Economia e Sociedade, Campinas 13(2) (23):81–105, July / December, p 83, 85

Fiatkoski ARFS (2009) A disputa entre Brasil e Canadá sobre subsídios à exportação de aeronaves. UniCeub, Brasília, p 5

Gonçalves EN (2001) A Tomada de Decisões Técnico-legais para o Mercosul: uma apreciação do dumping sob o enfoque da análise econômica do Direito. Thesis (Doctorate in Law) - Postgraduate Course in Law, Federal University of Minas Gerais, Belo Horizonte, p 123

Gonçalves EN, Stelzer J (2010) Economia e Direito para o Rompimento de Barreiras ao Comércio Internacional: a disciplina jurídica do GATT a OMC. http://www.conpedi.org.br/manaus/arquivos/anais/fortaleza/3755.pdf, pp 2409–2410

Goyos Jr DN (1994) A OMC e os Tratados da Rodada Uruguai. Observador Legal, São Paulo, pp 13–14

Granados J (2003) Export processing zones and other special regimes in the context of multilateral and regional trade negotiations. Intal, Buenos Aires, p 12

Harada K (2011) Incentivos fiscais: limitações constitucionais e legais. http://www.fiscosoft.com.br/a/5pf2/incentivos-fiscais-limitacoes-constitucionais-e-legais-kiyoshi-harada

Hoekman B (2014) Supply Chains, Mega-Regionals and Multilateralism: a roadp map for the WTO. http://papers.ssrn.com/sol3/papers.cfm?abstract_id=2406871, pp 41–42, 44

Hoekman B, Kostecki M (2009) The political economy of the world trading system: the WTO and beyond. Oxford, New York, Position 2306, 2499

Jackson JH (2000) The Jurisprudence of GATT and WTO: insights on treaty law and economic relations. Cambridge University Press, Cambridge, pp 8–9

Kolosky AB (2014) A OMC e sua Influência na Política Legislativa Brasileira de Defesa Comercial: o caso dos subsídios. Monograph (Law) - Graduate Course in Law, Federal University of Santa Catarina, Florianópolis, p 68, 169

Krugman P (2008) Dead Doha. http://krugman.blogs.nytimes.com/2008/07/30/dead-doha/?_r=0, p 177, 182

Krugman P, Obstfeld M (2010) Economia Internacional: teoria e política. 8ª ed. Pearson Prentice Hall, São Paulo, pp 141–142, 145

Lamy P. L'Organiseation mondiale du commerce. Disponível em: http://entempsreel.com/wp-content/uploads/2014/07/Pascal-Lamy-En-temps-r%C3%A9el.pdf

Leonetti CA (1998) A Contribuição de Melhoria a partir da Constituição de 1988. Dissertation (Master of Laws) - Postgraduate Course in Law, Federal University of Santa Catarina, Florianópolis, p 62

Lobo MJ (2004) Direitos antidumping (crítica de sua natureza jurídica). Dissertation (master's degree) - Law School of the Pontifical Catholic University of São Paulo, São Paulo, p 186

Machado HB (2008) Tax law course, 29th edn. Malheiros, São Paulo, p 137

Magalhães LRP (2007) Subsídios na disciplina da Organização Mundial do Comércio. Forense, Rio de Janeiro, p 127

Maia JM (2011) Economia Internacional e Comércio Exterior. Atlas, São Paulo, pp 155–156

Mankiw GN (2009) Introdução a economia. Cengage Learning, São Paulo, pp 75–76

Martins AMS (2007) Subsídios e medidas compensatórias na OMC. São Paulo, Customs, p 30, 44, 68

Pires AR (2007) Brief reflections on the issue of tax incentives in Brazil. In: Martins IGS, Elali A, Peixoto MM (Coord.) (2007). Incentivos Fiscais: questões pontuais nas esferas federal, estadual e municipal. São Paulo, MP, pp 18–19, 27

Prazeres TL (2003) Comércio internacional e protecionismo: as barreiras técnicas na OMC. Customs, São Paulo, p 43

Presser MF (2006) As negociações em NAMA na OMC: Impasses e desafios. BRIC, p 63, 66

Reich A (2009) Bilateralism versus multilateralism in internacional economic law: applying the principle of subsidiarity. http://ec.europa.eu/education/jean-monnet/doc/confglobal06/contribution_reich.pdf

Reis M, Santarossa ET, Azevedo AFZ. A OMC continua promovendo o comércio de forma desigual: novas evidências a partir dos anos 1990 http://www.anpec.org.br/sul/2013/submissao/files_I/i5-f863ffba99f341d2f0f1f52c344169ae.pdf

Rose AK (2012) Protectionism isn't counter-cyclical (anymore). http://www.nber.org/papers/w18062.pdf

Saldanha E (2012) Desenvolvimento e Tratamento especial e diferenciado na OMC. Direito Econômico Socioambiental Magazine, Curitiba 3(2):297–333, July/December, pp 298–299, 303

Sanchez MR (2004) Demandas por um novo arcabouço sociojurídico na organização mundial do comércio e o caso do Brasil. Tese apresentada a Faculdade de Direito do Estado de São Paulo, pp 62–63, 71, 87–89

Schoueri LE (2005) Normas Tributárias Indutoras e Intervenção Econômica. Forense, Rio de Janeiro, pp 43–44

Schwab SC (2011) After Doha: why the negotiations are doomed and what we should do about it? https://www.foreignaffairs.com/articles/2011-04-09/after-doha

Sella LF (2010) A Organização Mundial do Comércio: histórico e aspectos a reforma. http://www.anima-opet.com.br/pdf/anima4-Estrangeiro/anima4-Luis-Felipe-Sella.pdf, p 19

Stichele MV (1998) Towards a World Transnationals' Organization? http://www.tni.org/archives/reports_wto_wto3

Stigler GJ (1977) A Teoria dos Preços. Atlas, São Paulo, p 183

Stigler GJ. The theory of economic regulation. http://web.mit.edu/xaq/Public/Stigler

Stiglitz JE. The Chinese Century. http://www.vanityfair.com/news/2015/01/china-worlds-largest-economy

Sumner DA (2006) Reducing cotton subsidies: the DDA cotton initiative. In: Anderson K, Martin W (eds) Agricultural trade reform and the Doha development Agenda. Palgrave Macmillan, New York, pp 271–292

Sykes AO (2003) The economics of WTO rules on subsidies and countervailing measures. Law and Economics Working Paper, n. 186, The Law School, University of Chicago

Thorstensen V (1999) A Organização Mundial do Comércio. Customs, São Paulo, pp 31, 123

Thorstensen V, Oliveira LM (2013) Releitura dos Acordos da OMC como Interpretados pelo Órgão de Apelação: efeitos na aplicação das regras de comércio internacional. http://ccgi.fgv.br/sites/ccgi.fgv.br/files/file/Publicacoes/11%20%20Acordo%20sobre%20Subs%C3%ADdios%20e%20Medidas%20Compensat%C3%B3rias%20%28SCM%29.pdf, pp 22–23, 38, 101

Viner J (2014) The customs union issue. Oxford University Press

Walter J.. O Brasileiro que Ressuscitou a Rodada Doha. http://dw.de/p/1AVWq

Wolfe R.. Letting the Sun Shine at WTO: how transparency brings the trading system to life. http://www.wto.org/english/res_e/reser_e/ersd201303_e.pdf, pp 8–13

World Bank (2008) Lessons from the World Bank Research on Financial crisis. Policy Research Working Paper, n° 4779. The World Bank, Washington DC, p 16

Chapter 4
Strategies for Political-Economic Use of Subsidies in the Multilateral Framework

Abstract The purpose of this study is to find the gaps under WTO' system that allows States to make use of illegal subsidies. In the negotiations to change rules, lack of representatives and technical conditions and the unanimous consent rule can be an obstacle in reaching an agreement. The gaps of the notification and review system is also a hindrance for transparency that hinder prompt actions. The problem of countervailing measures as they cannot be imposed in a third country also creates spaces that encourages subsidies when parties compete in a third market, especially in a world with quite fragmented production. Some diplomatic characteristics of the dispute settlement system is explored to show how it enables subsidies practices and the fact that the State is condemned to withdraw the subsidy only at the end of the entire process also enhance ways for subsidies' strategies. In this sense, the discrepancy of economic power of members must be considered. By the end, the study suggests a cross retaliation system to restrain political and economic use of illegal subsidies.

It is true that targeted subsidies distort trade by reallocating resources inefficiently, causing world prices to fall, and preventing fair competition from taking place. However, even in the hypothesis of full free trade, the perfect market situation does not exist. Moreover, the first 5 years of the WTO have been enough to confirm that trade openness alone does not generate development.

Based on this reality, States need to implement policies that correct externalities and promote economic and social development in their respective territories. For this reason, other criteria besides economic ones are considered when defining State intervention in the economy. Therefore, the States must be attentive beyond merely economic issues, and must observe social and human rights, disciplined in their constitutions and in international treaties.

For a long time, governments had a wide margin to contain market failures, as well as to promote national industry and the realization of constitutional social rights. This space has been reduced by the GATT and, mainly, by the WTO, which, in turn, has an extensive legal framework that limits unfair trade practices.

By condemning the use of certain subsidies, the WTO imposes limits on government maneuvers. This has caused States to seek political and economic strategies to

© The Author(s), under exclusive license to Springer Nature Switzerland AG 2024

J. Marteli Fais Feriato, *Legal, Political and Economic Strategies of Subsidies within the World Trade Organization*, European Yearbook of International Economic Law 40, https://doi.org/10.1007/978-3-031-73869-2_4

manage negative externalities, promote domestic social policies, and increase domestic production. In this sense, it is considered that:

> [...] the reality of the international trading system today does not correspond to rhetoric. Instead of open markets, there are many barriers that conspire, stifle and deprive. And instead of global rules negotiated by all, in the interests of all, and enforced by all, there is too much decision-making behind closed doors, too much protection of vested interests, and too many broken promises.[1]

The restriction of State intervention in the economy by international rules, as well as the opening of the market conducted within the framework of the WTO, while it caused the decrease of state power, increased the use of subterfuges as political-economic strategies for the concession of subsidies.[2]

The WTO provides its members with mechanisms to counter the use of illegal measures, such as prohibited subsidies. However, their effectiveness is questionable, given the existence of loopholes that allow for the use of political-economic strategies to circumvent its rules and achieve any desired result.

The scope of this chapter is to present the main regulatory gaps that enable the use of specific subsidies in the WTO. First, the difficulties encountered by members during the negotiations to change the rules will be addressed, and only then will we move on to the analysis of the system that somehow limits the use of subsidies. This way, the instruments of control and inspection of the SCM will be approached, as well as the impasses of the compensatory measures and their effects, and the problems of the dispute settlement system, with emphasis on the procedural deadlines and its implementation mechanism.

4.1 Difficulties in Negotiations

Since the Uruguay Round, WTO members meet formally in ministerial conferences,[3] which are multilateral negotiations held periodically with the aim of improving the organization's rules. All members are represented at these meetings, where it is possible to deliberate on any matter within the scope of the organization's objectives.

Besides these conferences, negotiations can occur, informally, at any time, involving two or more States, which can agree, bilaterally or plurilaterally, on access

---

[1] Free adaptation from: "[...] the reality of the international trading system today does not match the rhetoric. Instead of open markets, there are too many barriers that stunt, stifle and starve. Instead of fair competition, there are subsidies by rich countries that tilt the playing field against the poor. And instead of global rules negotiated by all, in the interest of all, and adhered to by all, there is too much closed-door decision-making, too much protection of special interests, and too many broken promises". In: Annan (2003). http://www.un.org/press/en/2003/sgsm8859.doc.htm.

[2] See: Bliacheriene (2006), pp. 118–119.

[3] In total, 12 conferences have been held, which are: Singapore (1996), Geneva (1998), Seattle (1999), Doha (2001), Cancun (2003), Hong Kong (2005), Geneva (2009), Geneva (2011), Bali (2013), Nairobi (2015), Buenos Aires (2017) and Geneva (2022).

to new markets. This is possible because the principle of non-discrimination guarantees for all members the extension of benefits granted by the members. They can also be realized by the parties during the entire dispute settlement procedure.

On average, there are more than fifty meetings a week at the WTO, which makes it difficult for developing countries to participate due to the lack of representatives and technical conditions to negotiate on various issues.[4]

Similar problems can occur at ministerial conferences. Before setting up a large conference such as the ministerial one, the themes are suggested by the members, who are organized in groups, known as the "catalysts", whose proposals are submitted to a prior negotiation. In this opportunity, the agenda will be established, the result of which will be subject to inspection to ensure its observance.[5]

Two WTO ground rules have a direct bearing on the difficulty of reaching agreement at the negotiating rounds: the unanimous consent rule and the principle of *single undertaking*. Thus, the agreement will only be obligatory for all members when unanimously approved.[6] This means that the opposition of a single member is enough to obstruct an agreement.

Although the consensus rule makes reaching agreements difficult, it is necessary because WTO Law is equivalent to *hard law,*[7] whose compliance can be enforced by the dispute settlement system. Therefore, the voting system would lead to an exodus of its members.

However, the difficulties in reaching unanimous consensus make it impossible to adapt the organization to the dynamic needs of the economy and to emerging challenges. In addition, it induces the formation of articulations and political pressures for the persuasion of members and the weakening of groups,[8] fostering the prevalence of power.

Several situations can be mentioned, occurring throughout the rounds, in which persuasion mechanisms were used. Soon after the terrorist attacks of 2001, the United States began to take a tougher attitude within the WTO as well. In the Doha Round, then-President George W. Bush announced: "Those who are not with us are against us".[9] This attitude was confirmed by a representative of a developing

---

[4] Those at the WTO point out that only one-third of the thirty least developed countries have permanent offices in Geneva. In: WTO Understanding the WTO: developing countries. https://www.wto.org/english/thewto_e/whatis_e/tif_e/dev1_e.htm.

[5] See: Hoekman and Kostecki (2013), position 2408–2410.

[6] Article IX of the Constitutive Agreement of the World Trade Organization states that: "Unless otherwise provided, where it is not possible to adopt a decision by consensus, the decision in question shall be decided by vote. At the meetings of the Ministerial Conference and the General Council, each Member of the WTO shall have one vote:". However, dissenting members will still be bound by the principle of *single undertaking*.

[7] Unlike the recommendations of the UN General Assembly, which are considered *soft law,* WTO rules are binding on its members and are therefore called *hard law.*

[8] To strengthen themselves in negotiations, members form alliances according to their common interests.

[9] In: Jawara and Kwa (2004), p. 63.

country, who stated: "[…]american negotiators are extremely arrogant and use the stick more than the carrot, compared to EU negotiators".[10]

Unfortunately, there are no mechanisms to control retaliation in International Law or in WTO rules.[11] and, in this sense, the developed countries benefit because of their greater power to enforce their interests.

The difficulty is exacerbated by the complex heterogeneity of the members' interests, which are no longer restricted to the classic North-South conflict. The divergence occurs due to geographical differences, variations in productive capacity, infrastructure, production capacity, as well as political, social, environmental issues, etc.

The multilateral framework of negotiations facilitates the creation of common interest groups, which expand their bargaining power and mitigate the differences between developed and developing countries. Nevertheless, interests within the same group can be overlapped, giving rise to new groups.

The principle of *single undertaking*, in turn, imposes obstacles for heterogeneous economic and social issues to be raised. The negotiation of the exceptions ends up prolonging the time for the conclusion of the rounds, bringing excessive fatigue to the negotiators.

It is important to note that, internally, States also suffer from conflicts of interest between their federated entities, departments, or between producers and consumers, or even between interest groups such as farmers' associations and their branches, industrial sectors, etc.

These groups, also known as lobbies, can trigger new complications by exerting political pressure on their respective governments, which in turn respond to their wishes in exchange for political support. This allows the dominance of the politics of favoritism in negotiations to the detriment of economic and social interests. In these situations, the use of economic and political power is more frequent, as is the application or maintenance of protectionist barriers.

Lobbies constitute externalities, similar to the distortions found in an imperfect market situation, which can only be corrected through cooperation. However, when states disregard the externalities that impact others, it will be difficult to reach an agreement by cooperative means, due to the lack of convergence of interests. The agreements are reached only between those countries that will benefit. In this sense:

> One implication of the terms of trade theory is that there is no prospect of cooperation for new rules or market access agreements if the large countries cannot agree on a mutually beneficial (balanced) solution of political compromises. Reforms in WTO procedure or institutional structure will make no difference. Calls to create mechanisms that will force these countries to "do the right thing" are irrelevant: the WTO is a self-enforcing agree-

---

[10] Free adaptation of: the American negotiators are more overtly arrogant and use the stick more than the carrot compared to those of the EC. In: Ibid, p. 85.

[11] Retortions are legal but unfriendly measures, backed by the principle of reciprocity. See: Accioly (2008), pp. 804–805.

ment; There is no central or supranational enforcement agency. Cooperation should be in the self-interest of all members.[12]

In view of the exposed, it can be noted the influence of the mercantilist ideology in the negotiations, to the extent that each member seeks to protect its less competitive sectors and open those with greater comparative advantage.

Nevertheless, the multilateral trading system has promoted what Krugman[13] calls "enlightened mercantilism," which he also calls *"GATT – thinking"*.[14] The adjective "enlightened" has to do with the progressive liberalization of trade through international agreements.

The lack of a higher objective, superior to individual interests, that guides all regulation of international trade, as occurs in the common market of the European Union (EU), makes the WTO a system aimed at managing the sum of interests of its members. "Hence, the obligations stipulated in the WTO Agreements constitute a network of obligations of a bilateral and reciprocal nature".[15]

Thus, negotiations must be guided by a higher principle, the Principle of Social-Economic Efficiency (PESE), which, encompassing the criteria of social justice, distributiveness of richness, eradication of unemployment, etc., aims to achieve a balance between the economic and social issues of the participants in each economic activity. According to Gonçalves and Stelzer, this principle establishes that:

> [...] the decision-making process must continue *ad infinitum* until the economic-social balance is established, no longer in the realm of utopia. This is the desideratum of humanity conscious from a juridical-economic point of view, which is, the world welfare, the global development of peoples and the maintenance of the human race under fraternal and, at least, sufficient living conditions, including, according to the internationalization of markets and capital, generating equalization, in the level of world employment, in the living conditions of people, in the achievement of social goals, etc.[16]

When trade is seen as a "zero-sum" game, that is, when the gain of one means, respectively, the loss of another, little effort will be expended to achieve cooperation. Thus, states tend to cooperate when the results are beneficial to them, such as

---

[12] Free adaptation from: "An implication of the terms-of-trade theory is that there is no prospect for cooperation on new rules or market access deals if the large countries cannot agree on a mutually beneficial (balanced) exchange of policy commitments. No possible reform of process or the institutional structure of the WTO will make a difference. Calls to put in place mechanisms that will force these countries to "do the right thing" are irrelevant: the WTO is a self-enforcing agreement; there is no central or supranational enforcement agency. Cooperation must be in the self-interest of all member". In: Hoekman and Kostecki (2009), p. 6.

[13] For Krugman *"[...] trade negotiations aren't driven by economists' calculations of welfare gains; they're driven by enlightened mercantilism, what has come to be known as GATT-thinking"*. Krugman. http://krugman.blogs.nytimes.com/2008/07/30/dead-doha/?_r=0.

[14] The GATT-*thinking* view represents the mercantilist ideas whereby imports are seen as bad while exports are welcomed. In: Krugman. http://krugman.blogs.nytimes.com/2008/07/30/dead-doha/?_r=0.

[15] Borges (2008), p. 273.

[16] Gonçalves and Stelzer (2007). http://www.egov.ufsc.br/portal/sites/default/files/anexos/25380-25382-1-PB.pdf.

the "prisoner's dilemma." Krugman[17] stresses that interest groups should seek to negotiate among themselves.

In this sense, the WTO should be seen as a forum, in which all members are encouraged to participate, under the auspices of a legal framework that will support fair play, to cooperate toward the realization of a higher purpose that goes beyond simple trade liberalization. Cooperation will be more present in the negotiations when they are guided by social criteria that promote economic activity and the inclusion of developing and least developed countries.[18]

It is emphasized that it is not the intention to eliminate the economic focus from the negotiations, but to include other criteria in consonance with the rights to freedom, drivers of development, considering that it is the expansion of these rights "the main end and the main medium of development".[19] Amartya Sen adopts as a criterion for identifying underdevelopment "[...] the deprivation of basic capabilities rather than merely as a low level of income [...]".[20]

For this, it is first necessary to consider the economic and social particularities of the members. The recognition of the diversity, multiplicity, and incompatibility of ideas promotes the inclusion of its members' micro-systems into the WTO's macrosystem, which often have divergent and often antagonistic characteristics. In this sense, Edgar Morin points out[21] that "[...] the organization of a system is the organization of difference".

It is true that the "invisible hand" of the market is incapable of promoting, by itself, the development of countries, especially in those that are still in the initial phase of insertion in international trade and, therefore, need more space for fostering measures.

In an attempt to balance the differences between members, the Swiss formula has been widely used to reach consensus in negotiations. Used for the first time in the Tokyo Round (1973–1979),[22] this model determines that the cut in tax barriers should occur in a non-linear way, that is, proportional to the import rates. This means that the cuts would be higher for the highest rates and lower for the lowest, which causes losses to developing countries, since their rates are higher than those of developed countries.

---

[17] In Krugman's words: "If trade negotiators want to take on well-entrenched interest groups, they have to find countervailing interest groups with an interest in liberalization". Krugman. http://krugman.blogs.nytimes.com/2008/07/30/dead-doha/?_r=0.

[18] See: Gonçalves and Stelzer (2012). http://revista.unicuritiba.edu.br/index.php/RevJur/article/view/412/0, p. 98.

[19] Sen (2000), p. 71.

[20] Ibid, p. 108.

[21] See: Idem (1987), p. 113.

[22] Until the Tokyo Round, the proposals were for linear tariff cuts. In: Vianna CC, Lima JPR (2010) Política Comercial Brasileira: possíveis impactos de uma redução nas tarifas de importação dos setores automotivo e têxtil. Revista Econômica, Rio de Janeiro, v. 12, n 2, pp. 157–186, December 2010.

For this reason, it was proposed by governments during the Doha Round to use two coefficients, one for developing countries and one for developed countries, allowing both to reduce their tax barriers proportionally.

However, there was an impasse regarding the coefficients, in view of that the elasticity of the good can influence the result. Thus, goods with high elasticity tend to show larger variations relative to the lowest coefficient. On the other hand, goods with low elasticity present little variation in relation to the coefficient.[23]

Although States did not reach a consensus on such coefficients in the Doha Round, the impasse reveals that homogeneous rules are not well accepted, especially those involving lowering tax barriers on more elastic goods, non-tax barriers, or spaces for industrial policy maneuvers.

In this scenario, reciprocity plays a fundamental role in circumventing the difficulties of negotiations, due to its capacity to neutralize externalities. It is through this that the convergence of interests can be reached.

The Doha Round is the result of a convergence of opinion among the poorest countries about the inability of the multilateral trade system to promote economic and social development. For its part, the United States also had an interest in the establishment of a new round, as a means of opposing the terrorist attacks of September 11, 2001, reaffirming values of the multilateral trading system, such as "free, peaceful, reciprocal, inclusive and regulated trade by norms established by agreements".[24]

It should be noted that despite the divergence in the reasons for having a new round, the need for it was not in question. However, it was the differences over the motivating causes for the round that prolonged it considerably.

This extension highlights the problems exposed here and the need for a multilateral trade organization more committed to human development and the inclusion of the interests of developing countries.

To this end, the structure of the organization must be readjusted so that it accompanies the dynamism of trade, starting with the recognition of the differences of the members to be inserted in the agreements. The fact is that this change can only be achieved by unanimous consensus, since any structural change in the WTO must comply with this criterion, which makes it even more difficult to achieve.

The impossibility of reaching new agreements places the WTO system at risk. According to Hoeckman, "The WTO is often compared to a 'bicycle' that has to keep moving in order not to fall over."[25]

For Simon Evenett,[26] professor of international business and development at the University of St. Gallen in Switzerland, "there is no alternative to unanimity. None of the great powers will ever accept being defeated in a vote". In Hoeckman's words,

[23] Vianna and Lima (2010).

[24] Hoekman and Kostecki (2013), position 2244.

[25] Free adaptation from: "the WTO is often likened to a "bicycle" that needs to keep moving if it is not to fall over". In: Hoekman (2011), p. 3.

[26] Evenett. In: Breuer. http://dw.de/p/1Bhqo.

"[…] the culture of negotiation and the mercantilist spirit often seems to dominate interactions between members."[27]

Therefore, working with the idea of a possible restructuring of the WTO is closer to utopia than to reality. On the other hand, a stiffening of the Organization in the sense of reducing cooperation among its members may bring even worst effects.[28] These and other difficulties, such as gaps in transparency mechanisms, lead to asymmetries in relations between WTO member States.

4.2   The Notification and Review System

Throughout the WTO agreements, there are more than two hundred notification requirements regarding the trade policies adopted by its members. Information is the cornerstone for the proper functioning of the Organization. Knowledge of the rules, of the trade policies practiced by members, and of their statistics contributes to the enhancement of negotiations, the monitoring of the trade policies adopted, and eventual responsibility, when illegal.

In order to fulfill these purposes, the WTO offers two mechanisms to promote transparency: the *Trade Policy Review* and mandatory notifications on the use of subsidies and countervailing measures. The first refers to the review of members' general trade policies, including subsidies. It is conducted by the Trade Policy Review Body, which is composed of all members and, with the cooperation of the secretariat, periodically reviews the trade policies of the countries. The periodicity is 2 years for developed countries, 4 years for the main developing countries and every 6 years for the others.

It is important to point out that this Body does not make any kind of value judgment, because it does not analyze the effects nor the legality of the practices, restricting itself to the mere gathering of data that will serve as a basis for possible questionings and complaints by the members.

Recently, the WTO Director-General, Roberto Azevedo, highlighted the importance of this tool for the promotion of transparency and the proper functioning of the Organization.[29]

Regarding notifications, Article 25 of the SCM obliges members to forward them annually to the Organization regarding the subsidy programs granted or maintained, containing sufficient details for others to evaluate their effects. Necessarily, the notification must address the form, the amount of the subsidy per unit or, where

---

[27] Free adaptation from: "the culture of negotiation and the mercantilist spirit that often appears to dominate interactions between members". In: Hoekman (2011), p. 22.

[28] See: Abbot and Snidal (2000), p. 421.

[29] See: Azevêdo. http://www.wto.org/spanish/thewto_s/dg_s/dg_s.htm.

Table 4.1 Average
expenditure on subsidies
according to separate sources
in billions of dollars,
1998–2002. Source: WTO[a]

States	National accounts data	Notifications
Canada	7.7	0.9
United States	43.5	16.3
Australia	4.7	0.3
Japan	34.3	4.2
Switzerland	10.8	0.7
India	12.2	–
South Africa	0.9	–
European Union	109	96.3
Korea	1.0	1.3
Brazil	2.0	1,7

[a]WTO (2006)

impossible, the total envisaged, the purpose, the duration, and statistical data for the evaluation of its effects.[30]

The deadline for notifications expires every June 30 of each year, but unfortunately, the number of delays and omissions is quite significant. The *World Trade Report* of 2006 revealed that Canada, the United States, Australia, Japan, Switzerland, India and South Africa significantly omitted their subsidy policies between 1998 and 2002, while the European Union, the Republic of Korea and Brazil had a high rate of notifications, as shown in Table 4.1.

Despite the efforts of the Committee on Subsidies and Countervailing Measures to encourage members to make notifications, the scenario has not changed. It was found that half of the members still fail to comply with the duty of notification.[31]

It can be observed that members tend to omit specific subsidies in more sensitive sectors. For example, Brazil has been assiduous in notifying its agricultural subsidies, which are considered legal, but, on the other hand, omits fiscal benefits in sectors such as automotive, which has raised questions from developed countries.

Considering the vagueness of the ASCM and that each member unilaterally determines which policies constitute reportable subsidies, it is easy to omit them. Therefore, proper compliance with notifications should be encouraged for better monitoring and control of specific subsidies.

Late notification, in turn, is also prejudicial to the proper functioning of the Organization. Due to the 2008 crisis, the General Council established a specific mechanism to monitor contingency measures applied by members, and it was found that the Secretariat could not count on up-to-date information.[32]

---

[30] In this regard, see Article 25 of the SCM. In: WTO. Agreement on Subsidies and Countervailing Measures. http://www.wto.org/english/docs_e/legal_e/legal_e.htm.

[31] Ibid.

[32] Free adaptation of: "The 2008-09 financial crisis revealed the importance of timely data on trade policies, trade finance and trade flows—and the fact that there were important lacunae in all three áreas". In: Hoekman (2011).

However, even if there is an omission in the notifications, the subsidy policies may be questioned by other members within the Committee on Subsidies and Compensatory Measures. This procedure is governed by Articles 25.8 to 25.10 of the SCM. Thus:

> Any Member may at any time request in writing from another Member information as to the nature and extent of any subsidy provided or maintained by another Member (including any subsidy referred to in PART IV) or request an explanation as to why a particular measure was considered to be excluded from the notification requirement.[33]

This instrument is known as the reverse notification system, which is applicable in the case of an omission, allowing any member to report illegal subsidy practices to the Subsidy Committee and Countervailing Measures. However, this does not occur due to lack of interest, given the fear that questions will be directed to the reporting member.

For example, Brazil has received notifications from the United States, Australia, Canada, and New Zealand, questioning alleged subsidies granted to the automotive industry. The most extensive notification was the North American, containing five questions only on the duty to inform, since Brazil has not notified the WTO since 2008, alleging the inexistence of notifiable programs.[34]

Thus, in reverse notification, the accused member has the obligation to provide the required information quickly and sufficiently so that the other members can evaluate the appropriateness of the required measure.

Members may also ask questions about the notified grant programs in order to clarify doubts for a better evaluation of their effects, which must be answered promptly. However, the SCM does not establish a response procedure, stipulating deadlines and imposing sanctions in case of omission or delays.

The difficulties in promoting transparency in relation to subsidy policy are numerous. Firstly, the complexity of the SCM makes it difficult to know the content of the notifications, such as the very concept of specific subsidies and their categories. The language issue is also an obstacle to the interpretation of the agreements and notifications, especially for those members who do not work in the official languages of the WTO: English, French and Spanish.

Another point to be highlighted is the fact that the investigation of subsidies is performed unilaterally by the members. Therefore, it is possible that, when elaborating the notification, the member understands that its policy does not fit into the SCM's concept of specific subsidy, as it happened in the case of Brazil, previously mentioned.

---

[33] Free adaptation from: "Article 25.8 SCM Agreement: Any Member may, at any time, make a written request for information on the nature and extent of any subsidy granted or maintained by another Member (including any subsidy referred to in Part IV), or for an explanation of the reasons for which a specific measure has been considered as not subject to the requirement of notification".

[34] Brazil answers to four countries' consultations on subsidies at the WTO. http://www.ictsd.org/bridges-news/pontes/news/brasil-responde-a-consultas-de-quatro-pa%C3%ADses-sobre-subs%C3%ADdios-na-omc.

The lack of knowledge internally also makes it difficult to fulfill the obligation to notify. Subsidies, in fact, for example, suffer from a lack of full transparency because they are not provided for in law.

In the same way, there is no uniformity in the notifications, being either prolix or more concise, which makes it difficult to interpret their content.[35] In this sense, emphasizes Order:

> [...] WTO notifications often fail to provide accurate and meaningful data on the economic advantages granted to producers. Countries have chosen to notify various policy measures in different ways - the categories are not uniform, nor is the estimation for calculating aid levels.[36]

The difficulty in gathering the necessary data for notification also corroborates its asymmetry and may even be the cause of procrastination. However, it is a fact that too much delay may be a government strategy to gain time, while the member country benefits from trade advantages.[37]

There are proposals to strengthen notifications and fill existing gaps. Among them, the following stand out: the direct collection of data by the Committee and the creation of a commission to examine and denounce unfair trade practices.[38] The North American proposal privileges the adoption of a specific procedure for article 25.8 of the SCM, with sixty-day time limit for answering the questions.[39]

Note that grant notification currently takes place *a posteriori*, that is, members notify subsidies already granted or maintained during the one-year period, allowing the State to gain time and trade until questioned and contested.

It should be noted that there is no provision for sanctions in the SCM in case of noncompliance or delay in the obligation to notify, which makes the system dependent on the cooperation of its members.

In this sense, the multilateral system of subsidy notifications and reviews is fragile, as it allows the use of political-economic maneuvers, based on the flaws presented here, to gain time and commercial advantages. Therefore, non-compliance with the rules on notifications cooperates with the perpetuation of subsidies in international trade relations.

This situation confirms the incompleteness of the WTO agreements and the asymmetry of information that retard the use of the dispute settlement mechanism

---

[35] See: Wolfe (2015). http://www.wto.org/english/res_e/reser_e/ersd201303_e.pdf, p. 17.

[36] Free adaptation from: "[...] the WTO notifications often fail to provide accurate and meaningful measurements of the economic support provided to producers. Countries have chosen to notify various policy measures in diverse ways—categories are not uniform and neither is the approach taken to calculate support levels". In: Order D et al. Wto Disciplines on Agricultural Support. Experience to date and assessment of Doha proposals. http://www.ifpri.org/sites/default/files/publications/rb16.pdf.

[37] Brink et al. http://onlinelibrary.wiley.com/doi/10.1111/1477-9552.12008/abstract.

[38] Hoekman (2011).

[39] See: Document G/SCM/W/557/Rev.1 of Sep. 22, 2014. In: WTO https://docs.wto.org/dol2fe/Pages/FE_Search/DDFDocuments/127132/q/G/SCM/W557R1.pdf.

and the imposition of countervailing measures to have the illicit act removed immediately, issues that are the subject of the following topics.

4.3 The Problematic of Compensatory Measures

Countervailing measures are imposed unilaterally by members against prohibited and actionable subsidies in accordance with the requirements disciplined in the ASCM and are intended to counteract the adverse effects of subsidies. Because they are optional, their use varies according to the convenience of economic and political criteria determined internally by governments. For Pires:

> The rights charged are intended to compensate for the inefficiency of other instruments, namely import duties. When taxation is insufficient to curb practices that are harmful to the economy, the correction mechanisms are used [...] that aim to compensate the difference between the real price of the goods in the country of origin and the export price. Countervailing rights restore the internal and external competitiveness of goods produced in the importing country.[40]

Countervailing measures are a faster way to inhibit the effects of subsidies, if compared to the WTO's dispute settlement procedure. This is because, despite the obligation to observe the requirements determined in the SCM, they are unilateral and depend on an internal procedure for their imposition. In the words of Pires, the unilateral investigation procedure:

> [...] aims to avoiding that the damages caused or that may be caused to the industry or to any other economic activity are prolonged for an undesirable period, provoking the retraction of the importing country's economic development process, which translates into a situation of transference of economic activity costs from one country to another.[41]

Thus, the countervailing measures can annul the damage caused by subsidies, as of their effectiveness, and may produce retroactive effects, compensating the damage caused by subsidies already conceded, when certain conditions are fulfilled. The SCM admits, in its article 20.6, the application of definitive countervailing measures with retroactive effect up to a limit of 90 days in case of damage difficult to repair caused by voluminous imports.

This situation does not apply to the DSB system, whose decisions have prospective effects. For this reason, countervailing measures are more advantageous and preferable in countering illicit subsidies.

In addition, unlike subsidies, notifications of countervailing measures occur *a priori* and can therefore be immediately challenged in front of the DSB. Moreover, those countries that impose such measures benefit from the fact that the onus of proof is on the party alleging illegitimacy. In this aspect, it is noted that it is easier

---

[40] Pires (2001), p. 214.

[41] Ibid, p. 211.

Table 4.2   WTO mechanisms to counter illicit subsidies. Source: Author

Subsidy Market	Prohibited	Actionable
Internal	Countervailing Measures DSB Procedure	Countervailing Measures DSB Procedure
Third	X DSB Procedure	X DSB Procedure

to impose a compensatory measure and, if necessary, wait for an eventual litigation, than to proceed to the WTO dispute settlement.

It should be noted that, notwithstanding the exceptions, the rule is that such measures do not affect past subsidies, only present ones, as was made clear in the Report of the *Panel* in the case *Japan—DRAMS Countervailing Duties*: "countervailing measures can only be imposed if the subsidy is present at the time of imposition".[42]

It is important to emphasize that subsidies produce three different effects:

(a) when country A subsidizes product X, increasing its exports in importing country B, harming its domestic producers;

(b) A's subsidies increase exports of product X in country C, harming country B's exports; and

(c) when A subsidizes its domestic producers by restricting imports similarly to tax barriers.[43]

Countervailing measures can only be applied by the country importing the subsidized goods. Therefore, only in the first case is its application possible, since country B does not have jurisdiction over the territories of countries A and C. Therefore, with regard to countering specific subsidies, the WTO lacks an expeditious measure for those that harm the exports of countries in third markets, as can be seen in Table 4.2.

In a world where production is fragmented into global value chains, competition is amplified in third markets,[44] preventing States from protecting themselves when countervailing measures can only be used in domestic competition.

It is noted that, faced with this situation, there is only one alternative for country B: to initiate a procedure in front of the DSB, which is expected to take at least 1 year and 3 months if all deadlines are strictly followed. WTO data confirm that the subsidy cases brought to the DSB "were motivated by a desire to restore

---

[42] Free adaptation from: "CVDs may only be imposed if there is present subsidization at the time of duty imposition". In: Report from the *Panel* in the case *Japan—DRAMs Countervailing Duties*, par 7.355.

[43] See: Bagwell et al. (2010), p. 54.

[44] For example, the Brazilian footwear sector, which as a result of the global chains model, besides losing the domestic market, had a 61.9% drop in the number of pairs and 55.2% in the value exported to UNITED STATES between 2000 and 2008, due to the invasion of Chinese products in this market. In: BNDES (2010) Indústria Calçadista e Estratégias de Fortalecimento de Competitividade.   http://www.bndes.gov.br/SiteBNDES/export/sites/default/bndes_pt/Galerias/Arquivos/conhecimento/bnset/set3104.pdf.

Fig. 4.1 Economic effects
of compensatory measures
in relation to subsidies.
Source: Author

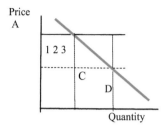

competitiveness on a global scale, rather than to stop subsidies from flooding domestic trade".[45]

Another issue worth raising is that countervailing measures, initially applied with the objective of neutralizing the effects of subsidies, can also be considered unfair, diverting trade in an unjustified manner, when their use is inappropriate.[46]

Pires warns that "the lack of criteria can transform the countervailing rights, contrary to what the GATT foresees, in an instrument of commercial protection".[47] This occurs due to the subjectivity of the subsidy calculation criteria,[48] which, although defined in the SCM, still offers margins for dubious interpretation.

For this reason, Brazil suggested in Doha that the procedure for the application of these measures should be more prudent, similar to the *antidumping* measures, in order to achieve greater standardization and avoid protectionism.[49]

Conversely, when countervailing measures are applied against and in proportion to the damage caused by the subsidy, it can be said that the market equilibrium is maintained, as shown in Fig. 4.1.

It can be noted that the countervailing measure moves the equilibrium from C to A, so that the importing country loses area 2 but gains area 1, while the exporting country gains areas 2 and 3 but loses area 1. The equilibrium will remain at A if the countervailing measure is effectively counterbalancing a subsidy.

Compliance with the proportionality criterion is indispensable for compensatory measures to fulfill their purpose without causing further detour and damage to trade. It is for this reason that such measures cannot be considered sanctions, but rather instruments to balance the deviations arising from the use of specific subsidies.

However, the ASCM makes clear, by requiring proportionality of measures to the injury caused by subsidies, that the reason for countervailing measures is to counterbalance the distortions caused by subsidies.

---

[45] Free adaptation from: "were motivated by a desire to restore the competitive playground on a global scale, as opposed to merely preventing subsidies from flooding the home market". In: Ehlermann and Goyette (2006), pp. 712–713.

[46] See: Gonçalves and Stelzer (2010). http://www.conpedi.org.br/manaus/arquivos/anais/fortaleza/3755.pdf, p. 2410.

[47] Pires (2001), p. 212.

[48] See: Pires (2001), p. 212.

[49] See: Munhoz (2005) http://www.iribr.com/hongkong/Defesa_Comercial_medidas_compensatórias.asp.

When disproportionate, countervailing measures lead to "detour of trade",[50] forming tax barriers against imports, raising the prices of imported goods. When this occurs, such measures can be contested in front of the DSB.

The imposition of countervailing measures must comply with the limits established in the SCM. They must be adopted for a period sufficient to counteract the subsidy and up to a maximum of 5 years, unless, after reviewing them, it is verified that the subsidy and its respective damage remain. This understanding is shares the OPA:

> Countervailing measures should be limited to the amount and duration of subsidies duly verified by the investigating authority, including in reviews (*positive determination*). The authority cannot ignore information/fact that suggests that the benefit no longer exists (in this case, change of state control to private control of the company).[51]

In this aspect, the use of countervailing measures should be cautious, since, due to their unilateral character, if used disproportionately, they can promote new distortions.

Nevertheless, part of the doctrine[52] argues that such measures may be useful to force States to eliminate their subsidy policies, another part[53] recognizes that such measures potentially aggravate trade tensions between States, rather than solve the problem.

Because of the observance of proportionality in relation to the damage and not in relation to the value of the subsidy, countervailing measures do not serve as a threat against developed countries. In this regard, the 2009 WTO report confirmed that the threat of using countervailing measures does not always discourage the practice of subsidies.[54]

In any case, countervailing measures have been little used and little challenged in the WTO, being the subject of a little less than one-third of the cases (out of 109 cases, 34 involve countervailing measures), since they cannot be imposed when the subsidy harms a State's exports in a third market.

4.4 Political-Economic Maneuvers in Dispute Settlement

So far, it has been seen that the dispute settlement system brought greater "jurisdictionalization" to the WTO as it established a specific procedure with pre-established deadlines. In addition, there is the possibility of cases being reexamined by the Appellate Body and, finally, the use of retaliatory measures when decisions are not implemented.

---

[50] Viner (1991).

[51] Thorstensen and Oliveira (2013), p. 184.

[52] See: Jackson (2000), p. 91.

[53] Munhoz (2005).

[54] WTO (2009) World Trade Report 2009, pp. 94–95.

The dispute settlement system is a central theme of the WTO, whose efficiency depends on the effective adjudication of rights and obligations. In this sense, Trachtman states that:

> It may seem strange that dispute settlement is at the center of world trade governance. In fact, it is worth asking why the focus on adjudication rather than legislation as the mainstay of legalism in world trade. [...] Dispute resolution is necessary for the enforcement of legislation. In this regard, dispute resolution is not important for itself, but as the place where legislation becomes obligatory and effective. Legislation without adjudication, at least, raises greater concerns in relation to its enforcement and effectiveness. It is only in this sense that dispute settlement can properly be considered the cornerstone of international law.[55]

It can be said that the effectiveness of WTO rules depends on the ability of its dispute settlement mechanism to adjudicate rights and obligations in an efficient manner, according to the PESE criteria. However, it will be found that the system has flaws that prevent efficiency.

Firstly, it is necessary to emphasize the diplomatic characteristic of the dispute settlement system, by encouraging the resolution of disputes through agreement, not only in its first phase, but throughout the procedure. According to Lafer, it is possible to verify these characteristics in the following situations:

> [...] for the recommended caution *before bringing a case*; by the explicit preference for negotiated solutions (DSU art. 3°, §7°); by recommending that the interpretation of WTO rules should be strictly, not constructively amplified (DSU 3°, § 2°) and especially the obligation to consult, as a mandatory preliminary step, before raising the constitution of a panel (DSU, art. 4°).[56]

According to the ESC, States should, before bringing a case to the DSB, reflect on its usefulness, bearing in mind that the relief granted by the system should have as its imperative the search for a positive solution, preferably acceptable to both parties and in consonance with the WTO agreements.[57] In this sense, Bliacheriene, points out that:

> For international law, the fact that the prevailing party does not retaliate or charge compensation does not mean that the WTO system is ineffective. This is a political composition and not a disobedience restricted to one *decisio,* as is normally done in domestic law.[58]

---

[55] Free adaptation from: "It may appear odd that dispute resolution is at the center of world trade governance. Indeed, it is worthwhile to wonder why the focus is on adjudication, rather than legislation, as the mainstay of legalism in world trade. [...] dispute resolution is necessary to the application of legislation. In this regard, dispute resolution is not important for its own sake but as the place where legislation becomes binding and effective. Legislation without adjudication at least raises greater concerns regarding the application and effectiveness of the legislation. It is only in this sense that dispute resolution may properly be considered the cornerstone of international law". In: Trachtman (1999), p 339.

[56] Lafer (1998), p. 130.

[57] See art. 3.7 of the Dispute Settlement Understanding.

[58] Bliacheriene (2006), p. 56.

Nevertheless, the reasons that lead governments to appeal or not to the DSB are varied, besides the analysis of the legal merit and its factual support, the probability of success and internal *lobbies*, as well as the interaction between private and public interests are able to influence such a decision.

In this sense, the dispute settlement procedure presents diplomatic and Public International Law characteristics, because it encourages the achievement of consensus between the parties, who, in turn, are subjects of Public International Law.

The opening for negotiations, within the procedure, is intended to encourage the resolution of international trade issues by diplomatic means. Priority is given to the agreement between the parties due to its ability to maintain the openness of trade, given that retaliation imposes obstacles. For this reason, throughout the dispute settlement procedure, agreement is encouraged.

Furthermore, it contributes to the negotiations that the DSB does not have the character of a tribunal, and that its decisions do not have the legal nature of a sentence, but rather of a recommendation. The execution of these decisions has a private law nature, and is therefore more flexible, admitting the optional nature of retaliation.[59] Silva Neto states that:

> The WTO dispute settlement mechanism is a technical-legal process with space for politics, unlike the predominantly technical-legal internal judicial process where politics is less present.[60]

Therefore, despite a certain "jurisdictionalization" of the WTO dispute settlement system, its procedure still presents spaces for the use of political-economic strategies of the States.

4.4.1 The Procedure

In this item, the general procedure of the ESC for the settlement of disputes will be addressed. Regarding subsidies, the SCM establishes procedural particularities that must prevail over the general procedure. Variations in terms and solutions, for example, are established according to the nature of the subsidy. Such specificities will be highlighted throughout the general explanation, which will follow in Fig. 4.2.

Before going into the procedure itself, it is important to emphasize that it is guided by procedural principles, among which are: due process of law, good faith and procedural fairness, equality, contradiction, burden of proof, celerity and procedural economy and effectiveness.

The principle of due legal process implies the correct application of the dispute settlement mechanism, in order to guarantee a fair process for both parties. This

---

[59] In order to have the characteristics of a tribunal, there must be a body responsible for providing solutions based on Law, and these solutions must be obligatory, and once provoked, the parties do not control the procedure.

[60] Silva Neto (2005), p. 173.

WTO legal disputes: the panel and appeal processes

The various stages a dispute can go through in the WTO. At all stages, countries in dispute are encouraged to consult each other in order to settle "out of court". At all stages, the WTO director-general is available to offer "good offices", to mediate or to help achieve a conciliation. Articles cited here are from the Dispute Settlement Understanding.

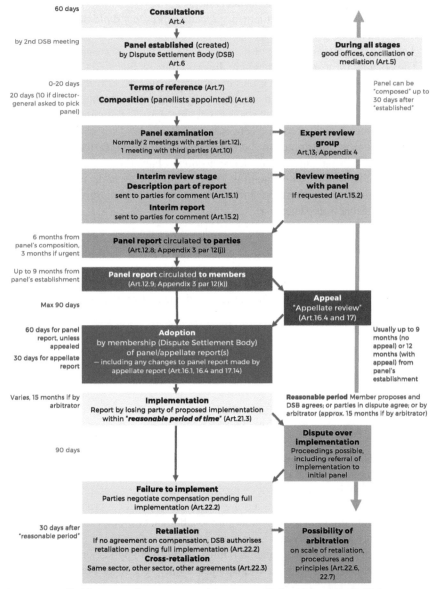

Note: some specified times are maximums, some are minimums, some binding, some not. **Source:** WTO

Fig. 4.2 WTO dispute settlement procedure. Source: WTO (http://www.wto.org/english/thewto_e/whatis_e/tif_e/disp2_e.htm)

entails ensuring the necessary balance according to the economic differences and technical defense capacity of the parties.[61]

Good faith and procedural fairness means that parties must abstain from practices that may cause frustration in the process, such as intentionally failing to provide important information. The principle of equality, on the other hand, aims to promote the access of all members to the DSB in an equal manner.

By the adversarial principle, the parties are granted, throughout the process, opportunities to express themselves in relation to the decisions of the *Panel* and the Permanent Appellate Body (OPA), as well as the right of reply in relation to the manifestations of the other party.

As for the burden of proof, the rule determines that it is up to the complainant to prove the facts constituting his right, and the defendant to prove the impeding, extinguishing or modifying facts. In relation to subsidies, it is up to the requesting to prove specificity, unless the subsidy is prohibited. In this case, the defendant must prove the inexistence of specificity or the causal nexus between the measure and the damage, since its specificity is presumed.

By the principle of speed and procedural economy, the process must be as fast as possible. According to Article 3 of the Dispute Settlement Procedure (ESC), "[…] it is essential for the effective functioning of the WTO and for maintaining the proper balance between the rights and obligations of Members to resolve situations promptly; […]". The procedural speed is of extreme importance, since there is no condemnation to indemnity.

The application of this principle implies the admission of plurality of parties and the fixing of tighter deadlines, which are even shorter when the case involves the concession of subsidies.

The limitation of the subject to be analyzed also derives from this principle and has been confirmed by previous *Panels*, which addressed only those issues that they considered necessary for the resolution of the merits.[62] Thus, some allegations are considered irrelevant and are not inserted in the motivations of the final report, which, in turn, will present only the arguments necessary to justify the decision.

The principle of effectiveness determines that the provisions of the agreements must be interpreted as a whole, making it necessary to perform a systemic analysis in consonance with the principles and rules of the organization. In addition, prompt compliance with the decisions of the DSB, especially in relation to developing and least developed countries, is required, as stated in Article 21 of the ESC:

1. Prompt compliance with DSB recommendations or decisions is essential to ensure effective resolution of disputes for the benefit of all members.
2. Special attention should be given to issues affecting the interests of developing countries with regard to measures that have been the subject of dispute resolution.[63]

---

[61] Cretella Neto (2003), p. 197.

[62] WT/DS33 United States—Measures Affecting Imports of Woven Wool Shirts and Blouses from India.

[63] Free adaptation from: "Article 21 DSC Proceeding: 1. Prompt compliance with recommendations or rulings of the DSB is essential in order to ensure effective resolution of disputes to the benefit of all Members. 2. Particular attention should be paid to matters affecting the interests of developing country Members with respect to measures which have been subject to dispute settlement".

In view of this, we now proceed to the study of the procedural steps for dispute settlement in the WTO. The first of these is called consultations, which begins with the requesting's complaint, focusing on the following grounds: (a) the violation of the agreements; (b) non-infringement, the practice of which has generated damages or annulment of benefits as a result of the breach of legitimate expectations of the advantages deriving from the agreements; and (c) for the situation, which did not involve any kind of violation, but resulted in damage or cancellation of benefits.[64]

The last two cases refer to measures that, although legal, cause imbalance in the rights and obligations agreed upon between the members. Because they are difficult to prove, they are rarely used, and on the occasions when they have been the subject of complaints to the DSB, they have not progressed.[65]

In this sense, any measure incompatible with WTO rules, such as specific subsidies, whether prohibited or actionable, or incompatible countervailing measures, can be questioned in front of the DSB.

Faced with any of these situations, the parties initiate the procedure by holding mutual consultations, for a period of 60 days, to seek a solution. This phase has an exclusively diplomatic characteristic and can be compared to the "conditions of the action",[66] without which the next step cannot be taken.

If an agreement is not possible, the State in question may request the DSB to institute a *Panel*, presenting the subject matter of the dispute and the respective legal basis. Even if the parties do not reach an agreement, this step is still important, serving to delimit the object of the controversy.

In the second stage, one can already identify the jurisdictional characteristic of the system, by which the dispute will be resolved by a body of arbitrators, between three and five, elected by the parties, observing the principles of due legal process and adversarial proceedings, according to the WTO rules.

If the parties do not reach consensus on the election of the arbitrators within 20 days, the WTO Director-General will be requested to appoint the composition of the *Panel.*

When the subject of the solicitation is the granting of a prohibited subsidy, Article 4 of the SCM determines that at the end of the consultation phase, before opening the Panel, the DSB may request the Permanent Group of Experts (GPE)[67] to perform a previous analysis to find out if this is really the case.

---

[64] Possibility provided for in Article XXIII: 1 (c), used for emergency cases, such as economic crises, high unemployment, etc., which never resulted in the establishment of a *Panel* due to the lack of criteria for invoking it.

[65] Benjamin (2013), pp. 36–37.

[66] See: Cretella Neto (2003), p. 109.

[67] 24.3 of the SCM The Committee will establish a Permanent Expert Group (GPE). Composed of five independent *experts*, highly qualified in the area of subsidies and trade relations. The experts will be elected by the Committee and one of them will be replaced every year. The GPE may be requested to assist the special group as provided in Article 4, paragraph 5. The Committee may also request an opinion on the existence and nature of any subsidy. Free adaptation from: "Article 24.3 SCM Agreement: The Committee shall establish a Permanent Group of Experts composed of five independent persons, highly qualified in the fields of subsidies and trade relations. The experts will

Based on the fundamentals presented, the *Panel* delimits the matter to be appreciated, which will serve as terms of reference for the purposes of procedural speed. Thus, the terms of reference have the objective:

> To examine, in the light of the relevant provisions in (indicate the covered agreement (s) cited by the parties to the dispute), the matter referred to the DSB by (name of party) in document [...] and to establish conclusions that support the DSB in making recommendations or issuing decisions provided for in that agreement(s)".[68]

When analyzing the *Panel* case it conducts at least two meetings with the parties and subsequently issues a preliminary report for internal review purposes and thus avoids making material errors. This report is sent to the parties for their considerations.

After this step, the report becomes definitive and is sent to the DSB for adoption. Only with the adoption, the report becomes binding. Although the decision is taken on the basis of WTO rules, one cannot affirm the international jurisdiction characteristic of the *Panel*, since that decision has an advisory nature, only becoming binding on the parties when adopted by the DSB.[69]

It is worth remembering that adoption occurs by means of the negative consensus rule, and it is sufficient that one member approves the report for it to be adopted. Thus, the adoption is practically automatic, since the party that wins will certainly vote in its favor. This procedure has political relevance, since, by promoting debate about the decision, it functions as a "thermometer" of its legitimacy.

Before the adoption of the *Panel*'s report, the parties may still recur to the OPA, for re-examination of the questions of law, with powers to reformulate, modify, or revoke the decision. The respective report will be sent to the DSB for approval, at which time the *Panel* report will also be adopted. The deadline for adoption of both reports is 30 days from the date of their distribution to the members.

It should be noted that the double degree of jurisdiction reinforces the "judicialization" of the system. Nevertheless, at any stage of the procedure it is possible for the parties to reach an agreement, including in the implementation phase of the decision.

The DSB decision may result in three different solutions, in the following order: a) the immediate or timely withdrawal of the incompatible measure or its harmful effects; b) the conclusion of a compensation agreement; and c) retaliation.[70]

---

be elected by the Committee and one of them will be replaced every year. The PGE may be requested to assist a panel, as provided for in paragraph 5 of Article 4. The Committee may also seek an advisory opinion on the existence and nature of any subsidy".

[68] Free adaptation from: "To examine, in the light of the relevant provisions in (name of the covered agreement(s) cited by the parties to the dispute), the matter referred to the DSB by (name of party) in document [...] and to make such findings as will assist the DSB in making the recommendations or in giving the rulings provided for in that/those agreement(s)". In: Article 7, of the WTO Dispute Settlement Understanding.

[69] See: Borges (2008), p. 423.

[70] The term 'retaliation' is used by American doctrine and is not found in the WTO agreements, which also have divergent terms. While Article 4 of the SCM refers to countermeasures, ESC deals

In fact, the first constitutes the only possible jurisdictional remedy, while the others constitute solutions that can be sought by the members in case the first one is not complied with. In this sense, Article 19 of the ESC provides that:

> Where a special group or Appellate Body concludes that a measure is incompatible with a covered agreement, it shall recommend that the Member concerned bring the measure into compliance with the agreement. In addition to its recommendations, the special group or Appellate Body may suggest ways in which the Member concerned can implement the recommendations.[71]

As a general rule, the respondent must present to the DSB the time and manner in which it intends to comply with the decision. In the case of prohibited subsidies, for the purposes of expediency, Article 4.7[72] of the SCM requires the *Panel* to immediately set a deadline for removal from the program.

In the case of actionable subsidies, the recommendation will first order the defendant to eliminate their harmful effects, and if this is not possible, it will recommend the removal of the subsidies within 6 months from the adoption of the DSB decision.

If it is impossible to remove the measure immediately, the member must do so within a reasonable period of time, to be discussed between the parties, since this varies according to the limits of its internal legislation. According to article 21.3 of the ESC, this period will be determined based on the following guidelines:

(a) the time frame proposed by the Member interested, provided that such time frame is approved by the DSB; or, in the absence of such approval;

(b) a deadline mutually agreed upon by the parties to the dispute within 45 days of the date of adoption of the recommendations and decisions; or, failing such agreement;

(c) a time limit determined by binding arbitration within 90 days of the date of adoption of the recommendations and decisions.[73]

---

with suspension of concessions. Daniel Damásio Borges calls them reprisals. Here, we have opted for the ESC terminology, in view of the great doctrinal divergence on the concept of reprisals and the wide range of possibilities for countermeasures. See: Borges (2008), pp. 57–62.

[71] Free adaptation from: "Article 19.1 Dispute Settlement Understanding: Where a panel or the Appellate Body concludes that a measure is inconsistent with a covered agreement, it shall recommend that the Member concerned bring the measure into conformity with that agreement. In addition to its recommendations, the panel or Appellate Body may suggest ways in which the Member concerned could implement the recommendations".

[72] Article 4.7 ASCM: If the measure under consideration is deemed to be a prohibited subsidy, the panel shall recommend to the granting Member to withdraw the measure without delay. In this regard, the panel shall specify in its recommendation the deadline by which the measure should be removed. Free adaptation from: "Article 4.7 SCM Agreement: If the measure in question is found to be a prohibited subsidy, the panel shall recommend that the subsidizing Member withdraw the subsidy without delay. In this regard, the panel shall specify in its recommendation the time-period within which the measure must be withdrawn".

[73] Free adaptation from: "Article 21.3 Dispute Settlement Understanding: (a) the period of time proposed by the Member concerned, provided that such period is approved by the DSB; or, in the absence of such approval; (b) a period of time mutually agreed by the parties to the dispute within 45 days after the date of adoption of the recommendations and rulings; or, in the absence of such agreement; (c) a period of time determined through binding arbitration within 90 days after the date of adoption of the recommendations and rulings. In such arbitration, a guideline for the arbitrator should be that the reasonable period of time to implement panel or Appellate Body recommendations should not exceed 15 months from the date of adoption of a panel or Appellate Body

The article further adds that the reasonable period to be determined by the arbitration may not exceed 15 months from the date of the adoption of the decision. In the case of prohibited subsidies, this time limit is predetermined by the *Panel*.

Article 21.6 determines that the DSB shall inspect compliance with the decision, based on receipt of periodic reports from the respondent on the stage of implementation. It is possible to have a dispute over implementation because of the range of possibilities for compliance with the decision.

In this case, it is important to verify whether the implementing measure is not in violation of the WTO agreements or whether compliance has been partial. It must be emphasized that this mechanism cannot be used in the absence of implementation measures, otherwise it would allow the defendant to use it to delay compliance.

The difficulties of the implementation phase stem from resistance on the part of members to comply with recommendations, especially when these involve more politically sensitive issues, such as subsidies.[74]

In any situation, whether of non-compliance, partial compliance, or replacement by another unlawful measure, the parties may negotiate a settlement or indemnification agreement. Compensation implies the opening of trade through the concession of benefits. In the case of subsidies, it seeks to neutralize the loss of market caused by them.

Considering the duty to comply with the WTO agreements, offsetting is a rarely used instrument because it implies the opening of a new market by the defendant. This makes it of little interest to the claimant, due to the most favored nation principle, whereby the benefits granted must be extended to all members. Thus, it will only be economically interesting in the case of a monopoly.

Compensation is not obligatory and must result from an agreement between the parties. In the case of subsidies, the claimant may immediately ask the DSB for authorization to initiate retaliation, which, unlike compensation, involves the suspension of concessions in order to force compliance with the decision.

Note that the ESC does not treat retaliation as an illicit act and neither as a sanction. However, Amaral Junior defends that retaliation has the legal nature of a sanction because it is "[…] coercive act, which is characterized by limited interference in the protected sphere of interest of another State, through the temporary deprivation of legitimately established rights".[75]

Borges[76] disagrees with this view due to the illicit nature of retaliation, as it qualifies them as reprisals, which, in turn, constitute violations of international norms, and are only admissible when there are motives to exclude their illegality.

On the other hand, for Amaral, the punitive function of retaliation is non-existent and can be proven by the requirement of proportionality in its application, that is, retaliation must be equivalent to the damage or the nullity of benefits.[77]

---

report. However, that time may be shorter or longer, depending upon the particular circumstances".

[74] See: Borges (2008), p. 431.

[75] Amaral Jr. (2008), p. 113.

[76] Borges (2008), p. 52.

[77] Amaral (2012), p. 94.

Unlike sanctions, retaliation, arising from the principle of reciprocity, represents an individual interest and is therefore optional, and its predominant function is to induce compliance with international norms. Sanctions, on the other hand, are institutional, in the collective interest, applied by States on behalf of the international organization and, therefore, obligatory.[78]

According to Pauwelyn,[79] retaliation expresses the mercantilist ideas of the organization. As Article 3.7 of the ESC states, the whole purpose of the dispute settlement mechanism is the regularization of the incompatible measure, while maintaining compliance with the agreements to safeguard the balance of concessions:

> If no mutually agreed solution can be reached, the first objective of the dispute settlement mechanism will normally be to achieve the elimination of the measures in question if they are found to be incompatible with the provisions of any of the included agreements.[80]

This device reflects the corrective function of retaliation, in order to restore the balance between the parties.[81] In the case of prohibited subsidies, retaliation is intended to induce the immediate removal of their program, and in the case of appealable subsidies, in the first instance, the goal is the elimination of the damage, if this is not possible, then the general rule of Article 3.7 applies.

For this reason, settlement and retaliation are optional and used only in the case of non-compliance with DSB recommendations. In this sense, the ESC makes clear in Article 22.1 the preference for implementation of decisions:

> Compensation and suspension of concessions or other obligations are temporary measures available if the recommendations and decisions are not implemented within a reasonable period of time. However, neither compensation nor suspension of concessions or other obligations is preferable to full implementation of a recommendation to adapt a measure to a covered agreement.[82]

This device is consistent with the provisions of Article 3.7 of the ESC, transcribed above, in prioritizing compliance with the *Panel*'s recommendations. However, this is the last resource, which is reached after a long period of time. In the meantime, political-economic maneuvers and trade gains operate, the spaces for which will be studied below.

---

[78] Ibid, pp. 55–56.

[79] Pauwelyn (2000), pp. 335–347.

[80] Free adaptation from: "Article 3.7 DSU: In the absence of a mutually agreed solution, the first objective of the dispute settlement mechanism is usually to secure the withdrawal of the measures concerned if these are found to be inconsistent with the provisions of any of the covered agreements".

[81] Borges (2008), p. 498.

[82] Translation by Vera Thorstensen and Luciana Maria de Oliveira. In: Thorstensen V, Oliveira LM (2013) Rereading the WTO Agreements as Interpreted by the Appellate Body: Dispute Settlement Understanding.   http://ccgi.fgv.br/sites/ccgi.fgv.br/files/file/Publicacoes/01%20Dispute%20 Settlement%20Understanding.pdf, p. 257.

4.4.2 Spaces for Political-Economic Strategies in Dispute Settlement

There is room for political and economic maneuvering throughout the WTO dispute settlement procedure. In the first phase, by virtue of its diplomatic character, it allows the exercise of political pressure, especially by developed countries against developing countries, for the conclusion of agreements.[83] Countries, especially rich ones, may threaten to suspend concessions,[84] blacklisting the State, making threats to government representatives, blocking a negotiation package, among others. Moreover, they may threaten not to comply with an eventual DSB decision, arguing the inefficiency of decision implementation mechanisms.

If the parties reach an agreement and there is subsequent non-compliance, the DSB has no mechanism to enforce compliance, as is the case with Panel and OPA decisions.[85] This means that the parties have to go back to square one, that is, a new dispute settlement procedure has to be opened to resolve the issue, starting again with consultations. In the meantime, the violating member gains time and market.

Another issue to be highlighted is the fact that the *Panel*'s and OPA's decisions produce prospective effects only, *ex nunc*, this contributes to the defendant seeking subterfuge and taking advantage of all the mechanisms provided by the DSB to prolong litigation.

It has been decided, in the case of subsidies, that the effects of DSB decisions should be retroactive, implying also the reimbursement of the financial contribution on which the subsidy was based, in addition to its removal.[86] However, this understanding was much criticized in the WTO, including by both parties involved in the case, and was not raised again, due to the difficulty of this effect being applied in the internal scope of the States.[87] This situation may trigger the producer's disinterest in having his State initiate a dispute settlement procedure in the WTO, since it will not be compensated for the damage already suffered.

It is important to remember that the WTO dispute settlement rules are neither restorative nor punitive in nature. Its objective is to restore the balance of trade relations, neutralizing the effects of incompatible measures.

---

[83] Silva Neto (2005), p. 179.

[84] With the exception of the most favored nation principle, the WTO allows developed countries to grant more favorable tax treatment to imports from developing countries. Known as the GSP - Generalized System of Preferences, developed countries often threaten to remove the concessions; after all, they are optional. Nevertheless, Daniel Damásio Borges understands that, once such benefits are granted, their removal suffers limitations. In this sense, see: Borges DD (2008) Represálias nos Contenciosos Econômicos na Organização Mundial do Comércio: uma análise na perspectiva dos países em desenvolvimento. São Paulo, Customs, pp. 253–256.

[85] Bliacheriene (2007), p. 107.

[86] Panel Report in the Australia case—Subsidies Provided to Producers and Exporters of Automotive Leather, par 6.39.

[87] Bossche and Zdouc (2013), pp. 205, 777–778.

Thus, in order for there to be full compliance with the recommendation, the defendant must remove the subsidies entirely, if prohibited, or their damages, when appealable. If some of these remain or are replaced by other subsidies, it is possible that the parties will reach a settlement agreement. If this is not possible, the claimant may ask the DSB to apply proportionate retaliation until the decision is fully complied with.[88]

During this period, States, in order to gain time and trade, use subterfuge arising from procedural flaws, such as time limits, the investigation of damages, and the manner in which retaliation is applied.

4.4.2.1   The Deadlines

Articles 4 and 7 of the SCM establish shorter timeframes for the resolution of subsidies disputes. Consultations take place within 60 days, with a maximum of 30 days for prohibited subsidies. In the case that the parties do not reach consensus, the Panel must be instituted immediately and will have 90 days, instead of 6 months, to analyze the case. On the other hand, the deadline for the adoption of the decision by the DSB will be 30 days and not 60, as is the general rule.

Likewise, the deadlines for the appeal procedure are special. Regardless of the nature of the subsidies, whether prohibited or actionable, the OPA has a period of 30 days to issue its decision, extendable for an equal period, unlike the general rule, which establishes a limit of 90 days. Finally, the other DSB deadlines not specified in this article must be reduced by half.

The deadlines for compliance with the recommendations are also different: 6 months to remove the damage caused by actionable subsidies, while for prohibited ones, their removal must be immediate. According to Wouters and Coppens, such differentiation about deadlines and retaliation reflects members' more negative position towards prohibited subsidies.[89]

If, on the one hand, the establishment of deadlines for each procedural phase guarantees the automaticity of the system, by impeding that one of the parties procrastinates the demand, on the other hand, despite being short, the deadlines are not followed to the letter, mainly in the more complex cases.

With regard to the recommendations, it was seen that the first solution is the removal of the incompatible measure without delay or within a reasonable period of time. It so happens that this period runs into the constitutional precepts of each member, in view of the need to make changes in its internal legislation, which may still be subject to discussion.

In addition to the disagreement over the deadline for implementation, the parties may not agree on the way the defendant intends to correct the incompatible

---

[88] In this regard, see: Appellate Body Report in the United States case—Tax Treatment for 'Foreign Sales Corporation', par 82.

[89] Wouters and Coppens (2010), p. 56.

measure. In principle, the conformation of the measure occurs unilaterally, determined internally by the defendant without any intervention by the DSB. This, in turn, will only manifest itself when the defendant demonstrates the impossibility of immediate compliance. Thus, the respondent must notify the DSB, within 30 days, of its intentions regarding implementation, which may be questioned by the complainant.

Both issues, both material and in relation to deadlines, can be discussed. For this, the procedure on the implementation is established, giving rise to a series of questions, further delaying its compliance. If there is no consensus on the implementation deadline, it will be decided by arbitration, which should be concluded in 90 days from the adoption of the report. In the meantime, it should be noted that the incompatible measure continues to produce its effects.

Once the deadline and the form of implementation are established, the possibility of non-compliance must still be considered, further extending the time for the demand to be solved.

Notwithstanding the short deadlines, when they are not complied with, it is necessary to open new procedures. The first, established in article 21 of the ESC, serves to analyze the partial fulfillment of the obligation. The second, provided in article 22, is used to request retaliation, in case of total or partial non-compliance, which, if not contested, will be authorized within 30 days.

If the complainant contests the *quantum* or the object of the retaliation, an arbitration procedure is initiated, with a period of 60 days, to ascertain the degree of retaliation, which must be proportional to the damage or the annulment of the benefit. In addition, there is also the arbitration procedure for the analysis of cross-retaliation, with a period of 60 days for its definition, as determined by Article 22.6 of the same device.[90]

As an example, one can cite the cases between Brazil and Canada[91] about subsidies granted by both countries to their respective aircraft industries (Embraer and Bombardier), which took 3 years until the final OPA decision (1997–2000). The emblematic cotton case between Brazil and the United States,[92] which started in 2002, only obtained the final OPA decision in 2005.

It is important to remember that after the decision, the compliance phase is initiated, which can generate new controversies, opening new arbitration proceedings.

---

[90] There is doctrinal divergence on whether it is possible to claim Article 22 retaliation before the *Panel* has pronounced on the implementation of Article 21. Borges, for example, says that it is incongruous to authorize retaliation before proven non-compliance with the decision. The jurisprudence of the WTO has not yet been pronounced in this sense, but it has accepted the request for retaliation even without verifying the conformity of the implementation. In this case, the request will be based on the data provided by the complaining party. See: Borges (2008), pp. 439–445.

[91] The imbroglio over subsidy programs for the aircraft industry has generated the following cases: DS46 *Brazil — Export Financing Programme for Aircraft (Complainant: Canada);* DS70 *Canada — Measures Affecting the Export of Civilian Aircraft (Complainant: Brazil);* DS71 *Canada — Measures Affecting the Export of Civilian Aircraft (Complainant: Brazil)* e DS222 *Canada — Export Credits and Loan Guarantees for Regional Aircraft (Complainant: Brazil).*

[92] DS267 *United States — Subsidies on Upland Cotton (Complainant: Brazil).*

Thus, the Bombardier case was defined in 2003 and the cotton case was only effectively resolved in October 2014, constituting the longest in the history of the WTO.

This time lapse for compliance with the decisions occurs because of the possibility of negotiations between the parties, especially with regard to compliance with the decision. In the case of cotton, for example, the final decision of the OPA took place in 2005, confirming the condemnation of the United States for illegal subsidies, which were to be removed immediately.

Faced with legislative obstacles, the United States claimed that it was not possible to immediately remove the subsidies, so it was agreed that it would take 15 months to adapt the U.S. legislation to the decision.

After this period, there was no compliance with the decision and, in August 2006, the Brazilian government claimed retaliatory rights, based on article 21.5, which establishes a Panel to solve controversies about non-implementation within 90 days. Due to the complexity of the work, this deadline was not achieved, and the dispute was only concluded in December 2007.

Given the evidence of non-implementation, Brazil pleaded the right to retaliation, which also went to arbitration to discuss its object and *quantum*. In 2009, the Brazilian government obtained the right to retaliate against the United States for up to eight hundred million dollars. With this, Brazil could suspend concessions regarding trade in goods, services, and intellectual property from the United States.

On March 8, 2010, CAMEX published resolution number fifteen, increasing the import tax rate of one hundred and two products originating from the United States. This resolution would only come into effect on April 7th, a period that provided the opportunity for new negotiations.

Although the WTO prioritizes negotiation over retaliation, the fact that it can be realized at any time allows the demand to be prolonged, even more so when the resulting agreement is not complied with.

This is exactly what happened between Brazil and the United States in the case of cotton: the parties reached an agreement whereby the United States committed itself: (a) to establish a fund to finance projects for the Brazilian cotton industry with an annual value of approximately one hundred and forty-seven million dollars; (b) the suspension of resources for the subsidy program, which guaranteed export credits; and (c) speeding up the process of sanitary recognition of pork and beef.

However, in October 2012, the United States suspended the payments, which led to a new agreement between the parties. This time, after many internal discussions between retaliating or renegotiating, in October 2014, the parties ended the dispute in a more cautious and diplomatic manner through a new agreement, in which the U.S. government agreed to immediately pay three hundred million dollars[93] to the Brazilian Cotton Institute (IBA).[94] In addition, they also agreed to limit export

---

[93] By the time the new agreement was reached, the US government had already paid 530 million dollars.

[94] Instituto Brasileiro do Algodão - IBA, a non-profit civil association founded in June 2010, to manage the resources from the payments made by the United States as a partial settlement of the

subsidies to up to 18 months. However, this new agreement was only possible through the Brazilian threat of cross-retaliation.

It is important to note that the parties may, by agreement, extend the deadlines, but without such an agreement, the deadlines apply, and the complainant is entitled to continue the procedure, preventing the defendant from blocking it.

Therefore, on the one hand, the thickening of the jurisdiction of the multilateral trade system ensures more security and predictability, but on the other hand, the presence of a diplomatic character is still noticeable, which demonstrates the interests of the States in maintaining room for maneuver.

The diplomatic character extends the deadlines and facilitates the exercise of pressure to desist from cases or to close agreements, especially when there is a significant economic disequilibrium between the parties. When Brazil initiated the demand on cotton, for example, the United States began to apply measures *antidumping*[95] on Brazilian orange juice. However, Brazil has the technical capacity and structure to return to the WTO litigation, which would be impossible for the more fragile countries.

Non-compliance with the deadlines, whether due to the complexity of the issue or the use of delaying subterfuges, contributes to the use of the dispute settlement mechanism in order to obtain commercial advantages, by perpetuating the illicit conduct. Added to this scenario is the lack of retroactive remedies to repair the damages resulting from subsidies, whose problems will be studied as follows.

4.4.2.2 Of the Damages

The current rules encourage the continuation of illegal subsidy programs, since as long as the deadline for complying with the recommendations has not passed, the violating member continues to divert trade and gain advantages without suffering any kind of penalty.

In the meantime, injured members must pay for the damage caused by subsidies until the end of this deadline in cases where compensatory measures are

---

cotton case. Aims to promote the development and strengthening of the Brazilian cotton industry, observing the best management, governance and transparency practices. http://www.iba-br.com.

[95] According to Article 2 of the *Antidumping* Agreement, a product shall be considered as object of dumping when it is introduced into the market of another country at a value lower than the normal value, that it, when the export price of the product from one country to another is lower than the price, if compared, in the course of trade, to the similar product when destined for consumption in the exporting country. Free adaptation from: "Article 2 Antidumping Agreement: For the purpose of this Agreement, a product is to be considered as being dumped, i.e. introduced into the commerce of another country at less than its normal value, if the export price of the product exported from one country to another is less than the comparable price, in the ordinary course of trade, for the like product when destined for consumption in the exporting country". When this occurs, a *antidumping* measure is applied to bring the price back to its normal value. See DS250 and DS382 cases.

impractical. In this sense, Amaral[96] warns of the possibility that the damage may become irreversible at the end of the litigation.

The legacy of GATT/47 increases the gravity of the problem, whose solutions are restricted to the mere removal of the illegal measure or damage. As in GATT/47, the WTO system does not admit condemnation for reparation of damages. This means that because of the prospective effect of the DSB decisions, what has already been achieved in terms of trade gains is irreversible.

With rare exceptions,[97] damages are only raised in dispute settlements when defining the *quantum* of retaliation. Before going into the polemical issues of retaliation, it is important to note that the concept of damage in international trade is specific and translates into *nullification or impairment of benefits*. The reason for this is the WTO's exclusive focus on fair competition among its members. Therefore, independently of the illicit act causes a reduction in the flow of trade, damages or the annulment of benefits are established when they cause adverse effects on trade. These effects can take many forms, such as increased transaction costs and changes in the conditions of access to markets.[98]

With regard to prohibited subsidies, their concession reallocates resources, causing distortions to the trade of States and, therefore, their analysis is independent from the ascertainment of damages for the responsibility of the granting State.

On retaliation, Article 22.4 states that "the degree of suspension of concessions or other obligations authorized by the CSO shall be equivalent to the degree of nullification or injury".[99] According to this device, retaliation, in general, should be equivalent to the damage caused by violations of the WTO agreements. In the case of prohibited subsidies, it is possible to exceed their amount to induce compliance with the DSB decision.[100] Considering that they can only be applied after the deadline established for implementation has expired, damages will only be computed from that date.

Such damages are estimated by the arbitrators in an approximate manner through the analysis of the *counterfactual situation*, that is, by investigating changes in demand and prices, we estimate what the net revenues would be if the illegal measure did not exist.

This approach has been criticized due to its subjectivity, the complexity and variables of the damage calculation method, mainly because it disregards the economic impacts that retaliation can generate in the different economic conditions in which States find themselves.

---

[96] Amaral (2012), p. 99.

[97] In the case of actionable subsidies, for example, the damages must be proven, as they are a requirement for the existence of the subsidy.

[98] See: Borges (2008), pp. 285–286.

[99] Free adaptation of: "Article 22.4 DSU: The level of the suspension of concessions or other obligations authorized by the DSB shall be equivalent to the level of the nullification or impairment".

[100] In cases *Brazil—Aircraft* and *Canada—Aircraft Credits and Guarantees*, the *Panel* clarified that, as a countermeasure, its ability to force the State to withdraw the illicit subsidy is considered.

This situation shows, once again, the WTO's homogeneous treatment, which disregards the different economic realities of its members. For Borges:

> The damages, whether resulting from the illicit act or from the reprisals, must be appreciated in light of the peculiar economic situation in which the injured State and the State responsible find themselves, otherwise there will be no real equivalence between them.[101]

This treatment diverges from the objectives prescribed in the preamble of the WTO Agreement, which places development as one of the pillars that must permeate the entire Organization and its agreements. Ignoring the impacts of retaliation on members can further deepen the differences between developed and developing countries, with the former having greater economic capacity to both retaliate and withstand retaliation.

Developing countries, in turn, because of their economic and social reality, may suffer even more from disproportionate retaliation. Therefore, this reality must be weighed when determining the *quantum* of retaliation.

In relation to prohibited subsidies, whose retaliations are disciplined in Article 4.10 of the SCM, damages have not served as a parameter for the application of retaliations. The decisions of the Panels show the adoption of two criteria: (a) the function of retaliation to induce the immediate withdrawal of the prohibited subsidy; and (b) the total amount of the subsidies, both of which are admitted for the sake of effectiveness.[102]

The adoption of these criteria has been a cause of disparities among members, as they often reveal disproportionate retaliation. In the case of the European Union on bananas,[103] the *Panel* made it clear that the purpose of the retaliations is to induce compliance with the decision and, therefore, they are temporary. However, it emphasized that their disproportionate application, going beyond the damage or the annulment of the benefit, is not justified.

In markets such as aircraft, competition is very fierce, and a small amount of subsidy can bring much higher losses. For this reason, Borges believes that the calculation of damages based on proportionality is the best criterion to be adopted to determine the *quantum* of retaliation.[104]

---

[101] See: Borges (2008), p. 327.

[102] In the case *Canada—Export credits and loan guarantees for regional aircraft*, the arbitrators concluded that the total value of the subsidies granted by Canada to its aircraft industry was not sufficient by way of retaliation to force immediate removal of the subsidy. Based solely and exclusively on this fundament, 20 percent was added to the value of the subsidy. See: Borges (2008), pp. 333–334.

[103] See: Panel Report in the EC Case—Regime for Importation, Sale and Distribution of Bananas, par 6.3.

[104] See: Borges (2008), pp. 342–343.

4.4.2.3 Of Retaliations

Retaliations constitute the last resource allowed by the DSB, in an attempt to induce compliance with the recommendation for the effective resolution of the controversy. It is at this moment that starts to quantify the damage, so that the retaliation is proportional to the amount of the subsidy when it is prohibited and, to the damage, when it is actionable.[105] However, independently of the nature of the subsidy, the retaliation will always be prospective, not reaching the reparation of damages before the decision.

When it comes to developing countries, Article 21.8 of the ESC determines that the DSB must analyze the impacts of retaliation not only on the agreements involved, but on the entire economy of the country.[106]

The problem is that the adverse effects of retaliation are often unavoidable. Because they are suspensions of benefits, they decrease supply, which in turn causes prices to rise, damaging the exporters affected by the measure, while favoring their foreign competitors, who now obtain the market that previously belonged to the defendant. For this reason, retaliation, even if applied bilaterally, produces multilateral effects.[107]

Retaliations must occur within the same sector[108] economic and of the same agreement affected by the incompatible measure. If it is not impractical or ineffective, the member may plead to be authorized to suspend concessions with respect to another sector within the same agreement. If, this would still be impractical or ineffective, the DSB may authorize, cross-retaliation, that is, the suspension of concessions under another agreement.

The analysis of the practicability and effectiveness of the retaliation is made by the arbitrators based on the party's request. By the first criterion, an analysis is made of the concessions made by the party within the agreement, which, if non-existent, will make the retaliation impracticable. The concept of effectiveness, on the other hand, implies in the analysis of its capacity to induce the State to comply with the Panel's decision and, in this case, it is necessary to investigate the asymmetries between the parties.

---

[105] See: Appellate Body Report on the Brazil case—Aircraft, par 3.48.

[106] Article 21.8: If the case has been submitted by a developing country, in considering the appropriate action to be taken the DSB shall take into consideration not only the commercial implications of the measures under discussion, but also their impact on the economy of the developing countries interested. Free adaptation from: "Article 21.8 DSU: If the case is one brought by a developing country Member, in considering what appropriate action might be taken, the DSB shall take into account not only the trade coverage of measures complained of, but also their impact on the economy of developing country Members concerned".

[107] See: Thorstensen and Oliveira (2013), pp. 115–117.

[108] Article 22.3 (f) (i) of the ESC prescribes that "sector, in relation to goods, means all goods". Free adaptation from: "Article 22.3 (f) DSU: for purposes of this paragraph, "sector" means: (i) with respect to goods, all goods".

In the banana controversy between the European Union and Ecuador,[109] the arbitrators understood that when the injured State is dependent on imports from the respondent, retaliation, which is nothing more than suspension of concessions, can be even more damaging.

Thus, retaliation is often unfeasible when applied by weaker countries, because it generates costs and little or no effect against richer countries. For Borges, there is a "close relationship between the dysfunctions of retaliation and the asymmetric distribution of economic power".[110]

For this reason, cross-retaliation has been used more often by developing countries against developed ones, since it can affect more sensitive sectors to the latter. The intellectual property agreement is one of the most requested in such cases, in view of its relevance for developed countries and the benefits of suspending it for developing and least developed countries.[111]

The downside of cross-retaliation is that most of the time, it does not reach the same economic sectors benefiting from the incompatible measure, causing sectors dissociated from the illicit to suffer. For this reason, the ESC has established a priority order to be followed.

There are cases in which retaliation, independently of the sector, does not even produce effects on the defendant, but generates costs for the claimant. This is the case of members whose trade is irrelevant to the other party because of their tiny share in world trade.

Less developed countries are economically weak to retaliate against developed countries. In Amaral's words:

> Even though the WTO dispute settlement mechanism is said to have teeth to bite members that do not comply with the decisions adopted, in reality the effectiveness of suspending trade concessions is challenged by the huge difference in market size that may be competing in the trade game.[112]

What we have seen after 20 years of operation of the WTO dispute settlement mechanism is its effectiveness before even reaching retaliations.[113] But this does not change its central problem: the reflection of the discrepancy of the economic power of the States in relation to the fulfillment of the obligations. In this sense, the respondent tends to comply with DSB decisions when it knows of the economic and politi-

---

[109] In this regard, see: Appeal of the European Community on the arbitration provided for in paragraph 6 of Article 22 of the ESC in the case *European Communites—Regime for the Importation, sale and distribution of banana*, par. 73–80.

[110] Borges (2008), p. 501.

[111] Developing countries, for example, can benefit from the suspension of patents on medicines, making them cheaper for the consumer. See: Ibid, p 360–361. The impacts, when considering private consumption, are positive in the area of intellectual property and negative in trade retaliation. See also: Amaral (2012).

[112] Amaral (2012), p. 95.

[113] In the 20 years of the WTO, 472 cases have been initiated, in only eight of which retaliation has been authorized. In: WTO Chronological List of Disputes. https://www.wto.org/english/tratop_e/dispu_e/dispu_status_e.htm.

cal potential of the claimant to retaliate. Therefore, when the government of the Member State does not intend to observe the decision of the DSB, the system proves to be weak.

Among developing countries, Brazil, besides being one of the pioneers, has a relevant role as a demanding country, although it is still behind the United States and the European Union. Next are China, Mexico, India, and Argentina. On the other hand, weaker developing countries, such as Bolivia, Venezuela, Peru, Ecuador, as well as most Caribbean countries, have minimal or no participation, since, due to their small economic power, their difficulties are not restricted to accessing the system. Even if that were possible, their retaliations pose little threat to the developed countries.

Many proposals have already been presented to reform the multilateral dispute settlement system, mainly regarding strengthening the instruments for the enforcement of decisions. The responsibility for repairing retroactive damages has been a frequent topic among developing countries since the GATT/47 era.[114]

Another possibility would be to allow members to unite in retaliation, making it more effective when developing countries are supported by developed ones.[115]

Thus, to solve this problem, a group of African countries proposed collective retaliation of developing countries against developed countries.[116] However, some less developed countries face difficulties in accessing the system, so well used by developed countries, since they can only retaliate, upon authorization from the DSB, after going through the procedure foreseen in the ESC. In this sense, Sella points out that:

> Despite the formal equality of all WTO members, they are neither technically equal nor equally capable of supporting the costs of the demands and the resulting reduction in diplomatic capacity. Each of these stages, by draining time, efforts, and human and material investments, directly prejudices the interested party in complying with the final decision issued by the Appellate Body. The sum of the frustrations, however, has even more damaging effects than just delaying the full pacification of a specific controversy. Indirectly, the slowness of the final decision implemented and the successive costs incurred promote a corrosion of confidence in the WTO dispute settlement mechanisms and accentuate the inequality of forces among its members.[117]

Proposals that make the dispute settlement system and the means of countering subsidies more rigid would hardly be accepted among the members. This is because, among other reasons, members do not want to be bound by stricter instruments when the rules are not very clear. In this sense:

---

[114] Hoekman (2011), pp. 16–18.

[115] For Borges, the junction of members at the time of retaliation is not possible due to the bilateral character of the WTO agreements and, for this reason, only the injured States are allowed to retaliate. Even because some States benefit from the subsidies, due to the lower prices of the subsidized product for consumers in importing States. See: Borges (2008), pp. 295–296.

[116] See: Amaral (2008), p. 114.

[117] Sella (2010), p. 26.

Table 4.3 List of the most active members and the number of cases as complainants and complainants, 1995–2023

Member	Claimant	Member	Claimed
United States	32	United States	43
European Union	26	European Union	20
Canada	15	Canada	11
Brazil	12	China	18
Korea	8	Brazil	7
China	7	Indonesia	5
India	6	India	5
Mexico	5	Mexico	3
Indonesia	5	Korea	3
Argentina	3	Argentina	2

Source: adapted from WTO data

> In summary, many proposals have been made to strengthen the dispute settlement system. A recurring theme in economic analyses of the relatively weak enforcement mechanisms in the WTO is that it is endogenous: it reflects the incomplete nature of the WTO contract. As a result governments do not want to submit themselves to a process in which they may be subject to penalties that they consider inappropriate, given the absence of ex ante specificity about the rules that will be applied.[118]

Thus, the margins for political-economic maneuvering were voluntarily targeted by member governments, which demonstrates the influence of mercantilist ideas in the WTO. On the other hand, it must be considered that the greater the rigidity in the settlement of disputes, the lesser the chances of cooperation, accentuating tensions among members, which, consequently, makes it difficult to sign new agreements.

This model, however, privileges developed countries, considering that they are, at the same time, the members that grant the most specific subsidies and impose the most compensatory measures, as well as being the biggest complainants in the dispute settlement system.

The data confirm that this competition is restricted to developed and emerging countries. Of the 130 cases involving subsidies and compensatory measures, the United States and the European Union lead among the main claimants and respondents, followed by Canada, as shown in Table 4.3.

It is observed that, in general, the system has exclusively served the rich countries and kept poor countries away. Most developing countries and all least developed countries are on the fringes of the WTO system. And when it comes to subsidies, whose social damage is irreparable, especially for poor countries, it is

---

[118] Free adaptation from: "Summing up, many proposals have been made to strengthen the dispute settlement system. A recurring theme in the economic analyses of the relatively weak enforcement mechanisms in the WTO is that this is endogenous: it reflects the incomplete nature of the WTO contract. As a result governments do not want to subject themselves to a process where they may be subject to penalties that they deem inappropriate given the absence of ex ante specificity on the rules that will apply". In: Hoekman and Kostecki (2009), p. 17.

necessary that measures be taken within the WTO to prevent such damage from occurring.

Even the strength of the emerging developing countries as demanders lags far behind that of the developed countries. As demanders, the emerging group is closer to the United States. Moreover, of all the cases between developed and developing countries in which an agreement was reached in the implementation phase, it is noteworthy that only in one of them was it necessary for the complaining State to request retaliation authorization. This case is emblematic in the WTO and became known as the cotton case between Brazil and the United States.

It should be noted that, after the reduction of tax barriers, subsidies are one of the few instruments[119] that are left to the States to achieve internal social-economic adjustments, knowing that the developed countries are more capable of doing so. In this sense, the reduction of tariff barriers can be illusory when countries make use of subsidies.

Knowing that developed countries have a greater political and economic ability to grant subsidies and make use of the WTO system, it cannot be forgotten that, in consonance with the principle of special differential treatment for developing and least developed countries, these are assisted by the WTO. However, the aid is not enough, when considers that these States can hardly bear the costs of competing in a trade distorted market using subsidies.

While the controversy is being discussed, trade detour produces concrete effects that often lead to the perishing of goods that are stranded in the warehouses of less developed countries. In this sense:

> Where there is no retroactive remedy, it is difficult for a government to refuse to exercise the full range of procrastinatory tactics when pressured by national interest groups with an interest in maintaining protection. Assuming that a measure exists because someone had enough political influence to pass it, the same someone is likely to fight for its maintenance. In many cases, even if the government, and therefore the national interest group, loses in the technical sense, they can be considered winners in the marketplace because of the effects of the unfair competitive advantage they obtained, temporarily, free of cost.[120]

At this juncture, the effects of subsidies are not sufficiently banned by retaliation, since they exceed its limits, given that retaliation is prospective, which can be advantageous to the violating government.

---

[119] Technical barriers are also used for producer protection purposes.

[120] Free adaptation from: "Where there is no retroactive remedy, it is difficult for a government to refuse to pursue the entire range of delay tactics when pressured by domestic interest groups with a stake in maintaining protection. Assuming a measure exists because someone had enough political clout to get it passed, the same someone will probably fight for its survival. In many cases, even if a government, and hence the domestic interest group, comes out a technical loser, it may already be a market winner because of the effects of its temporary cost-free unfair competitive advantage.". In: Horlick (2002). In: Kennedy and Southwick (2002), p. 640.

4.5   Using Subsidies to Counter Subsidies

The WTO regulations as they stand encourage the practice of specific subsidies among its members. In effect, the loopholes studied above are used to counterbalance the agreements that reduce tax barriers, to solve problems caused by negative externalities, or to prevent the effects of other subsidies.

Faced with the existence of a specific subsidy, WTO members can: (a) apply unilateral countervailing measures when possible; (b) appeal to the DSB; (c) do nothing, according to Adam Smith's theory, since the subsidies would be financing another country's consumption which, for him, would be the purpose of all production; or (d) apply specific subsidies to gain time to maneuver until they are challenged.

The first possibility cannot be applied if the harmed State is competing with the subsidized product in a third market. In the second, the DSB may authorize the harmed government to retaliate against the grantor, however, this only occurs after verification of noncompliance with the decision, which may take too long, benefiting the lender with the gain of trade. The DSB may also authorize, under Article 4.10 of the SCM, the claimant to apply new subsidies to counterbalance the effects of the illicit subsidies, but if they are licit and affect only the defendant. Furthermore, because they depend on the authorization of the DSB, the concession of new subsidies does not solve the problem in an *a priori* way either.

In the third scenario, the member would have to tolerate such a situation, believing in the "invisible hand" of the market, which is in imperfect conditions. Although the latter option is illicit under WTO rules, it is the quickest way to avoid the effects of subsidies when there is competition in a third market.

In this way, members take advantage of the fait accompli strategy, applying subsidies and gaining time while waiting for such measures to be contested before the DSB.

The scenario is even more dramatic for the less developed countries, which, faced with technical and financial incapacity for proper access to the system, are doomed to lose their production and their market. For developed countries, it is worth countering specific subsidies by applying new ones, even if they are illicit. Despite running the risk of being contested in the WTO until the controversy is effectively resolved, the market gain was obtained.

It is in this sense that the multilateral trade system encourages the practice of subsidies among its members since it is the quickest way to neutralize their effects when operating in the third market.

The doctrine has called this situation "*race to the bottom*". Although the terminology is more used for subsidy competition in search of foreign investment, it still makes sense for the issue presented here. Jackson warns of this phenomenon because, according to him:

The unrestricted use of subsidies in international trade can lead to the use of counter-subsidies, and counter-counter-subsidies in an increasing progression, of which can seriously damage world welfare. This has already been demonstrated in the agricultural sector.[121]

This situation occurred in the case between Brazil and Canada,[122] in which both countries subsidized their aircraft industry, respectively Embraer and Bombardier. In these circumstances, the *Panel* has made it clear that "counter-subsidy" measures, that is, the application of illicit subsidies as a means of countering illicit subsidies, cannot be admitted:

Brazil's approach to item (k), however, would effectively allow a member to elevate the offer of export subsidies -or in fact, any subsidies- by complaining members as a defense to justify its own provision of export subsidies. This would imply a race to the bottom, as each WTO member would justify the granting of export subsidies by claiming that other members were doing the same.[123]

In this regard, the only legal subsidies are those that are in line with the SCM. Therefore, when specific subsidies are used as a countermeasure, they are considered illegal and can be complained about in front of the DSB. However, until they are challenged, the grant program may have already fulfilled its purpose.

Canada's attitude in relation to the case confirms this premise. Despite being authorized by the DSB to retaliate against Brazil, the Canadian government also chose to subsidize its industry by providing Bombardier with a loan of three billion US dollars, on the grounds that they would lose market due to Brazil's resistance to implement the *Panel's* recommendations.

The same happened in the case *EU—Measuring Affecting Trade in Commercial*[124] *Vessels* against the Republic of Korea, in which the European Union's granting of subsidies was at disagreement with the ASCM, which does not permit the unilateral imposition of illegal subsidies to counteract other subsidies.

However, due to the high burden of subsidies, developing and least developed countries are excluded from this possibility. Considering that the higher a country's

---

[121] Free adaptation from: "The unfettered use of subsidies in international trade can lead to counter-subsidies, and counter-counter-subsidies in an escalating progression, all of which can seriously damage world welfare. This has already been demonstrated in the agricultural sector." In: Jackson (2000), p. 90.

[122] DS46 *Brazil — Export Financing Programme for Aircraft (Complainant: Canada);* DS70 *Canada — Measures Affecting the Export of Civilian Aircraft (Complainant: Brazil).*

[123] Free adaptation from: "The Brazilian approach to item (k), however, would effectively allow a Member to raise the provision of export subsidies –or indeed of any subsidy — by the complaining Member as a defense justifying its own provision of export subsidies. This would entail a race to the bottom, as each WTO Member sought to justify the provision of export subsidies on the grounds that other Members were doing the same". In: *Panel's* Final Report on the Brazil case— *Export Financing Programme for Aircraft*, WT/DS46, par. 7.26.

[124] Case DS301.

GDP, the greater its economic capacity to provide subsidies,[125] when applied against specific subsidies, the system reverts to then model *power-oriented*, extremely harmful to the least developed countries.

When the member makes use of unilateral measures of specific subsidies as a form of retaliation against subsidies without proper WTO supervision, the system reverts to the *power-oriented*, extremely harmful to economically fragile countries. These countries need instruments to counter subsidies, because if they too start subsidizing their production, whether through direct investment or by exempting economic activity, the social costs will fall on their population, whose welfare is already damaged.[126]

In the face of failures to protect established rights, reprisals were justified by GATT members. This means that, in the absence of guarantees of their rights, States have begun to adopt illicit measures to counter noncompliance with their foreseen obligations.[127] In the case of subsidies, this translates into the application of illicit subsidies to counterbalance the effects of equally illicit subsidies.

In this scenario, subsidy competition, that is, the use of subsidies against subsidies, is the worst form of response to the problem, since it results in new distortions.[128]

Governments have found space in the WTO system for political-economic maneuvering to promote political interests, preventing trade from being entirely free. Schwartz and Sykes point out that: "[…] the WTO system operates on contractual principles designed to permit breaches of contract when the political gains from defection are greater than the political costs to the harmed States".[129]

In this aspect, WTO members have several informal trade policy tools at their disposal, which do occur. Among them are subsidies and noncompliance with agreements as a subterfuge with commitments made.[130]

In this case, the lengthy WTO dispute settlement system allows the current government to pass on the costs of adjusting illicit subsidies to the next government. The fact that the system blames States that make their subsidy policies compatible with the rules only at the end of the procedure also induces opportunistic behavior. In Brewster's words: "Delay is important in the WTO context because none of the damage caused during the dispute settlement process is appealable."[131]

---

[125] Of the notified and known subsidies, the WTO Secretariat concluded in the 2006 *World Trade Report* that more than eighty percent belonged to developed countries. In: WTO (2006) World Trade Report 2006: exploring the links between subsidies, trade and the WTO. Geneva: WTO, 2006. http://www.wto.org/english/res_e/booksp_e/anrep_e/world_trade_report06_e.pdf.

[126] Jackson (2000), p. 90.

[127] Borges (2008), pp. 381–382.

[128] Schwartz and Sykes (2002). http://www.law.uchicago.edu/files/files/143.AOS_.wto_.pdf.

[129] Sykes (2003).

[130] Schropp (2009), p. 4.

[131] Free adaptation from: "Delay is important in the context of the WTO because none of the damage done during the dispute resolutions process is subject to a remedy". In: Brewster (2011), pp. 102–158.

In this way, injured States are left for years at the goodwill of the offending States until retaliation is authorized, although they are not offered any instruments to force the removal of subsidies or even to coerce agreements.

Considering that the benefits of non-cooperation are greater for developed countries, capable of taking better advantage of the loopholes in the system, the WTO has served as an instrument for the promotion of inequalities among its members.

Therefore, the analysis of governments' choice to use subsidies takes place in the incentive structure of the system. This, in turn, allows countries to maintain violations of agreements until the last recourse of the dispute settlement procedure. As Gary Horlick puts it[132]:

> Assuming that, charitably, the complainant discovers on the day of the Appellate Body decision that it has been acting inconsistently with a WTO agreement, at least 15 months have already passed in the inconsistent situation, or even more, since a Member would be unlikely to request consultations on the first day of the inconsistent measure's existence. However, even with all the resources finished, the only incentive to comply is enlightened or diplomatic self-interest, because the DSB allows a free opportunity to delay compliance for several months.[133]

In pursuit of maximizing their individual interests, members find in the flaws of the WTO system space for maneuvering in the granting of subsidies. By analyzing the cost-benefit of all available alternatives for the realization of your interests, we verify that the system encourages developed countries to non-compliance with the agreement, since the gain obtained with the subsidies is higher than the cost of non-compliance.

The same doesn't occur with developing and least developed countries, which, lacking economic capacity, are unable to bear the effects of subsidies until the dispute is resolved by the DSB, nor is it convenient for them to concede new subsidies to counterbalance the effects of the first ones.

In this scenario, countries have found more space for trade policy enforcement in the gaps in the SCM and the dispute settlement system. It is true that "the current system sets misplaced incentives for those who cause damage and undercompensates the victims of subterfuge".[134] This situation induces the use of retaliatory subsidies, leading to a real subsidy competition between developed countries, leaving poor countries at the margins of the system.

---

[132] Horlick (2001).

[133] Free adaptation from: "Assuming, charitably, that the losing member finds out on the day the Appellate Body decision is released that it has been acting inconsistently with a WTO Agreement, it has already spent at least fifteen months in the state of inconsistency, but probably more since it would be unlikely for a Member to request consultations on the first day of existence of an inconsistent measure. Yet, even with all appeals exhausted, the only incentive to comply is enlightened (or diplomatic) self-interest, because the DSU allows a cost-free opportunity to delay compliance for several months". In: Ibid, p. 3.

[134] Free adaptation from: "the current system sets the wrong incentives for injurers, and undercompensates victims of escape". In: Schropp (2009), p. 6.

It should be remembered that the use of unilateral measures has been avoided by the WTO since its formation. For this reason, the organization does not allow the use of subsidies against subsidies unless authorized and lawful.

In this sense, with regard to subsidies, the WTO has changed little from the previous reality, and has flaws that persist and exclude, in fact, fragile countries from the system. As it stands, the system has induced developed countries to take advantage of regulatory loopholes for the granting of illegal subsidies.

Thus, the mechanisms provided by the WTO to counter specific subsidies, when inefficient, deprive members of the expected development, favoring those with greater economic power, who, in turn, take advantage of the strategy of the fait accompli.

At this juncture, the role of the multilateral trade system, reinforced by a "jurisdictionalized" mechanism, is to prevent the use of unilateral illicit practices. Even so, the time factor and the lack of precautionary and retroactive remedies have been determinant for the achievement of a reality different from the expected, making a new perspective urgent: the necessity to strengthen the system to counter illicit subsidies to promote equality between rich and poor countries, ensuring compliance with the rules.

4.6   Proposals

There are several proposals presented by the doctrine and by jurists in order to promote greater effectiveness of the system that oversees subsidy policies and holds accountable those considered illegal. The main ones add damages as a possible condemnation of the DSB or change the retaliation by adopting the unconditional and retroactive form.

Liability for retroactive damages has been a frequent topic among developing countries since the GATT/47 era.[135] Another possibility would be to allow members to unite in retaliation, making it more effective when developing countries are supported by developed ones.[136] This proposal, put forward by the African countries, became known as collective retaliation.[137]

---

[135] Hoekman (2011), pp. 16–18.

[136] For Borges, the junction of members at the time of retaliation is not possible due to the bilateral character of the WTO agreements and, therefore, only the injured States are entitled to retaliate. Even because some States are benefited with the subsidies due to lower prices of the subsidized product for consumers in importing States. See: Borges (2008), pp. 295–296.

[137] Amaral (2008), p. 114.

4.6.1   Indemnity

According to the economic theory of contracts, from the perspective of EAL, compliance with the agreement will occur when its costs are less than the costs of the liability for the breach. In turn, the party fails to comply with the agreement if the costs of its breach are greater.

Regarding optimal compliance, efficiency requires the party to internalize them if they are less than the benefits obtained by the other party. Thus, when the liability for the breach is equivalent to the lost benefit, its costs are internalized.[138]

When analyzing WTO rules, Trachtman[139] notes that "WTO law is distinct from the prohibition of war and therefore should not be complied with at any cost, but only to the extent that it increases welfare". For this reason, the remedies provided by the system should be compensatory in nature, allowing the member to violate agreements whenever this situation produces more gain than the loss of the prejudiced member.

The indemnity should cover all the damages caused by the breach of the agreement, both retrospective and prospective. Therefore, "perfect indemnification, creates incentives for efficient compliance and breach".[140]

However, compensation is only recommended in the case of substitutable goods, which does not seem to be the case of subsidies, since the trade detour caused leads to irreparable social damage. That is, the damages are irreversible and difficult to calculate, as determined by the PESE.

For Lawrence,[141] subsidies seem like a crime and not like a breach of contract. For this reason, retaliation plays an important role in forcing governments to adjust illicit subsidy policies. Given this, it is possible to state that, when it comes to subsidies, there is no space for efficient breach.

4.6.2   Unconditional and Retroactive Retaliation

It is true that retaliation has been little used by WTO members. Seventeen retaliations have been authorized to date, of which eight have been granted to developing countries, only one of which has applied it.[142] This data may mean that retaliation

---

[138] Cooter and Ulen (2010), p. 214.

[139] Free adaptation from: "After all, WTO law is not like the international law prescription of genocide or aggressive war: it does not normatively demand compliance at all costs. Rather, WTO law is better understood largely as instrumental law that is only worthy of compliance to the extent that compliance makes people better off". In: Trachtman (2006). https://doi.org/10.2139/ssrn.815844.

[140] Cooter and Ulen (2010), p. 215.

[141] Lawrence (2003).

[142] See list of cases available at: https://www.wto.org/english/tratop_e/dispu_e/dispu_status_e.htm.

fulfills its role as a means of political pressure to settle the dispute by agreement, or that it is not always efficient, resulting in its low use.

In this way, it is proposed to make retaliation unconditional, also covering retroactive damages. This means that retaliation would not be conditional on the breach of the obligation.

However, this alternative diverges from the main objective of retaliation, which is to force the infringing State to adapt the illicit subsidy to WTO rules. The calculation of retroactive damages is more interesting because the State would be obliged to respond for all the damage caused, if it were not for the difficulty of calculating irreparable damage.

In both cases, the solution is in the last phase of the procedure and does not stop States from using political-economic strategies to gain time and trade.[143]

All proposals aim at correcting the failures of the DSB by means of solutions to be applied after its final decision. In the case of illicit subsidies, because of their capacity to divert trade and eliminate competition, such proposals are inefficient, because by the end of the procedure, the subsidies have already produced harmful effects on society.

Thus, all the proposals come back to the same problem: dependence on cooperation. Now, if the government's desire is to fulfill its obligations, it will hardly adopt an opportunistic behavior, even facing the possibility of being held accountable in the future. On the other hand, those who have no intention of complying with WTO rules tend to adopt opportunistic behavior, even if they must indemnify the injured party for loss and damages or even suffer retaliation.

This debate fails to take into consideration the biggest problem that these solutions can generate: the strategy of paying for non-compliance with the agreements, which is more easily adopted by the developed countries due to their economic conditions. For this reason, it is necessary to reinforce the WTO system in order to prevent subsidy strategies from causing irreparable damage to society, in the sense of imposing higher costs on developed countries that use illegal subsidies and granting greater bargaining power to less developed and developing countries.

4.6.3 Tradable Retaliation

The tradable retaliation was proposed by Mexico to reinforce the threat of retaliation, especially when authorized for fragile countries. In this case, the right to retaliate would be transferred to the member with the greater economic capacity for such action.

Nevertheless, Mexico does not present the form by which this negotiation would take place. Authors such as Bagwell, Mavroids and Staiger[144] add that the right to

---

[143] See: Brewster (2011), pp. 102–158.
[144] Bagwell et al. (2003).

retaliate can be auctioned off to interested member countries, which in turn are better able economically to promote retaliation.

However, such a measure would cause increased use of the WTO dispute settlement system unnecessarily, driving bilateral political disagreements into the multilateral arena, making costs exceed the benefits.[145]

Moreover, this solution also does not solve the problem of the economic-political strategies of subsidies that postpone the responsibility of the State to the next government.

As can be seen, none of the alternatives are aimed at immediately preventing the use of subsidies, since they restrict themselves to changing the ESC's last resource, allowing rich countries to take advantage of the loopholes in the system. In this vein, this thesis proposes that preventive cross-retaliation be granted to developing and least developed countries, as explained below.

4.7 Cross-Compensatory Measures Applied by Developing and Least Developed Countries Against Developed Country Subsidies When Competing in a Third Market

Economic differences among members not only remain but are also accentuated when it comes to political-economic subsidy strategies, since they derive from government policies that depend on the government's economic capacity to be implemented. Whereas the imposition of technical or sanitary barriers of a protectionist nature is independent of significant economic capacity and the practice of *dumping* comes from private institutions, subsidies vary according to the economic capacity of States, since they are granted through direct financial aid or tax incentives, implying fiscal resignation. And also, because they are more difficult to identify, subsidies are a disguised form of protectionism.

Furthermore, the loopholes in the system function as spaces for maneuvers by developed countries to gain time until they are forced to remove illicit subsidies, which hardly occurs, since "non-compliance with the decision by a developed country makes it difficult for the 'winning' developing Country to apply compensatory measures or suspend economic advantages".[146]

The WTO has already recognized this asymmetry among its members by establishing the principle of special and more favorable treatment for developing and least developed countries. In addition, the SCM still allows the use of subsidies to counter subsidies, as long as they are licit. However, poor countries lack the economic power to do so, and in practice, differences in economic power are accentuated by the system.

---

[145] Bagwell (2007) In: Janow et al. (2008), pp. 754–760.
[146] Silva Neto. In: Mercadante and Magalhães (1998), p. 207.

For this reason, it is necessary to reinforce the mechanism to counter subsidies in situations of power imbalance, that is, when subsidies from developed countries directly affect the social welfare of less developed and developing countries. In the current model, when exports are damaged by subsidies, these countries can only complain to the DSB, bearing its harmful effects while waiting for the dispute to be resolved.

It is important to point out that, notwithstanding the similarity of rationality between public and private agents in relation to cost-benefit analysis, their logics operate differently. While private entities immediately assimilate the costs of liability for violation of rules, public representatives transfer these costs to the next government. Assim, a concessão de subsídios deve ser custosa para o governo que o concede. Thus, subsidies must be costly to the government providing them. This means that the WTO system must transfer the costs of maintaining illicit or actionable subsidy programs to developed countries. As it stands, poor countries are most heavily burdened.

It should be noted that all the previous proposals presented still allowed the granting government to gain time, since they sought to resolve the issue *a posteriori*, by proposing changes only on the last resource of the dispute settlement procedure. In this case, cross-retaliation, when compared with retaliation in the same sector, has proven to be the most threatening option, within the mechanisms capable of making governments comply with DSB decisions.

The benefits of cross-retaliation have already been proven, as in the case of cotton, between Brazil and the United States, in which the agreement was only reached after Brazil threatened to retaliate in intellectual property. In this regard, at Workshop 2, conducted by the WTO's Legal Affairs Division, which discussed the future of the dispute settlement system, the following conclusion was reached:

> The group noted that retaliation in the same sector is often impractical. This observation led to a discussion about the usefulness of cross-retaliation. Cross-retaliation was considered superior to same-sector retaliation because it allows Members to retaliate with greater leeway to minimize injury to their domestic industries. The group noted that the level of compliance could be improved if the DSB preference for retaliation in the same sector were abandoned.[147]

Analyzing cases involving Brazil, Amaral[148] concluded that cross-retaliation can be the way for the least developed and developing countries to assert their rights vis-à-vis developed countries. In addition, this modality, especially when it involves intellectual property matters, promotes development and social well-being. As an

---

[147] Free adaptation from: "The group observed that retaliation in the same sector is often impracticable. This observation prompted a discussion on the usefulness of cross-retaliation. Cross-retaliation was considered superior to same-sector retaliation because it provides retaliating Members with greater leeway to minimize injury to its domestic industries. The group observed that the compliance level might be improved if the DSU preference for same-sector retaliation were abandoned." In: WTO PUBLIC FORUM 2012. https://www.wto.org/english/res_e/booksp_e/public_forum12_e.pdf.

[148] See: Amaral (2012).

example, the author cites the suspension of pharmaceutical patents that, by allowing the production of generics, decreases the value of medicines for consumers.[149] In addition, *lobbying* by the pharmaceutical industry eventually forces the government to seek an agreement rather than suffer cross-retaliation.

However, cross-retaliation, admitted only as a last resource, is not able to prevent that subsidies generate economic and social damage to the injured Country. In fact, prolonging the use of prohibited subsidies causes irreparable damage, since their effects are perpetuated even after the measure is removed. In the unsubsidized market, by unduly reallocating economic resources, subsidies prevent investment in the sector and eliminate competition, generating social costs.

As can be seen, such damage cannot simply be annulled at the end of the dispute settlement procedure under the PESE precepts; it is necessary that the damage be stopped from occurring. For this reason, when it comes to subsidies there is no such thing as efficient breach. "Subsidies are crimes, not breaches of contract, and the role of retaliation seems to be more towards inducing compliance than facilitating efficient breach.".[150]

As they are similar to crimes, there is no need to talk about an efficient break in subsidies, as it would be equivalent to "sentencing an individual guilty of stealing a car two years ago to simply return it to its owner within a year and not commit the crime again".[151] For this reason, preventive measures are now necessary to immediately stop the damage caused by subsidies.

Note that the proposals presented do not enforce Article 21 of the ESC, by which countries must comply promptly with DSB decisions, especially regarding the interests of developing countries.

To this end, this thesis proposes an alteration in the SCM to allow the use of countervailing measures, in cross modality, that is, in the scope of another agreement of the WTO, when competition also occurs in a third market, that is, when subsidies practiced by rich countries are reallocating exports from less developed and developing countries.

The intention is to prevent that the only option for the most fragile countries is the long wait until retaliation is authorized in a dispute settlement procedure, thus avoiding that this serves as an even larger space than the spaces admitted by the safeguards measures.[152]

---

[149] In the same direction follow: Rachel Brewster, *The surprising Benefits to Developing Countries of Linking International Trade and Intelecctual Property*. Henning Grosse Ruse-Khan, *A Pirate of the Caribbean? The Atraction of Suspending TRIPS Obligations*. Arvind Subramanian, Jayashree Watal, *Can Trips Serve as an Enforcement Device for Developing Countries in the WTO?*

[150] Free adaptation from: "Subsidies are crimes not breaches and the role of retaliation appear to be more about inducing compliance than about facilitating efficient breach". In: Bagwell (2007). In: Janow et al. (2008), p. 762.

[151] Free adaptation from: "This is equivalent to a court ruling that an individual found guilty of stealing a car two years ago must simply return the car to its owner within a year and not steal again". In: Davis (2012), p. 291.

[152] According to BREWSTER, differently from the spaces found in the dispute settlement procedure, the conditions for the application of safeguard measures are restricted, in addition to being

In this case, least developed and developing countries would be authorized to initiate domestic and unilateral subsidy investigation proceedings, as established under the ordinary procedure for the imposition of countervailing measures against prohibited and actionable subsidies.

Regarding the procedure and the evidence, the cross countervailing measures will be imposed by developing and least developed countries against prohibited or actionable subsidies from developed countries, following, basically, the rite determined in articles 10,11 and 12 of the SCM and, in the case of Brazil, together with Decree no. 1.355 of December 30, 1994, as well as Decree no. 1.751 of December 19, 1995 and, in accordance with the circulars and ordinances of SECEX and resolutions of CAMEX.

The investigation will be initiated, unilaterally, in the competent organ of each State, in the case of Brazil, in SECEX, in order to investigate the existence, the degree and the effect of the supposed subsidy. In attention to the principles of transparency, due legal process, contradictory and ample defense, the grantor Country must be notified to manifest itself and present evidence, whose confidentiality must be respected.

It is important to mention Article 12.6 of the SCM, which allows the investigating authority to search for evidence in the territory of other Members, including their industries:

> 12.6 The investigating authorities may carry out investigations in the territory of other Members as necessary, provided that they have notified the Member concerned in advance and unless the latter opposes the investigation. In addition, investigating authorities may conduct investigations at a company's premises and examine a company's records if (a) the company agrees and (b) the member in question notified does not oppose it. (...)[153]

Since we are dealing with competition in a third market, this article should be enhanced to make its use feasible. To this end, it is necessary to add the duty of member States to cooperate with the production of evidence to better determine the subsidies and their volume.

When the subsidy competes with the domestic industry in the domestic market, it is easier to prove its impact on domestic production. In the case of competition in a third market, it is necessary to prove the damage caused to exports of the similar product manufactured by the national industry that would be destined to the third market, which means determining how much of exports have been diverted as a result of the use of prohibited or actionable subsidies.

For this reason, international cooperation is essential for the lawfulness and proportionality of the compensatory measure, whose purpose is to counterbalance the

---

limited in time. In: Brewster (2011).

[153] Free adaptation from: "Article 12.6 SCM: The investigating authorities may carry out investigations in the territory of other Members as required, provided that they have notified in good time the Member in question and unless that Member objects to the investigation. Further, the investigating authorities may carry out investigations on the premises of a firm and may examine the records of a firm if (a) the firm so agrees and (b) the Member in question is notified and does not object".

effects caused by specific subsidies. The consequences of not cooperating are described in the following article:

> 12.7In cases where any interested member or interested party refuses access or in other ways fails to provide the necessary information within a reasonable time or significantly impedes the investigation, preliminary or final determinations, positive or negative, may be made on the basis of the data available.[154]

This article promotes the interest of the parties to cooperate so that the compensatory measure imposed is licit and proportional to the subsidy, avoiding arbitrariness. By "parties" we mean not only the governments of the States but also exporters or importers, producers and their respective associations.

In fact, developing and less developed countries also face difficulties regarding the knowledge of the subject, for lack of qualified professionals. In this case, the Subsidies Committee may be asked to provide technical assistance to these countries, which, by virtue of the principle of special and differential treatment, have the right to make use of technical assistance.

Once the requirements determined between articles 10 to 12 of the SCM are met, the countervailing measure will be applied on imports of any goods from the subsidizing country to the limit of the amount of damage caused by the subsidies. To this end, the country imposing the measure will notify the WTO in advance, divulging the list of goods whose measures will be imposed, which may occur in different sectors and agreements, including intellectual property.

In this case, not being possible or unfeasible to impose compensatory measures in different sectors, due to the small market share shared by the least developed or developing country, these may, similarly to cross-retaliation, impose, by the same procedure, compensatory measures in other agreements, as in intellectual property. It is worth pointing out what Amaral says:

> (...)cross-retaliation under TRIPS, if well planned and executed, can contribute significantly to increasing the welfare of society and to increasing innovation in the country that is suspending concessions of intellectual property rights, while allowing access to information that would be used in favor of the domestic industry of the complaining member.[155]

However, it should not be forgotten that the cross-retaliation applied at the end of the dispute settlement procedure does not avoid the irreparability of the damage caused by subsidies. For this reason, it is necessary to concede, in attention to the principle of special and differential treatment to least developed and developing countries, the benefit of applying, unilaterally, the countervailing measure in other agreements, if the use of countervailing measures in the same sector is not feasible. This possibility should be ascertained during the investigative procedure.

---

[154] Free adaptation from: "SCM Article 12.7In cases in which any interested Member or interested party refuses access to, or otherwise does not provide, necessary information within a reasonable period or significantly impedes the investigation, preliminary and final determinations, affirmative or negative, may be made on the basis of the facts available".

[155] Amaral (2012). http://www.barralmjorge.com.br/pagina.php?id=807.

It is important to emphasize that the cross-compensatory measure concedes greater bargaining power to the least developed and developing countries, which will be better able to conclude agreements that best suit their interests.

The advantage is that it encourages governments to adjust prohibited or actionable subsidy measures, since it will no longer be possible to prolong the dispute settlement procedure repeatedly in order to gain trade.

If the compensatory measure imposed is unlawful, the developed country may seek recourse to the DSB, since it has better conditions to do so, including to bear the effects of the disproportionality or illegality of the measure applied.

In this way, the costs of developed countries violating WTO subsidy rules will no longer be passed on to the next government but will be effectively borne by the granting government, making the case quickly resolved.

This system makes it possible to transfer to developed countries the costs of waiting for the final decision on the dispute settlement procedure. For poor countries, the costs of cross-compensatory relief may be less than the burden of waiting for the effective resolution of the dispute. Applying countervailing measures or initiating disputes in front of the DSB should be optional for governments, similar to what happens when the imported subsidized product competes with the national one. To this end, governments consult with their industries on the best strategy to adopt.

In effect, the cross-compensatory measure is not capable of covering all the spaces of political-economic maneuvering of subsidies in the WTO, but at least it can reduce the differences between rich and poor countries, providing the latter with greater bargaining power to negotiate efficient solutions in a *Pareto* sense.

Moreover, by raising the costs of breaking commitments for developed countries, it discourages opportunistic behavior and encourages compliance with obligations under the SCM, or at least will make governments more cautious about political-economic subsidy strategies.

Considering that the proposal of this thesis implies an amendment to the SCM, it is necessary that it be approved by consensus of all members of the organization, which can be very difficult, mainly due to the divergence on the category of developing countries.

Countries such as Brazil, China, and India, also known as emerging countries, call themselves developing countries. Brazil due to its relevant role in the DSB as a subsidy complainant, China as the largest target of countervailing measures in addition to its strong presence as a complainant in the DSB, and India is the second largest target of countervailing measures. This demonstrates the economic potential of these countries, either to provide subsidies or to force the extinction of subsidy programs.

For this reason, WTO members are unwilling to grant even greater powers to these countries. There are two alternatives to reach consensus: (a) allow all members to make use of cross-compensatory measures or (b) restrict their imposition to least developed and developing countries, except emerging countries.

The first alternative would not solve the problem of the imbalance of power between rich and poor countries, since the first ones would still be the biggest users of this measure. The second alternative, on the other hand, shows itself to be a viable option, since it would meet the interests of those smaller countries whose economies depend exclusively on exports.

The intention of the proposal is to make it easier for poor countries to counter targeted subsidies by rich ones by providing them with one more instrument and reversing the time burden of the process.

In fact, the cross-compensatory measures are not free of costs for the government that imposes them, however, such costs are lower if compared to the dispute settlement procedure, that after long waiting for the result, the harmed country will be left to impose cross-retaliation, which are still costly. Therefore, the idea is to reduce inequality among WTO members by giving poor countries more bargaining power, because for free trade, the agreement will always be more advantageous than any dispute.

References

Abbot WK, Snidal D (2000) Hard and soft law in international governance. Int Organ 54:421
Accioly H (2008) Manual de Direito Internacional Público, 16th edn. Saraiva, São Paulo, pp 804–805
Amaral A Jr (2008) A Solução de Controvérsias na OMC. Atlas, São Paulo, pp 113–114
Amaral RV (2012) Retaliação Cruzada na OMC: disciplina e desafios para o sistema multilateral de comércio. Thesis (Doctorate in Law) - Postgraduate Program in Law, Federal University of Santa Catarina, Florianópolis, pp 55, 56, 94–95, 99
Annan K (2003) Message to WTO Conference: secretary—general calls on trade ministers to address needs of world's poorest. http://www.un.org/press/en/2003/sgsm8859.doc.htm.
Azevêdo R.. Mensaje del Director General. http://www.wto.org/spanish/thewto_s/dg_s/dg_s.htm.
Bagwell K (2007) Remedies in the World Trade Organization: an economic perspective. In: Janow M, Donaldson V, Yanovich A (coord) (2008) The WTO: governance, dispute settlement and developing countries. Juris Publishing, New York, pp 754–760, 762
Bagwell K, Mavroidis PC, Straiger RW (2003) The case for auctioning countermeasures in the WTO. National Bureau of Economics Research, Cambridge
Bagwell K, Bermann GA, Mavroidis PC (2010) Law and economics of contingent protection in international trade. Cambridge University Press, New York, p 54
Benjamin DA (Org) (2013) O Sistema de Solução de Controvérsias da OMC: uma perspectiva brasileira. FUNAG, Brasília, p 36–37
Bliacheriene AC (2006) Emprego dos Subsídios e Medidas Compensatórias na Defesa Comercial: análise do regime jurídico brasileiro e aplicação dos acordos da OMC. Thesis (Doctorate in Law)—Post-graduation course in Law. Pontifícia Universidade Católica de São Paulo, São Paulo, pp 56, 118–119
Bliacheriene AC (2007) Defesa Comercial. Quartier Latin, São Paulo, p 107
Borges DD (2008) Represálias nos Contenciosos Econômicos na Organização Mundial do Comércio: uma análise na perspectiva dos países em desenvolvimento. Aduaneiras, São Paulo, pp 52, 57–62, 273, 285–286, 295–296, 327, 333–334, 360–361, 381–382, 342–343, 423, 431, 439–445, 498, 501
Bossche PV, Zdouc W (2013) The law and policy of the World Trade Organization. 3rd edn. Cambridge University Press, pp 205, 777–778
Brewster R (2011) The remedy gap: institutional design, retaliation, and trade law enforcement. George Washington Law Review, pp 102–158

Brink L et al. BRIC Agricultural policies through a WTO lens. http://onlinelibrary.wiley.com/doi/10.1111/1477-9552.12008/abstract

Cooter R, Ulen T (2010) Direito e Economia. 5ªed. Bookman, Porto Alegre, pp 214–215

Cretella Neto J (2003) Direito Processual na Organização Mundial do Comércio. Forensic, Rio de Janeiro, pp 109, 197

Davis CL (2012) Why adjucate?: enforcing trade rules in the WTO. Princeton University Press, Princeton, p 291

Ehlermann CD, Goyette M (2006) The interface between EU state aid control and the WTO disciplines on subsidies. Eur State Aid Law Q 5(4):712–713

Evenett S. In: Breuer R. OMC reaches the age of 20 in the middle of an identity crisis. http://dw.de/p/1Bhqo

Gonçalves EN, Stelzer J (2007) O Direito e a Ciência Econômica: a possibilidade interdisciplinar na contemporânea Teoria Geral do Direito. Berkely Program in Law & Economics. http://www.egov.ufsc.br/portal/sites/default/files/anexos/25380-25382-1-PB.pdf

Gonçalves EN, Stelzer J (2010) Economia e Direito para o Rompimento de Barreiras ao Comércio Internacional: a disciplina jurídica do GATT a OMC. http://www.conpedi.org.br/manaus/arquivos/anais/fortaleza/3755.pdf, p 2410

Gonçalves EN, Stelzer J (2012) Eficiência e Direito: pecado ou virtude; uma incursão pela análise econômica do direito. Unicuritiba, n. 28. http://revista.unicuritiba.edu.br/index.php/RevJur/article/view/412/0, p 98

Hoekman B (2011) Proposals for WTO reform: a synthesis and assessment. The World Bank Policy Research Working Paper 5525, Jan, pp 3, 16–18

Hoekman B (2014) Supply chains, mega-regionals and multilateralism: a road map for the WTO. http://papers.ssrn.com/sol3/papers.cfm?abstract_id=2406871

Hoekman B, Kostecki M (2009) The political economy of the world trading system: the WTO and beyond. Oxford University Press, Oxford, p 6

Hoekman B, Kostecki M (2013) The political economy of the World Trading System. Oxford University Press, Oxford, position 2244, 2408–2410

Horlick G (2001) Confusing trade sanctions with trade remedies. Cordell Hull Institute. Trade Policy Analysis 3(8):3

Horlick G (2002) Problems with the compliance structure of the WTO dispute resolution process. In: Kennedy DM, Southwick J (2002) The political economy of international trade law. Cambridge University Press, Cambridge, p 640

Jackson JH (2000) The Jurisprudence of GATT and WTO: insights on treaty law and economic relations. Cambridge University Press, Cambridge, pp 90–91

Jawara F, Kwa A (2004) Behind the Scenes at the WTO. Zed Books, New York, p 63, 85

Krugman P. Dead Doha. http://krugman.blogs.nytimes.com/2008/07/30/dead-doha/?_r=0.

Lafer C (1998) A OMC e a Regulamentação do Comércio Internacional. Lawyer's Bookstore, São Paulo, p 130

Lawrence RZ (2003) Crimes & Punishment? Retaliation under the WTO. Institution of International Economics, Washington DC

Munhoz CPB (2005) Defesa comercial: medidas compensatórias e de salvaguarda na rodada Doha. Revista de direito econômico internacional: RDEI, Florianópolis, n. 8, Aug. http://www.iribr.com/hongkong/Defesa_Comercial_medidas_compensatórias.asp

Order D et al. WTO disciplines on agricultural support. Experience to date and assessment of Doha proposals. http://www.ifpri.org/sites/default/files/publications/rb16.pdf

Pauwelyn J (2000) Enforcement and countermeasures in the WTO: rules are rules—toward a more collective approach. Am J Int Law:335–347

Pires AR (2001) Práticas Abusivas no Comércio Internacional. Forensic, Rio de Janeiro, pp 211–212, 214

Schropp S (2009) Trade policy flexibility and enforcement in the WTO: a law and economics analysis. London, Cambridge University Press, p 4, 6

Schwartz WF, Sykes AO (2002) The economic structure of renegotiation and dispute resolution in the WTO/GATT system the law school. University of Chicago. http://www.law.uchicago.edu/files/files/143.AOS_.wto_.pdf

Sella LF (2010) A Organização Mundial do Comércio: histórico e aspectos a reforma. http://www.anima-opet.com.br/pdf/anima4-Estrangeiro/anima4-Luis-Felipe-Sella.pdf, p 26

Sen A (1987) O Método I: a natureza da natureza. Publicações Europa-América, Lisboa, p 113

Sen A (2000) Desenvolvimento como Liberdade. Companhia das Letras, São Paulo, 2000, pp 71, 108

Silva Neto OC (1998) The dispute settlement mechanism of the World Trade Organization: case analysis—Litigation Brazil and Venezuela vs. the United States. In: Mercadante A, Magalhães JC (eds) Solução e prevenção de litígios internacionais. NECIN, São Paulo, p 207

Silva Neto OC (2005) Análise Econômica do Procedimento de Solução de Controvérsias da OMC: os conflitos entre exceções legítimas de políticas públicas e regras substantivas dos acordos. Tese (doutorado em Direito)—Programa de Pós-graduação, Faculdade de Direito da Universidade de São Paulo, São Paulo, p 173, 179

Sykes AO (2003) The economics of WTO rules on subsidies and countervailing measures. Law and Economics Working Paper, n. 186, The Law School, University of Chicago, 2003

Thorstensen V, Oliveira LM (2013) Releitura dos Acordos da OMC como Interpretados pelo Órgão de Apelação: efeitos na aplicação das regras de comércio internacional. http://ccgi.fgv.br/sites/ccgi.fgv.br/files/file/Publicacoes/11%20%20Acordo%20sobre%20Subs%C3%ADdios%20e%20Medidas%20Compensat%C3%B3rias%20%28SCM%29.pdf, pp 115–117, 184

Trachtman JP (1999) The domain of WTO dispute resolution. Harv Int Law J 40:339

Trachtman JP (2006) Building the WTO Cathedral. https://doi.org/10.2139/ssrn.815844.

Vianna CC, Lima JPR (2010) Política Comercial Brasileira: possíveis impactos de uma redução nas tarifas de importação dos setores automotivo e têxtil. Revista Econômica, Rio de Janeiro, 12(2):157–186, December

Viner J (1991) Dumping: a problem in international trade. Reprints of economic classics. Augustus M. Kelly Publishers, Clifton

Wolfe R (2015) Letting the sun shine at WTO: how transparency brings the trading system to life. http://www.wto.org/english/res_e/reser_e/ersd201303_e.pdf, p. 17

Wouters J, Coppens D (2010) An overview of the agreement on subsidies and countervailing measures—including a discussion of the agreement on agriculture. In: Bagwell KW (ed.), Bermann GA, Mavroidis PC (2009) Law and economics of contingent protection in international trade. Cambridge University Press, New York, p 56

WTO (2006) World Trade Report 2006: exploring the links between subsidies, trade and the WTO. WTO, Geneva. http://www.wto.org/english/res_e/booksp_e/anrep_e/world_trade_report06_e.pdf

Chapter 5
Conclusion

The ineffectiveness of the WTO system of countering developed country subsidies by the least developed and developing countries has placed the latter at the margins of the organization, contrary to the objectives for which it was created, which basically boil down to efficiency and welfare.

Subsidies are government financial contributions, which, when specific, that is, when they confer a benefit to a company or sector, distort trade by reducing prices in the international market, increasing its demand, and causing the rival to lose market by not being able to compete with the prices of the subsidized product. For this reason, it is necessary to provide governments with instruments to prevent the harmful effects of subsidies from materializing.

At first, subsidies, by reducing product prices, can be beneficial to income distribution in the importing country, but at the macro level and in the long term, they can end international competition, generating perverse social effects. They can also be useful in countering negative externalities caused by trade, but for this they cannot be specific. In addition, they are important for the promotion of infant industry in poorer countries. The line is thin, and the challenge is therefore to distinguish the various types of subsidies and their purposes.

The WTO is concerned about specific subsidies, as these are capable of unduly allocating economic resources. General subsidies, granted horizontally, are allowed, which leaves room for governments to adopt economic policies according to their interests. For example, the exemption of exports, when intended for all exporters, without distinction, do not constitute subsidies to be challenged in the WTO.

Throughout history, governments have used subsidies for political and economic purposes to protect interests, whether to protect nascent industry or to boost exports in search of wealth, or to remain in power. Until the appearance of the World Trade Organization, in 1995, the regulation of such practices at the international level was little explored since the use of subsidies was linked exclusively to the sovereign wish of States.

© The Author(s), under exclusive license to Springer Nature
Switzerland AG 2024
J. Marteli Fais Feriato, *Legal, Political and Economic Strategies of Subsidies within the World Trade Organization*, European Yearbook of International Economic Law 40, https://doi.org/10.1007/978-3-031-73869-2_5

The regulation of subsidies at the multilateral level is important to avoid opportunism, because if one government does not cooperate and grants subsidies, it will have advantages over the others. In this sense, the system to counter subsidies must be effective in promoting the cooperation of all its members in order to be efficient.

In light of this, the WTO brought in a regulatory framework for subsidy practices considered illicit, as well as added a system of monitoring and accountability for its member States. The SCM divided the subsidies into prohibited, actionable and permitted, the latter having been repealed in 1999. By prohibiting specific, export-linked or import substitution subsidies, the WTO has restricted the economic policy space of member States. However, States have found the dispute settlement mechanism to be a fundamental pillar for maintaining the multilateral trading system and space for granting subsidies.

The flaws of the system favor the developed Countries, which adopt political-economic strategies of subsidies to gain time and trade, until they effectively have to eliminate them. Developing and least developed countries, on the other hand, find it difficult to access the system and, when they do, cannot tolerate the delay until the dispute is effectively resolved.

Therefore, this thesis sought to verify how the failures of the WTO dispute settlement mechanism induce the use of political-economic strategies that further unbalance the relations between rich and poor countries, proposing, in the end, an alternative for the latter, in order to inhibit the opportunistic behavior of the first ones and prevent the effects of subsidies from materializing.

To do so, it was shown that, for a long time, International Law did not care about regulating subsidies, which only came to occur after GATT/47, although in an incipient way, since it was an international agreement, guided by the power of governments. Compared to the GATT, the WTO brought a robust structure, guided by the rules of Law, providing its members with instruments to enforce compliance, such as the negative consensus rule and the *single undertaking* principle. However, contradictions of interest remain, when governments encourage free trade on foreign territory while protecting the internal market.

It has been shown that subsidies are governmental interventions in the economic domain that, from mercantilism to neoliberalism, serve as instruments of governments to achieve specific interests. Because of their distorting effects, it has been proven that subsidies should be regulated at the multilateral level to avoid opportunistic behavior. However, the current reality of production is fragmented, making governments more susceptible to market pressures, and making them use subsidies to expand their participation in trade.

The behavior of governments in the face of international rules was studied, in the second chapter, from the standpoint of the Economic Analysis of Law, a movement that adopts microeconomic premises to understand the reality of Law. The PESE was highlighted as the guiding principle of the analysis conducted in this thesis, due to the importance of including negative externalities in the economic calculation so that the efficiency of the system generates the lowest possible cost to society.

It was found that opportunistic behavior is encouraged by the failures of the system, when considering that governments, as well as individuals, make a cost-benefit analysis when adopting certain behavior, such as breaking with WTO rules. However, the interests of governments differ from those of individuals, because while the latter seek to maximize well-being, the former do not always act in favor of the common good, but rather in the specific interest of staying in power. In this sense, the pattern of government behavior revealed a tendency to transfer to others the costs resulting from the responsibility for the practice of subsidies.

Game theory analyzes the players and their respective strategies adopted according to the rules of the game and the decision making of the others, in this case, the member countries are the players, and the rules are the WTO agreements. The theory teaches that the tendency to cooperate is lower the greater the economic power of governments while less powerful governments are more cooperative. Therefore, Law must take these differences into account and ensure full cooperation, discouraging opportunistic behavior.

It is important to highlight the role of the WTO institution, which, by establishing the rules of the game, causes the reduction of transaction costs, but the failures of its mechanisms to counter subsidies, trigger new costs, which need to be avoided, especially when distributed differently, burdening developing and least developed countries. In this sense, the WTO has created more costs for developing and least developed countries, which cannot afford the long wait for the effective, removal of the subsidy program.

Furthermore, it is not conceivable that the SCM will be efficiently broken, because subsidies are like crimes and not like contracts. For this reason, the harmful effects of subsidies must be prevented from occurring. As the system stands, which condemns the government to remove its subsidy program only at the end of the entire dispute settlement procedure, it is like condemning the robber to return the car he stole two years ago, that is, the solution is inefficient.

To better understand the problem, the third chapter is dedicated to studying the structure of the WTO, its rules and principles, with emphasis on the principle of special and differential treatment to developing and least developed countries, which recognizes the difficulties faced by these countries, establishing certain privileges, such as, for example, the reduction of procedural deadlines for matters of subsidies, technical assistance, and the principle of prompt compliance with the decisions of the DSB, especially when the matter is of interest to developing and least developed countries.

In this vein, the problem of the category of developing countries was highlighted, since they call themselves as such, which has blocked the negotiations of the Doha Agenda, because, in the conception of developed and less developed countries, Brazil and China are strong economies, with good performance in the WTO and, therefore, could not enjoy more beneficial treatment.

Another problem to be considered is the concept and definition of subsidies, which still generate divergences, which have been clarified by the jurisprudence of the DSB. This has repercussions on the imposition of countervailing measures, requiring greater cooperation among members to determine subsidies, mainly because such measures are imposed unilaterally by the importing country, whose domestic legislation follows the guidelines of the ASCM.

Thus, it was found that the WTO provides its members with two mechanisms to counter subsidies: countervailing measures and the dispute settlement procedure, whose issues were studied in the fourth chapter.

Countervailing measure's function, economically, as taxes, increasing the price of the subsidized product to the point of returning the supply curve to its equilibrium status. As their purpose is to counterbalance the effects of subsidies, countervailing measures must be proportional to the subsidies, and may be contested in front of the DSB when disproportionate.

In Brazil, a subsidy investigation procedure is opened at SECEX, which, in turn, will verify, among other requirements, the existence of the subsidy, which can be both prohibited and actionable, the evidence of damage to domestic production and the causal nexus. It is emphasized that the procedure respects transparency, the due legal process, the ample defense, and the adversary, therefore, the investigated party is given the opportunity to manifest itself and produce evidence. Even the assistance of third countries or industries may be requested to provide data for the investigation.

Countervailing measures are the fastest way to counter subsidies. The entire investigation procedure takes no more than a year and it is imposed immediately and can even be retroactive. It has the legal nature of a special right, and its function and advantage is to induce the recovery of the parties at any time.

It was found that the use of countervailing measures is restricted to the main trading partners and that in a world of fragmented production, the tendency is to intensify competition in the third market. However, countervailing measures can only be applied in the importing market and are not an instrument to counter subsidies that divert exports to a third market.

When this happens, the only thing left for the government to do is to use new subsidies or to contest the subsidies before the DSB. The first option is unfeasible because it is extremely costly to the government, which can only grant non-specific subsidies. The DSB, on the other hand, has flaws that induce the use of political-economic subsidy strategies. The main problem of the system lies in the fact that the mechanism against non-compliance is equivalent to compliance, since, at the end of the procedure, the government will only be condemned to remove the subsidy.

Moreover, the possibility of opening new proceedings to, respectively, discuss the implementation of the decision, to verify it, to authorize retaliation, and to discuss the amount of retaliation prolongs noncompliance with the decision. The longer the time for compliance, the greater the incentives to use the DSB for procrastination and protectionist purposes.

It was sought to show which States and how they take advantage of these loopholes in favor of the perpetuation of subsidies. It was found that the system has been used exclusively by developed countries and has placed developing and less developed countries on its margins, except for those considered emerging.

Therefore, the rules of the game instituted by the WTO generate opportunistic behavior on the part of the governments of developed countries, which take advantage of all mechanisms to transfer the eventual responsibility to the next government. Meanwhile, the sectors for which the subsidies have been granted gain trade and their competitors lose it.

Following the logic of the EAL, it was decided to create new costs for rich countries and, at the same time, promote the social welfare of poor countries, according to the PESE. In this sense, the present thesis presents as an efficient measure to prevent the use of subsidies, the possibility of using cross-compensatory measures.

All the proposals presented so far by governments at the WTO: compensation, cross and unconditional retaliation, and negotiable retaliation, are *a posteriori* solutions, which do not solve the problem of the irreparable consequences of subsidies.

EAL determines specific execution as a *Pareto*-efficient solution. From this premise derives the principle of bargaining, which considers that the parties are best able to determine the solution that best serves their interests.

It turns out that the differences accentuated by the WTO system regarding subsidies do not put the least developed and developing countries in a bargaining position equivalent to that of developed countries.

For this reason, it is necessary to reinforce the WTO system so that developing countries are included and can assert their rights, preventing opportunistic behavior by developed countries, in order to maximize the results of international trade with the lowest possible costs to society.

Studies have proven the effectiveness of cross-retaliation and its benefits to social welfare, as has been seen in the intellectual property sector. However, cross-retaliation, as a last resource, does not restrain opportunism, on the contrary, it encourages the adoption of political-economic strategies. For this reason, the possibility is proposed for weaker States to impose countervailing measures in other sectors or agreements, reversing the time burden of the procedure.

The procedure for imposing these measures will follow the one determined in the SCM and the respective domestic legislation, adding the necessity to prove the damages resulting from export detour caused by illicit subsidies, both prohibited and actionable. To this end, the duty of cooperation among members to produce evidence must be added.

This mechanism frontloads the costs to the subsidizing government and provides an incentive to adjust immediately. In fact, the cost of waiting for the final decision in the dispute settlement process is much higher for poor countries than the cost of the cross-compensatory measure to be borne by developed countries. In fact, what is intended to be avoided is opportunistic behavior and, by granting greater bargaining power to poor countries, it is intended to encourage agreement between the parties. At the very least, developed countries are expected to be more cautious about subsidy policies.

Nevertheless, in the current scenario, the proposal will find it difficult to reach consensus in the WTO, mainly because emerging countries such as Brazil and China enjoy this privilege because they call themselves developing countries. But if the cross-compensatory measure is admitted for all members, without distinction, the system would continue to be used by the strongest. Therefore, the WTO urgently needs to adopt new development criteria, so that the countries that need it most can enjoy the principle of special and differential treatment.